Ancient Mines and Quarries

A Trans-Atlantic Perspective

Ancient Mines and Quarries
A Trans-Atlantic Perspective

edited by

Margaret Brewer-LaPorta, Adrian Burke and David Field

peer reviewed by

Martyn Barber, Hetty Jo Brumbach, Christopher J. Ellis,
Pierre M. Desrosiers, Gilles Gauthier, Patrick J. Julig,
Xavier Mangado Llach, Jean-François Moreau,
Jacques Y. Perreault, Jean Revez,
Duncan Ritchie, and Gillian Varndell

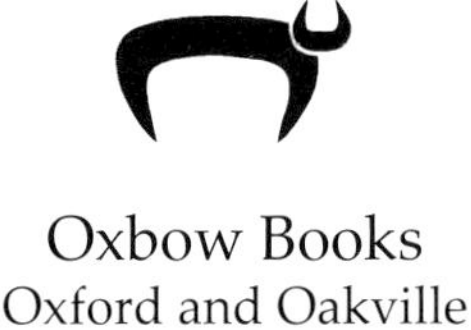

Oxbow Books
Oxford and Oakville

Published by
Oxbow Books, Oxford

ISBN 978-1-84217-401-2

A CIP record for this book is available from the British Library

This book is available direct from

Oxbow Books, Oxford, UK
(Phone: 01865-241249, Fax: 01865-794449)

and

The David Brown Book Company
PO Box 511, Oakville, CT 06779, USA
(Phone: 860-945-9329; Fax: 860-945-9468)

or from our website

www.oxbowbooks.com

Front cover: Earthwork remains of Neolithic flint mine shafts and spoil heaps at Grimes Graves, Norfolk, UK. Photograph taken from a helicopter in early morning light © Pete Topping.

Back cover: The Pike of Stickle, Great Langdale, Cumbria, UK, where quarrying has taken place on dangerously narrow ledges on the face of the mountainside. The group of figures provide scale. Photograph: Dave Field.

Printed in Great Britain by
Short Run Press, Exeter

Contents

List of Contributors

Elizabeth Bloxam Inst. of Archaeology, University College London.
e.bloxam@ucl.ac.uk

Margaret Brewer-LaPorta LaPorta Associates, L.L.C., Geological Consultants, 5 First Street #73, Warwick, New York, 10990, USA
and
Department of Chemistry and Physical Sciences, Dyson School of Arts and Sciences, Pace University, Pleasantville, New York USA
mbrewer-laporta@laportageol.com

François Bon Laboratoire TRACES (UMR 5608 du CNRS), Toulouse, France

Robert Boszhardt Mississippi Valley Archaeology Center, University of Wisconsin-La Crosse, 1725 State Street, La Crosse, WI 54601
boszhard.robe@uwlax.edu

Laurent Bruxelles INRAP et Laboratoire TRACES/CRPPM (UMR 5608 du CNRS), 13 rue du Négoce, 31650 St-Orens-de-Gameville, France
laurent.bruxelles@inrap.fr.

Adrian Burke Département d'anthropologie, Université de Montréal, C.P.6128, succursale Centre-ville, Montréal QC H3C 3J7
adrian.burke@umontreal.ca

Dillon Carr Department of Anthropology, Michigan State University, 354 Baker Hall, East Lansing, MI 48824
carrdill@msu.edu

Pierre Chalard Laboratoire TRACES (UMR 5608 du CNRS), Toulouse, France
chalard@univ-tlse2.fr

Richard Ciszak LMTG, Université de Toulouse, CNRS, IRD, OMP; 14 av. E. Belin, F-31400 Toulouse, France
ciszak@lmtg.obs-mip.fr.

Sylvain Ducasse Laboratoire TRACES (UMR 5608 du CNRS), Toulouse, France
sylvain.ducasse@orange.fr

Isabelle Duval Laboratoire d'archéologie et Laboratoire de géochimie, Université du Québec à Chicoutimi, Québec, Canada, G7H 2B1
Isabelle_Duval@uqac.ca or puzicalito@yahoo.ca

Thomas E. Emerson Illinois Transportation Archaeological Research Program (UIUC), 209 Nuclear Physics Laboratory, 23 East Stadium Dr., Champaign Il 61820

John C. Erwin Department of Archaeology, Memorial University of Newfoundland, St. John's, Newfoundland, A1C 5S7
jerwin@mun.ca

Kenneth B. Farnsworth Illinois Transportation Archaeological Research Program (UIUC), 209 Nuclear Physics Laboratory, 23 East Stadium Dr., Champaign Il 61820

David Field English Heritage, Kemble Drive, Swindon, Wiltshire SN2 2GZ, UK

Ivan Gatsov New Bulgarian University, National Archaeological Institute and Museum. igatsov@yahoo.com

Philippe Gardere Université de Toulouse III, France

Patricia Guillermin Laboratoire TRACES (UMR 5608 du CNRS), Toulouse, France
patriciaguillermin@yahoo.fr

Tom Heldal Geological Survey of Norway, N-7491 Trondheim
tom.heldal@ngu.no

Randall E. Hughes Illinois State Geological Survey, 121 Natural Resources Building, 615 E. Peabody Ave, Champaign IL 61820

Patrick J. Julig Anthropology Department, Laurentian University, Sudbury, Ontario, Canada, P3E 2C6

Adel Kelany Supreme Council of Antiquities, Aswan, Egypt
adelkelany@hotmail.com)

Philip C. LaPorta LaPorta Associates, L.L.C., Geological Consultants, 5 First Street #73, Warwick, New York, 10990, USA
plaporta@laportageol.com

Sébastien Lacombe Laboratoire TRACES (UMR 5608 du CNRS), Toulouse, France

Mathieu Langlais Laboratoire TRACES (UMR 5608 du CNRS), Toulouse, France et SERP, Barcelone, Espagne

David Leblanc Laboratoire d'archéologie, Université du Québec à Chicoutimi

Darrel Long Department of Earth Sciences, Laurentian University, Sudbury, Ontario, Canada, P3E 2C6

Romain Mensan Centre archéologique de Karnak, Egypte

Scott A. Minchak LaPorta LaPorta Associates, L.L.C., Geological Consultants, 5 First Street #73, Warwick, New York, 10990, USA

Jean-François Moreau Laboratoire d'archéologie, Université du Québec à Chicoutimi

Christian Normand Laboratoire TRACES (UMR 5608 du CNRS), Toulouse, France

Caroline Renard Laboratoire ARSCAN (UMR 7041 du CNRS), Nanterre, France et Laboratoire TRACES (UMR 5608 du CNRS), Toulouse, France

Robert Simonnet Laboratoire TRACES (UMR 5608 du CNRS), Toulouse, France

Per Storemyr Geological Survey of Norway, N-7491 Trondheim
per.storemyr@bluewin.ch

Andoni Tarriño Université du Pays Basque, Vitoria, Espagne

Nicolas Teyssandier Laboratoire TRACES (UMR 5608 du CNRS), Toulouse, France

Pete Topping English Heritage, Brooklands Avenue, Cambridge, UK
peter.topping@english-heritage.org.uk

Sarah Wisseman Program on Ancient Technologies and Archaeological Materials, University of Illinois at Urbana-Champaign (UIUC), 704 S. Neil St., Champaign IL 61820
wisarc@illinois.edu

Preface

This volume has its origins in a series of meetings on prehistoric mines and quarries held at the Society for American Archaeology Annual Symposium in San Juan, Puerto Rico in 2006. These included symposium and poster sessions that investigated a variety of aspects of recent work along with a workshop to discuss international nomenclature and were among the first events arranged by the Prehistoric Quarries Interest Group of the SAA. The interest generated a resolve to establish further workshops and events in future years in order to encourage and stimulate new ideas and provide a catalyst for new areas of research. Some of the contributions made were to be published elsewhere, but others have been brought together as a follow up to a similar set of papers from an earlier meeting *The Cultural Landscape of Prehistoric Mines* edited by Peter Topping and Mark Lynott in 2005 and published by Oxbow Books. Essays are loosely grouped into matters dealing with the old world, ancient world and the new world rather than by rock or quarry type, or by period. The contributions range from those dealing with ethnography to those with a geochemical approach, from excavation to survey and conservation, all of which serve to reflect the wide ranging approaches currently being applied to the subject.

Margaret Brewer-LaPorta, Adrian Burke and David Field
August 2008

Acknowledgements

We are extremely grateful to a number of individuals for undertaking the difficult and time consuming task of peer reviewing each paper. Our thanks to Gillian Varndell and an unnamed individual at the British Museum and Martyn Barber of English Heritage as well as, to Xavier Mangado Llach, Pierre M. Desrosiers, Hetty Jo Brumbach, Duncan Ritchie, Christopher J. Ellis, Jean-François Moreau, Patrick J. Julig, Gilles Gauthier, Jacques Y. Perreault and Jean Revez. Copyright lies with the individual authors.

Our thanks go to La Porta Associates for provision of a grant to support the publication.

Foreword

Pete Topping and myself met for the first time at the 1999 SAA Annual Meeting in Chicago, which ultimately led to the concept of the Prehistoric Quarries and Early Mines Interest Group (PQEMIG) being discussed at the New Orleans Annual Meeting amongst a group of by now frequent contributors to annual symposia on mines and quarries and whose enthusiasm led to the publication of *The Cultural Landscape of Prehistoric Mines* edited by Pete Topping and Mark Lynott in 2005. However, it was not until the 2005 Annual SAA Meeting in Salt Lake City that the nuts and bolts of the machinery of PQEMIG were assembled. After being proposed directly to Dean Snow, the formative meeting of PQEMIG was placed on the SAA agenda by Tobi Brimsek for the 2006 Annual Meeting in San Juan, Puerto Rico.

"Ancient Mines and Quarries: A Trans-Atlantic Perspective" is PQEMIG's inaugural volume. As indicated by the editors in the Preface, this volume contains papers and posters presented at the first PQEMIG-sponsored sessions at the 2006 SAA Annual Meeting in San Juan. This monograph includes a cross section of quarry studies, including research in the Canadian sub-arctic, the southwestern and northeastern United States, the British Isles, France, the Balkans and Egypt. The two investigations from France (Bruxelles *et al.* and Chalard *et al.*), are the results of long-standing regional researches that utilize geology to understand the quarries being examined. Thin section and isotopic work, that is appropriate to the rock type under investigation, is presented in Dillon and Boshardt, Wisseman *et al.*, and LeBlanc *et al.* Select papers focus on the *chain du opertoire,* while others are involved in the task of extracting cultural inference from bedrock (Topping, Burke, Julig and Long, Minchak, and LaPorta *et al.*). A common theme in this monograph is the emphasis on physiography, topography, and the conversion of natural space to political reference points and even places of ideological worship (Topping, Gatsov). Some studies are in their planning stages (Gatsov), while others are focused on policy making and the construction of management reports, especially in the development and tourism sectors (Storemyr *et al.*).

Traditional thematic venues in the study of ancient quarries continue to be addressed in this volume. Several of the papers focus on prospection, extraction technology, refinement sequences, chemical signatures, trade and exchange, the recycling of quarries, and the use of quarries as places of worship. These themes reach back more than 100 years. However, some of the papers in the monograph reflect a shift in how quarries are perceived, that is in no short part due to new techniques now available to archaeologists that allow workers to revisit quarries, many in classic reference sections, and allow them to reevaluate extraction technology and production systems (*i.e.* Erwin). Several of the papers (Bruxelles *et al.*, Chalard *et al.*, Minchak, LaPorta *et al.*) utilize geological data to better understand ancient quarries. Of particular interest is the use of stratigraphic and structural geology, mineralogy, petrology, isotopic analysis and petrofabric analysis in order to derive cultural inference from the examination of quarries and mines.

What these geologically buttressed papers show is the axiom that quarries and mines are geological resources first and archaeological entities second. Understanding the geological nature of quarries should be the first task of the quarry researcher. Prior to the initiation of archaeological excavation work, and before cultural inference is drawn from quarry locations, the necessary stratigraphic and structural (tectonic) geology should be compiled and tabulated. Archaeological investigations which have the strongest resultant cultural inferences, and the most convincing conclusions concerning prehistoric behavior, are those which have committed the time, energy, and expertise to conduct the background geology first. It has been difficult to convince the archaeological community that quarries are a geological issue first; however the time well spent constructing detailed stratigraphic sections, and elucidating rock geometry and architecture, pays off considerably when constructing excavation methodologies and research strategies. Those quarry studies that are built on a strong geological foundation are the investigations which survive, win funding, and are the studies that produce the most gratifying results.

This begs the question, what is left to examine in the field, given the geological nature of the quarry landscape? There is little, if anything, yet written on the role of fabric and diagenesis towards raw material selection, extraction, and the development of production systems. Quarry excavation methodology needs revision, as the bedrock quarry face is generally missed in quarry investigations. Excavations still take place on flat terraces great distances from quarry faces and the focus is on bifaces, cores and production systems. Little is said for quarry tools and mining instruments employed in extraction, sedimentation rates or site formation process at quarries, and the geological constraints or parameters that define quarries and quarry districts. Quarries are locations where mine tailings occur in astronomical numbers. Few, if any, studies address the analysis of quarry and mine tailings. The chain of operation, so important to the understanding of production and allocation systems, is genetically related to fabric in rock and even diagenesis. Yet, the inexhaustible volume of quarry tailings is rarely analyzed. Lastly, and possibly most importantly, a quarry is a place of repetitive extraction. It is a location which is oftentimes backfilled and whose face changes radically depending on need. Therefore, the search for intact context can be in many cases a futile exercise. Having said this, quarry investigators need to develop methods for analyzing large numbers of mine tailings, both quickly and efficiently. The intact cultural context may be in many cases the last extraction that took place at the quarry face. Therefore, with the exception of the upper level of sites, most quarry activity is backfilled, and with rare exceptions preserved.

The content of this monograph, and the above statements, touch on the vision of PQEMIG and the enormous task that lies before it. There will be signs in the future of the success of this interest group; however, it will not be in the form of the production of numbers of volumes, or publications from the group. It will be seen, as hinted in this volume, in a shift in perspective which is ushered in through a better understanding of bedrock quarry faces. When quarry and mine studies have a universal and acceptable terminology, one which can be transmitted across present-day cultural boundaries to intellectuals investigating quarries world wide, then PQEMIG will have made a substantial accomplishment. When raw materials are treated as an ore, with a unit value associated to it, then the importance of quarries in lithic-based economies will become salient. If the extraction of flint and chert, and other raw materials, could be placed in an economic context, eventually the variations of raw material value can be treated in a similar fashion to modern-day economics of correlative industries, such as coal extraction and transport. When these items have been accomplished, PQEMIG will have been successful in establishing the umbilical relationship between quarry and site. Until then, a quarry is simply anything you would like to make of it, and that is most unfortunate. This is my personal view.

Philip C. LaPorta, Ph.D.
President, Prehistoric Quarries and Early Mines Interest Group
and President, LaPorta and Associates, L.L.C., Geological Consultants

1 Geoarchaeological Prospecting and Palaeolithic Exploitation Strategies of the Bajocien Flints in Haut-Quercy, France

(Prospection géoarchéologique et stratégies d'exploitation paléolithiques des silex bajociens du Haut-Quercy, France)

Laurent Bruxelles, Pierre Chalard, Richard Ciszak, Sylvain Ducasse et Patricia Guillermin

---

Summary

The authors present a geoarchaeological study of the geological formations containing silica-rich rocks in the Haut-Quercy region of France. The purpose is to better understand the prehistoric use and distribution of local flints, cherts and jaspers, and in particular to reconstruct the territories of Palaeolithic hunter-gatherer groups. A brief history of geological work related to archaeological questions in southwestern France and the development of the research project is presented. This is followed by the geographic and geological setting of the bedrock formations studied in the Causses de Quercy of the Haut-Quercy region. The authors discuss the need for more fieldwork on the flint-bearing outcrops of the Dogger series formations. The lack of geoarchaeological information is particularly noticeable when trying to understand the prehistoric use of the Quercy flint compared with the better known Bajocien flint from other regions. The fieldwork methods and preliminary results constitute the main body of the text. Field methods include: 1) geological reconnaissance to identify and map outcrops of flint using GPS and technical datasheets, 2) detailed geological mapping and construction of reference stratigraphic columns and, 3) compiling these data in a GIS database and the creation of digital elevation models. A synthesis of the geological stratigraphy of the formations making up the Dogger series is presented. A more detailed description of the Presque section is provided explaining the genesis of the flint and its geological setting. This is supported by figures of the stratigraphic sections and maps. Thirty new outcrops containing silicified members have been located and their distribution is described in relation to the geography of the region and their prehistoric accessibility. A specific example of the use of Bajocien flint during the Palaeolithic is given using the Upper Palaeolithic levels from the site of Les Fieux, Quercy. An analysis of the chaînes opératoires for each raw material, presented in graphic form, shows that Bajocien flint from Quercy is used extensively at the site but most tools produced were exported. This contrasts with the use of other local and non-local materials at the site.

Résumé

L'exemple du site des Fieux a montré que le silex bajocien a été abondamment utilisé sur les Causses du Quercy au cours de la Préhistoire. Pourtant, celui-ci, rarement observé en place, n'a fait l'objet que d'études succinctes. Récemment, nous avons repris l'étude de ces silicifications en couplant une approche de terrain (prospection, lever de coupes, inventaire des gîtes) et l'utilisation de SIG afin de confronter ces données à celles de la géologie, de la géomorphologie et de l'archéologie. Ce travail a notamment permis de mieux connaître les modalités d'exploitation de ces silex au cours de la Préhistoire.

Introduction

L'ampleur des territoires d'approvisionnement en silex des hommes préhistoriques peut être appréhendée, entre autres, au travers de la détermination des zones d'exploitation et de circulation de ce type de matériau. Ces dernières peuvent être perçues selon deux axes de recherche : la reconnaissance des indices archéologiques sur les gîtes de matières premières et la caractérisation pétroarchéologiques des séries lithiques mises au jour dans les gisements fouillés.

Les caractéristiques géologiques et géographiques du Haut Quercy confèrent à cette région un potentiel réel en gîtes à silex. Les recherches concernant des affleurements siliceux, dans une perspective d'étude archéologique, y ont débuté il y a plus d'une vingtaine d'années (Demars 1982). Elles se sont alors largement inspirées du travail incontournable de cartographie géologique effectué notamment par J.-G. Astruc (BRGM). Par la suite, la publication de M. et M.-R. Séronie-Vivien (Séronie-Vivien 1987) sur les silex du Mésozoïque nord aquitain, a constitué une avancée remarquable dans ce domaine de recherche. Les résultats présentés ont été repris et précisés dans des travaux ultérieurs de doctorat (Demars 1994; Turq 2000). Ces études ont permis d'identifier de nombreuses silicifications dont les plus connues sont appelées communément les chailles (cherts) du Dogger. À cet ensemble, qui regroupe en fait plusieurs types, il convient d'ajouter les silex jaspéroïdes situés sur la bordure liasique (Limargue) qui borde les premiers contreforts du Massif Central (Ségala) ainsi que les accidents siliceux tertiaires, sporadiques sur les causses mais abondants dans les petits bassins lacustres cénozoïques localisés dans la frange orientale du Haut-Quercy.

A la suite de ces travaux, d'autres prospections ont été engagées dans le cadre d'un projet collectif de recherches (1994–1999) ayant pour objectif principal l'élaboration d'une lithothèque en Midi-Pyrénées. Ces opérations ont ainsi largement contribué à la connaissance des ressources siliceuses disponibles dans cette région (Briois *et al.* 1999: Chalard *et al.* 1995). Ces investigations de terrain ont permis de mieux circonscrire les zones d'affleurements (*op. cit.*), sans toutefois offrir un degré de précision suffisant dans la caractérisation géologique et géographique de chacun des types de silicifications, s'agissant notamment de ceux du Haut Quercy. L'inventaire exhaustif des indices d'exploitations archéologiques des gîtes identifiés restait également à faire. De nouvelles investigations se sont donc avérées nécessaires (prospection thématique en 2006) afin d'améliorer la résolution des données disponibles sur les différents silex en présence et plus particulièrement les silicifications du Bajocien.

Contextes geographiques et geologiques du Haut Quercy

Le Haut Quercy correspond à l'ensemble des plateaux calcaires formant la bordure orientale du Bassin d'Aquitaine. Leur surface présente des morphologies karstiques caractéristiques : dolines, grottes, gouffres et réseaux de vallées sèches qui sillonnent la surface du plateau entre les buttes isolées. D'une altitude moyenne de 350 mètres, ils sont incisés par deux vallées principales : la Dordogne au nord, entre le Causse de Martel et le Causse de Gramat, et le Lot au sud, entre le Causse de Gramat et le Causse de Limogne (Fig. 1.1). La confluence des cours du Célé et du Lot isole le petit causse de Gréalou.

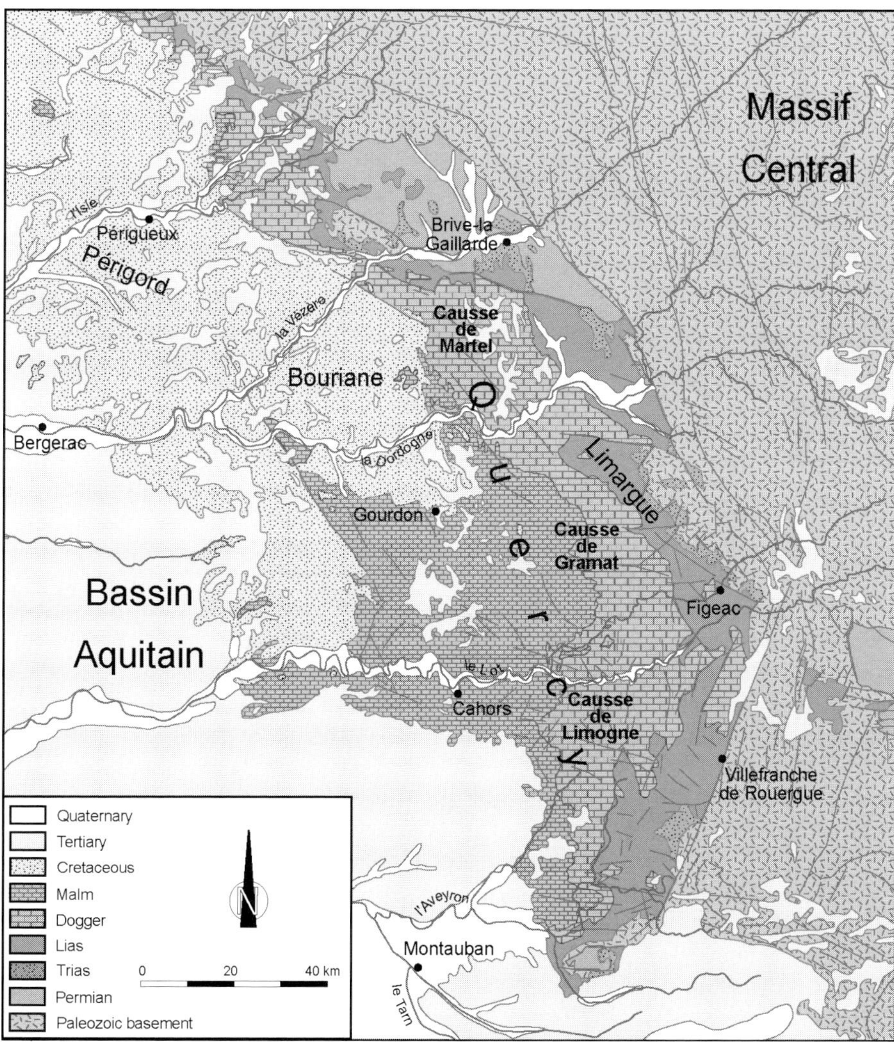

Figure 1.1. Simplified geology map of the Causses du Quercy (taken from the geology map of France, 1/1000000 scale produced by the BRGM). Carte géologique simplifiée des Causses du Quercy (d'après la carte géologique de la France au 1/1000000 du BRGM).

De part et d'autres des Causses du Quercy, deux régions naturelles contrastent avec les paysages caussenards : la Bouriane à l'ouest et le Limargue à l'est. La première est constituée de terrains argilo-sableux (crétacés et tertiaires) qui recouvrent le Jurassique et supportent une végétation à dominante silicicole (châtaigniers, pins). Le Limargue est une étroite bande de calcaires marno-argileux, aux sols profonds et aux paysages bocagers, coincée entre les ségalas sur roche cristallophyllienne et le causse calcaire.

Les terrains mésozoïques quercynois constituent la couverture du socle cristallin dans le secteur du Limargue, et de celui du Rouergue occidental avec lequel il est en contact par la faille de Villefranche-de-Rouergue, à l'est du Causse de Limogne (Fig. 1.1). Ils constituent ainsi une ceinture arquée, concave vers l'ouest. Du fait de la structure globalement monoclinale, l'ensemble carbonaté s'ennoie vers l'ouest sous les formations crétacées du Périgord, puis tertiaires du Bassin d'Aquitaine. Le Dogger, qui comprend les calcaires bajociens étudiés ici, affleure sous forme d'une bande orientée NO-SE localisée dans la partie orientale du causse, entre le Lias et le Malm. Ces formations constituent souvent les contreforts du plateau caussenard.

Au point de vue géologique, les nombreux travaux effectués depuis 1830, se sont attachés à décrire avec précision la série stratigraphique du Dogger en Haut Quercy. Néanmoins, la présence de silex, rarement observés en coupe, n'a fait l'objet que d'études succinctes. Dans l'Aaléno-Bajocien par exemple, la seule coupe dans laquelle la présence de silex a été relevée est celle de la Poujade (Guillot *et al.* 1992; Lezin 2000). Ce sont des silex que l'on retrouve dans des calcaires massifs, plus ou moins dolomitisés et recristalisés, situés dans la partie supérieure de l'Aalénien.

Utilisation des silex quercinois au cours de la Prehistoire Ancienne

Les publications des travaux effectués dans des gisements préhistoriques quercinois ont démontré l'utilisation, à des degrés divers, de différents matériaux locaux durant le Paléolithique, comme dans les abris du Cuzoul de Vers (Chalard *et al.* à paraître a et b, Ducasse 2003, Lelouvier 1996), des Peyrugues (Allard *et al.* 2005), dans les grottes des Fieux (Chalard *et al.* 2006: Faivre 2004 et à paraître: Guillermin 2004) ou de Pégourié (Séronie-Vivien dir. 1995), ainsi que dans les gisements de Coudoulous (Jaubert *et al.* 2005) ou d'Espagnac (Jaubert dir. 2001). L'utilisation de ces différentes ressources s'est poursuivie à l'Epipaléolithique (Valdeyron *et al.* 1998) et au Mésolithique (Chalard and Briois 2002; Chalard and Servelle 2003; Chalard *et al.* 2002). L'abondance de ces études ne doit pas cacher un manque de précision dans notre connaissance des silex autochtones qui font l'objet d'un renouveau d'intérêt dans la recherche actuelle et dont l'analyse précise permettra d'en distinguer les différents types au premier rang desquels on peut placer le silex du Bajocien. Les publications concernant l'utilisation de silex quercinois au cours de la préhistoire, insistaient principalement sur les chailles du Dogger (étage Bajocien principalement) dont les gîtes semblaient les plus abondants, mais aucune coupe stratigraphique précise de Bajocien contenant des silicifications n'avait été présentée et étudiée.

La prospection thematique : principes methodologiques et premiers resultats

Afin d'apprécier au plus près l'extension géographique maximale des silicifications, notamment celles présentes dans le Bajocien, et donc d'évaluer les possibilités d'approvisionnement en silex offertes aux hommes préhistoriques au cours du Pléistocène et au début de l'Holocène, il est indispensable de connaître très précisément les contextes géologiques de formation des silex (genèse), les conditions d'affleurement ainsi que leur évolution au cours du temps (aspects géomorphologiques). De plus, l'analyse pétrographique fine des échantillons géologiques constitue également une priorité pour améliorer le degré de précision des études pétroarchéologiques. Plusieurs approches complémentaires sont menées dans le cadre de notre prospection thématique pour atteindre ces différents objectifs. La première étape concerne un important travail d'acquisition des données géologiques et archéologiques comprenant les points suivants :

- une prospection pédestre systématique des affleurements aaléno-bajociens aboutissant à la réalisation d'un inventaire le plus exhaustif possible des gîtes à silex. Ce travail de terrain concerne notamment l'identification des affleurements calcaires, la cartographie des formations superficielles contenant des silex et la détection des vestiges archéologiques. Chaque point est relevé au GPS et des fiches d'inventaires ont été établies méthodiquement ;
- dans le même temps, des coupes stratigraphiques de référence sont levées avec pour objectif la définition précise de la localisation des silex dans la série lithologique et l'établissement des corrélations entre les différents affleurements siliceux. Au besoin, des déterminations micropaléontologiques seront réalisées sur lame mince ;
- Au fur et à mesure du levé de terrain, les informations recueillies sont saisies dans une base de données et intégrées dans un système d'information géographique (SIG). Les résultats issus des travaux précédents ont également été pris en compte.

L'intégration des données dans un SIG nous a permis d'établir un premier modèle prospectif. Il contribue notamment à orienter nos recherches vers d'autres gîtes et d'éventuels sites archéologiques (indices de débitage épars ou véritables ateliers de taille). Le repérage précis des différents niveaux de silicifications au sein de la série stratigraphique permet, à partir des points déjà connus, de positionner les affleurements de silex par rapport à la cartographie des calcaires bajociens. Il deviendra donc possible, en fonction de la structure géologique et de la morphologie, de repérer assez précisément les secteurs où l'on est susceptibles de trouver des silex en surface. Le report de l'ensemble de ces informations sur les cartes topographiques ou sur les Modèles Numériques de Terrain constitue un outil prédictif pertinent qui guide efficacement nos prospections (Fig. 1.2).

Stratigraphie synthétique des formations du Dogger

Tout le long de la bordure orientale du Quercy, le Dogger forme la base d'une corniche plus ou moins importante. Elle repose sur les marnes toarciennes du Jurassique moyen (Fig. 1.3). Depuis la base vers le sommet, on distingue les formations suivantes (observations personnelles et T. Pélissié 1982) :

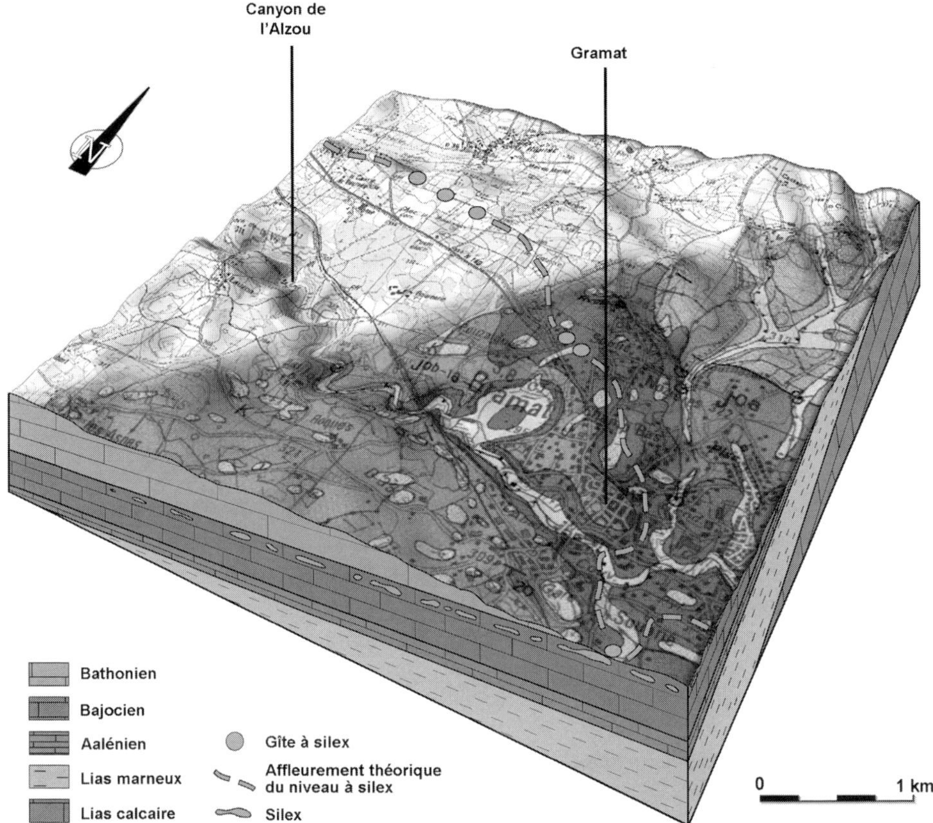

Figure 1.2. 3D model and geologic section which allows us to predict the location of flint outcrops according to geologic structure and landscape morphology. Exemple de bloc 3D permettant d'associer les données altitudinales, morphologiques, géologiques et structurales. Outre une bonne visualisation du secteur étudié, cette approche permet également de définir plus précisément les secteurs à prospecter.

- les "Calcaires marneux à oncolithes" (60m) rapportés à l'Aalénien, sont tronqués par une discontinuité sédimentaire régionale. Cette formation géologique, quelquefois soumise à la karstification, est le siège de nombreuses pertes au contact entre le Limargue et le causse. Elle constitue la base, souvent boisée, des principales corniches du Causse ;
- des calcaires massifs à oolithes admettant vers le sommet plus ou moins dolomitisé de nombreuses chailles (Formation d'Autoire, Delfaud 1970) d'âge bajocien. Ils sont suivis par des calcaires massifs à grain fin, à intercalations marneuses voire ligniteuses, vers le sommet (Formation de Cajarc) rapportés au Bathonien inférieur. Cet ensemble (30 à 150m) est largement karstifié ;
- une puissante assise calcaire (80m) à faciès variés (à grain fin, argileux ou à oolithes), en partie bréchique, ou/et dolomitisés, constitue le Bathonien supérieur. Elle est couronnée par une discontinuité sédimentaire majeure, marquée à l'échelle régionale ;

- des calcaires massifs ("Formation de Rocamadour") qui occupent l'intervalle Bathonien terminal-Callovien (80m). Le célèbre sanctuaire de Rocamadour est bâti sur les calcaires attribués encore au Bathonien, alors que la corniche supérieure sur laquelle repose le château est déjà callovienne. C'est aussi dans cette formation que s'expriment les plus belles morphologies de canyons des cours de l'Alzou et de l'Ouysse.

La coupe de Presque (Saint-Jean-Lagineste) : éléments de précision stratigraphique sur les silicifications bajociennes

Située à quelques kilomètres au sud de Saint-Céré, la coupe recoupe la formation d'Autoire. Elle est datée de l'Aalénien inférieur par l'ammonite *Leioceras opalinum* pour sa base et rapportée au Bajocien pour sa partie supérieure (Cubaynes *et al.* 1989a et b), souvent dolomitique, sur la foi de la présence de foraminifères (*Protopeneroplis striata* Weynshenk).

On distingue successivement (Fig. 1.3) :

- à la base, le membre des "calcaires à oncolithes de la Toulzanie" (Pélissié 1982), dans laquelle s'ouvre la grotte de Presque, correspond à une succession de calcaires marneux bioclastiques, riches en oncolithes ovoïdes millimétriques. Cet ensemble s'achève par un fond durci représenté par une croûte ferrugineuse matérialisant une discontinuité régionale (D10) ;
- le membre des "calcaires oolithiques dolomitisés de Calvignac" (35m) (Pélissié 1982). Il s'agit essentiellement de calcaires grainstones à larges structures obliques, qui renferment dans leur partie sommitale des niveaux à gros oncolithes centimétriques, irréguliers, bien représentés près du village de Calvignac. Sur cette coupe, la partie supérieure de ce membre (15m) admet des passées dolomitiques souvent rubéfiées et riches en accidents siliceux (Fig. 1.4).

  Cet ensemble est couronné par la discontinuité régionale D11 correspondant à une surface de réactivation ;
- la coupe s'achève par le membre des "Dolomies bréchiques du Pech Affamat", ici représentée par des calcaires micritiques à pseudomorphoses de gypse.

Le milieu de dépôt correspond à un complexe de dunes oolithiques inter à subtidales passant vers le haut à un milieu intertidal à supratidal avec des tendances à l'émersion de la plate-forme.

Ainsi, on rapporte :

- en milieu intertidal les niveaux dolomitiques rubéfiés et les dolomies à oncolites ;
- en milieu inter à supratidal, les grainstones à pellets constituant des levées entre lesquelles s'insinuent des chenaux de marées (grainstones à petites oolithes et laminations obliques) ;
- en milieu supratidal les dolomies bréchiques ou cargneulisées témoignant de faciès évaporitiques.

Par ailleurs, la présence de niveaux décimétriques très rubéfiés indique la présence d'hématite libérée par l'altération d'une zone émergée proche.

Les chailles siliceuses ou les rognons de silex sont concentrées dans les dépôts intertidaux à supratidaux, au sein des dolomies rubéfiées. De teintes grise à blanchâtre,

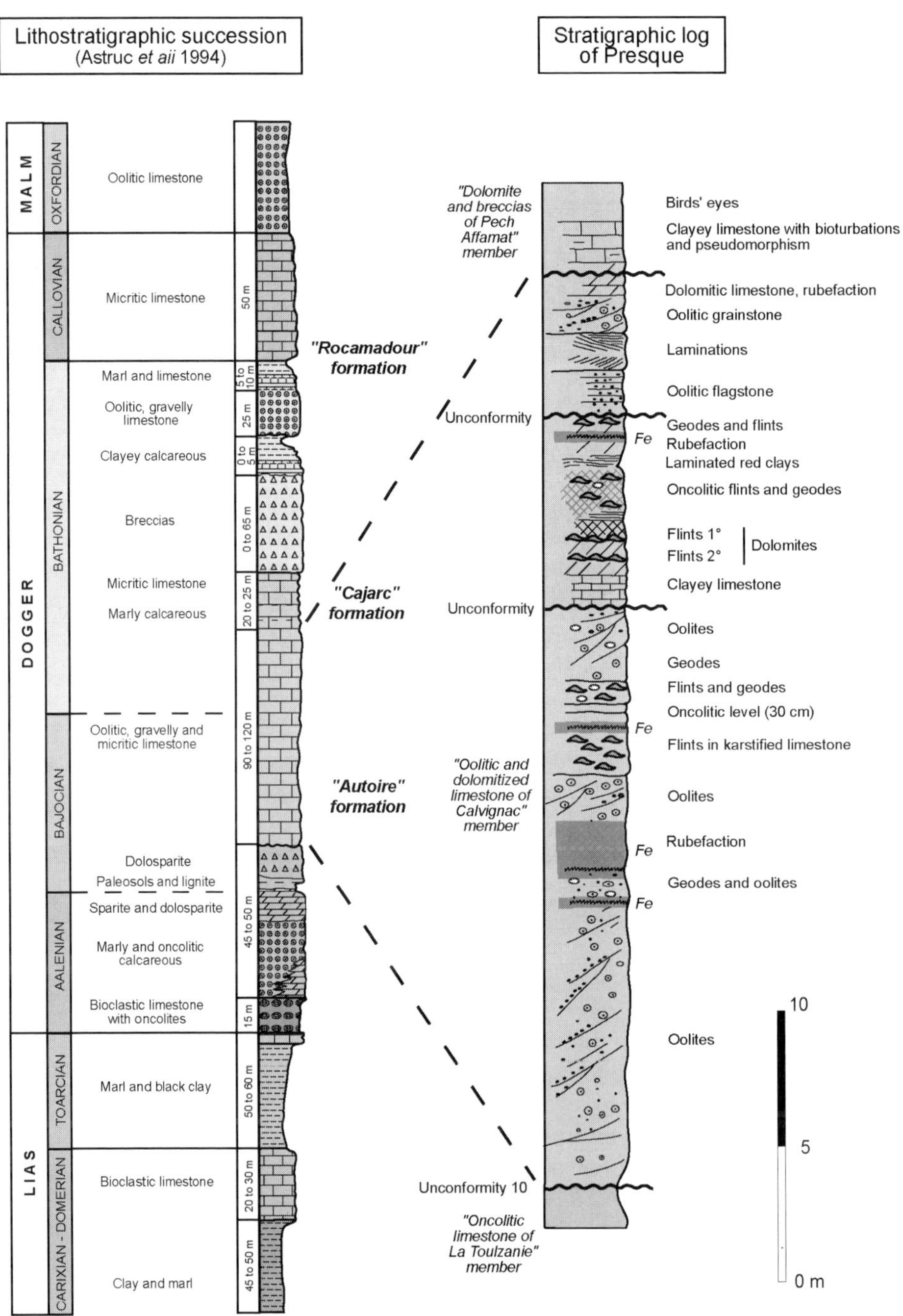

Figure 1.3 a) left – Stratigraphic log of the Dogger series, Causses du Quercy (from Astruc et al. *1994) and b) right – detailed stratigraphic log of the Presque section (Causse de Gramat). a) gauche – Log stratigraphique synthétique du Dogger dans les Causses du Quercy (d'après Astruc* et al. *1994) et b) droite – Log stratigraphique détaillé relevé le long de la coupe de Presque (Causse de Gramat).*

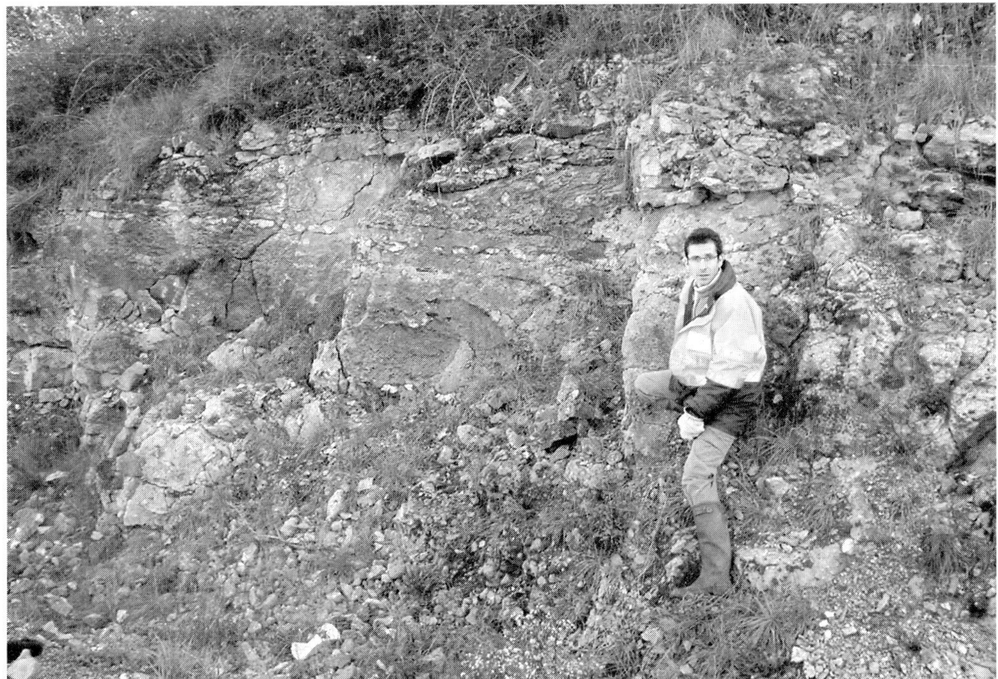

Figure 1.4. Several flint-bearing layers visible in the Presque section, western part of the Causse de Gramat. Vue d'une partie de la coupe de Presque. Derrière le personnage, plusieurs niveaux de silicification sont visibles.

les rognons de silex centimétriques à pluri-décimétriques renferment pour certains de nombreuses oncolithes centimétriques. Leur origine est vraisemblablement due à une remobilisation diagénétique de la silice, contenue dans les structures sédimentaires de bioturbation, en milieu tidal.

Répartition des gîtes à silex bajociens dans le Quercy : état de la question

Ce travail de recherche est en cours et nous sommes encore loin d'avoir prospecté l'ensemble des causses du Quercy. Mais la découverte de plus d'une trentaine de nouveaux gîtes à silex permet, avec l'appoint des résultats des travaux antérieurs, de donner une première vue d'ensemble de la répartition des zones à silex dans le secteur étudié. Ainsi, les silicifications sont abondantes sur la bordure orientale du Causse de Martel et au NE du Causse de Gramat. Néanmoins, dans le détail, elles ne sont pas réparties de manière uniforme. Elle sont par exemple absentes dans la reculée d'Autoire alors que plusieurs niveaux de silex bajociens superposés (cf. supra) ont été observés dans les mêmes niveaux recoupés par la reculée de Presque, à moins de deux kilomètres de là. En direction du sud, les silex deviennent de plus en plus rares et ont semble-t-il disparu à partir de Thémines. Le gîte que nous avons observé en coupe dans la vallée du Célé à Corn (d'après communication orale de T. Salgues), devra faire l'objet d'une étude plus poussée pour déterminer sa localisation précise dans la séquence du Dogger.

Sur le Causse de Limogne, entre Figeac et Villefranche-de-Rouergue, l'observation de plusieurs coupes couvrant tout le Bajocien tend à montrer qu'il n'y a quasiment pas de silicifications bajociennes dans tout ce secteur. Mais l'existence de silicifications signalée dans les environs de Cajarc (Turq 2000), demandera également des investigations complémentaires pour être catégorique.

Si l'essentiel des affleurements de Bajocien est contingenté à la partie orientale des causses, suivant une orientation nord-sud conforme à la structure du Quercy, quelques anticlinaux associés aux failles majeures font affleurer le Bajocien un peu plus à l'intérieur des plateaux. Ainsi, à l'ouest de Gramat, le canyon de l'Alzou recoupe toute la série bajocienne. L'examen détaillé des affleurements nous a permis de retrouver un seul petit niveau discontinu de silex. Pourtant, à quelques kilomètres à peine plus à l'est, les silicifications sont nombreuses, disposées en plusieurs lits plus ou moins massifs.

Ces différentes observations mettent en évidence la grande variabilité dans la répartition des silicifications. Seule une prospection ciblée et détaillée peut permettre de réaliser un inventaire exhaustif de ces gîtes à silex. Ces investigations de terrain offriront la possibilité de détecter les indices d'exploitation préhistoriques sur les affleurements siliceux, exploitation confirmée par le biais de nombreuses études pétroarchéologiques dont celles effectuées sur les séries en silex provenant du gisement quercinois emblématique des Fieux.

Exemple d'exploitation du silex Bajocien au Paléolithique supérieur : la couche E des Fieux (Lot, France)

Ainsi, l'inventaire en Quercy et sur ces marges, des gisements archéologiques contenant des industries en silex bajociens, donne des indications précieuses sur les modalités d'exploitation de ces silicifications au cours de la Préhistoire. Plusieurs sites moustériens de plein air ont été localisés sur les gîtes de silex Bajocien (Demars 1982; 1994; Turq 2000). Ce matériau utilisé fréquemment au Paléolithique moyen, se retrouve également dans des gisements de la fin du Pléistocène. Ainsi, de récentes études sur le gisement des Fieux, ont démontré que le silex Bajocien, loin d'être un matériau délaissé, a été abondamment utilisé au Gravettien. Ce site, situé au nord du Causse de Gramat, se présente sous la forme d'une galerie karstique effondrée. Les niveaux archéologiques qu'il renferme, concernent une fourchette chronologique très large (du Paléolithique moyen à l'époque médiévale). Le Paléolithique supérieur y est avant tout marqué par des niveaux aurignaciens et gravettiens. En ce qui concerne la couche E, attribuable à un Gravettien « moyen/récent » (Guillermin 2004; 2006), la détermination des principales sources d'approvisionnement en matières premières siliceuses (Chalard *et al.* 2006), témoigne, grâce à sa mise en perspective techno-économique, de l'anticipation et de l'adaptation des chasseurs-cueilleurs gravettiens à un environnement visiblement bien connu. Alors que les matières premières allochtones (Sénonien *sensu lato*), polyvalentes dans leurs objectifs (armatures et outils domestiques), arrivent sur le gisement sous des formes variées, du bloc précortical à l'outil, l'exploitation du silex bajocien trouve son intérêt dans la reconstitution d'un « stock de voyage ». Le débitage laminaire effectué dans ce matériau permet la production de supports relativement robustes, dont certains, par leur régularité et leur rectitude, sont des candidats potentiels pour la confection de pointes de la Gravette. Si le silex bajocien est la matière première la plus représentée au sein des éléments bruts, il est par contre très peu présent dans l'outillage et quasiment

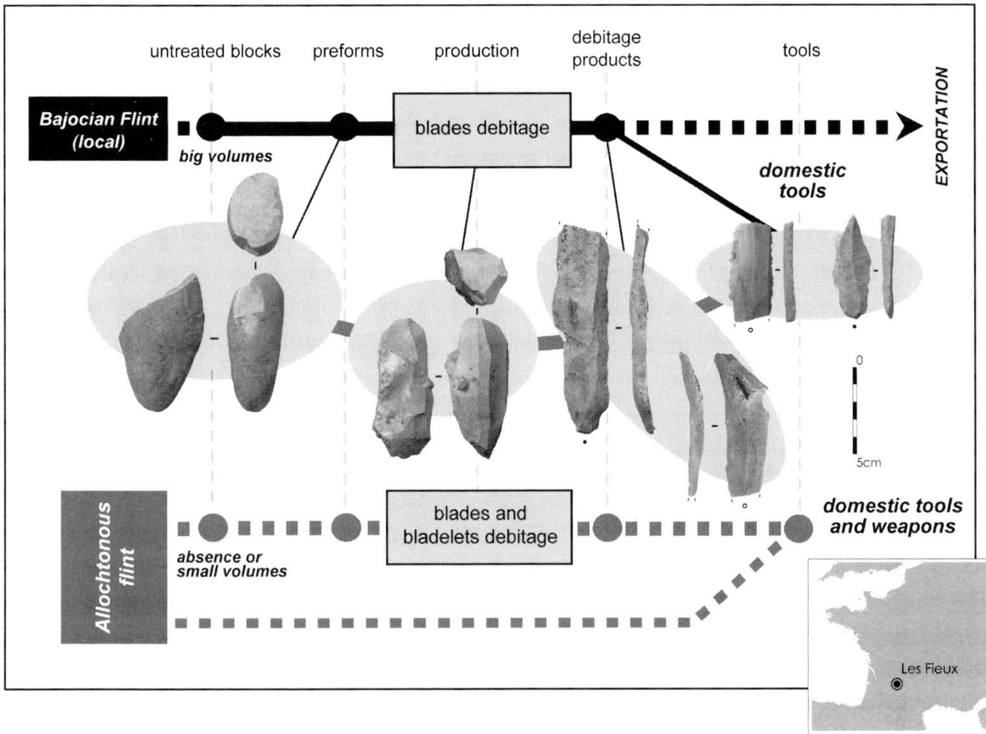

Figure 1.5. Chaîne opératoire reconstructed for the archaeological site of Les Fieux (Miers). Chaîne opératoire des Fieux (Miers)

absent des armatures. Seuls quelques outils à usage domestique, réalisés à partir de sous produits, témoignent de la transformation et de l'utilisation sur place de ce matériau. Il semble donc que la majeure partie de la production soit absente. Le fractionnement de la chaîne opératoire illustre le statut particulier du silex bajocien voué en grande partie à l'exportation (Fig. 1.5).

Conclusion

Ces premiers résultats mettent en exergue la pertinence d'une étude détaillée des silicifications bajociennes du Quercy. Les prospections systématiques de certains secteurs ont conduit à la découverte de nombreux gîtes à silex inédits. En parallèle, l'étude détaillée des coupes stratigraphiques contenant ces silicifications nous a permis de mieux connaître leur position au sein des séquences, mais aussi de définir les paléoenvironnements concourant à leur formation. Par exemple, l'association de ces silicifications avec des niveaux dolomitiques rubéfiés constitue un guide précieux lors des prospections. Il suffit alors de repérer ces dolomies dans les affleurements de Bajocien pour y trouver des accidents siliceux (Fig. 1.6).

Figure 1.6. In the Carennac quarry (Causse de Martel), reddish dolomitic levels help us to find several unknown flint-bearing layers. Dans une carrière de Carennac (Causse de Martel), la présence de niveaux dolomitiques rubéfiés nous a permis de repérer plusieurs niveaux de silex jusque-là inconnus.

L'intégration de ces données dans un système d'information géographique permet en outre de définir avec précision la localisation des secteurs à explorer. Il s'avère alors un outil prédictif avec lequel, par extrapolation des résultats de nos observations, il est possible de localiser ou de suivre les niveaux à silex.

Les implications en terme de recherche archéologique et plus spécifiquement dans le domaine de la caractérisation des silex locaux du Quercy sont également importantes. La localisation géologique et géographique précise contribue à mieux cerner l'étendue des territoires d'approvisionnement des groupes de chasseurs-cueilleurs. L'étude gîtologique (accessibilité, abondance et volume des rognons en présence) ainsi que l'analyse des caractères intrinsèques des silex du Bajocien (taillabilité, structure, fonds micropaléontologique..) ont d'ores et déjà apportés des renseignements précieux. Notre regard sur la richesse des gîtes découverts et le potentiel réel d'exploitation de ces matériaux a bien évidemment évolué. Les recherches devront se poursuivre et seront étendues aux affleurements siliceux du Bathonien et aux silicifications jaspéroïdes de l'Infralias.

Remerciements/Acknowledgments

Une partie des missions de prospection de l'un d'entre nous (L. B.) ont été réalisées dans le cadre de l'ACR Quercy dirigée par Marc Jarry (INRAP).

2 Chalosse-type Flint: Exploitation and Distribution of a Lithologic Tracer during the Upper Paleolithic, Southern France

Diffusion et exploitation d'un traceur lithologique au cours du Paléolithique supérieur dans le sud de la France : l'exemple du type Chalosse

Pierre Chalard, Sylvain Ducasse, François Bon, Laurent Bruxelles, Nicolas Teyssandier, Caroline Renard, Philippe Gardere, Patricia Guillermin, Sébastien Lacombe, Mathieu Langlais, Romain Mensan, Christian Normand, Robert Simonnet and Andoni Tarriño

---

Summary

The authors propose a petroarchaeological approach to understanding the exploitation of the environment and its resources by prehistoric groups. Petroarchaeology broadly defined includes the geological field study of formations containing lithic raw materials; the characterisation of these lithic materials and the study of their circulation. Most of the silica-rich rocks found within the Aquitainian basin were exploited during the Upper Palaeolithic. Some of these are well known, especially the Bergeracois flint from western Perigord which contains the fossil Orbitoides media. *This flint is often used as a 'tracer' to study the circulation of lithic raw materials in the Upper Palaeolithic of southwest France. Recent work in the Pyrenean Piedmont has identified several other flint sources that offer similar potential as 'tracers'. This article focuses on the flint-bearing formations of the Chalosse region that contain the fossil* Lepidorbitoides *sp. The authors provide a brief overview of the archaeological and geoarchaeological work done in the region of La Chalosse. Four main geological areas contain flints and were targeted: the Tercis, Saint-Lon-les-Mines and Audignon anticlines, and the Bastennes-Gaujacq dome-diapir. Geological maps for the region, outcrop photos and thin section images of fossil species are provided. Archaeological research demonstrates that the Maastrichtian age silicified members of the Chalosse region were clearly used throughout the Upper Palaeolithic. A preliminary survey of archaeological sites from the Aquitainian-Pyrenean region that have produced the Chalosse* Lepidorbitoides *sp. type flint is presented and mapped. The Chalosse flints are shown to travel over considerable distances along the Pyrenean Piedmont and northeast to the Aquitainian basin. In order to study the technological use of the Chalosse flint, the Solutrean-Badegoulian lithic assemblage from the Abri du Cozoul de Vers in the Quercy region was analysed. The chaîne opératoire of the Chalosse flint is diversified, and differs from that of other non-local flints which together make up a small proportion of the lithic assemblage (10%–15%). According to the authors, more geological fieldwork is needed and the fossil markers for Chalosse flint needs to be more precisely defined; however, the Chalosse* Lepidorbitoides *sp. type flint already shows great promise as a 'tracer' for understanding prehistoric group mobility, territory and interaction.*

Résumé

En France, l'exemple des silex Maastrichtiens à Lepidorbitoïdes *sp. provenant de Chalosse permet d'aborder la question de la circulation des matières premières siliceuses au cours du Paléolithique supérieur. En effet, en tant que « traceurs » lithologiques, ces derniers permettent, associées à la caractérisation géologique et géographique ainsi qu'à l'analyse technologique de l'ensemble des matériaux composant les industries, d'acquérir l'image, certes partielle, du territoire d'un groupe. Par leur large diffusion, ces matériaux semblent avoir joué un rôle constant pendant toute la durée du Paléolithique supérieur. Leur exploitation au Badegoulien récent (*c. *18.500 BP) n'en est qu'un exemple, le statut de cette zone d'approvisionnement ayant du varier avec le temps.*

Presentation

La compréhension des modalités d'exploitation de l'environnement mises en œuvre par les hommes préhistoriques constitue l'une des problématiques privilégiées par l'archéologie d'aujourd'hui. Parmi les différentes disciplines qui participent à cette appréhension globale de l'espace investi au cours de la préhistoire, la pétroarchéologie, dans son acception large (gîtologie, caractérisation des matières premières, notion de circulation des matériaux), s'avère une approche fondamentale dans la définition des territoires d'approvisionnement. Le degré de précision auquel l'archéologue peut prétendre dans sa quête d'une appréciation pertinente des espaces parcourus par les groupes de chasseurs-cueilleurs, est conditionné par deux facteurs déterminants : une excellente connaissance du potentiel gîtologique de la région (au sens large) concernée par son étude mais aussi l'identification de matériaux aux qualités intrinsèques spécifiques, permettant de les isoler dans les séries archéologiques mises au jour au sein de gisements, parfois éloignés de plusieurs centaines de kilomètres des points de prélèvements. Pour les pétroarchéologues, ces matières premières particulières sont considérées comme de véritables traceurs. Elles témoignent, en effet, de la circulation de biens entre deux lieux – les gîtes et les sites archéologiques – dont l'emprise géographique est bien circonscrite.

Au sein du Bassin aquitain, la plupart des ressources siliceuses exploitables a été utilisée au cours du Paléolithique supérieur. Parmi ces différents matériaux, des silex aux qualités remarquables ont retenu l'attention des archéologues. En effet, leur aspect, leur texture, mais surtout leur contenu micropaléontologique, confèrent à ce type de matière première le statut de traceur lithologique. L'exemple des silicifications du Maastrichtien est de ce point de vue emblématique (Fig. 2.1). Pour nombre d'archéologues, le silex du Bergeracois (ouest du Périgord), souvent identifié par la présence d'*Orbitoides media* (Séronie-Vivien

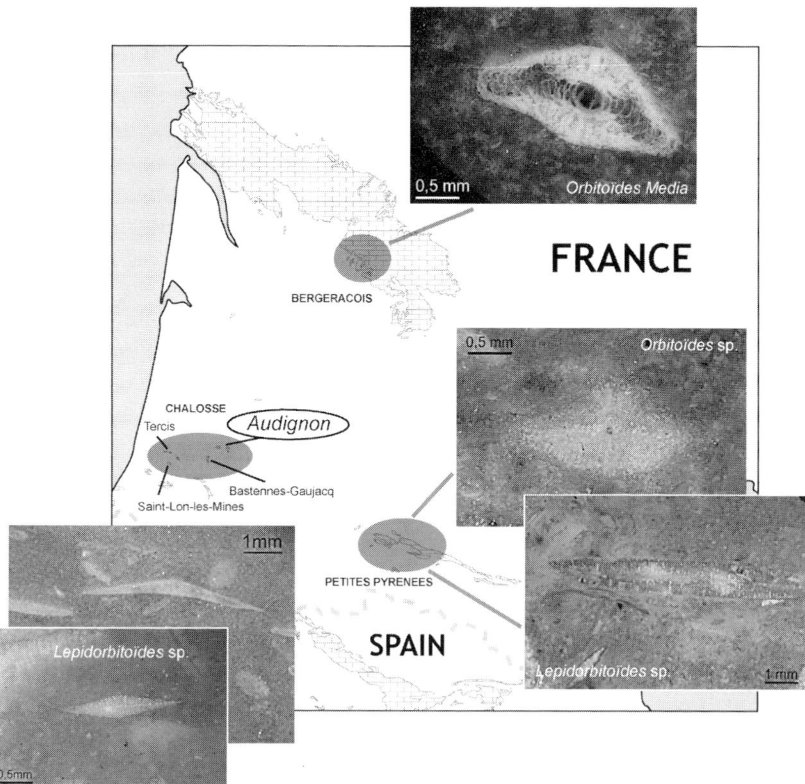

Figure 2.1. (upper) The silicified members of the Maastrichtian in the Aquitain Basin and Pyrenean piedmont with their micropaleontological characteristics. Les silicifications maastrichtiennes du Bassin Aquitain et du piémont pyrénéen et leur cortège micropaléontologique.

1987, 76; Turq 2000, 134), a été considéré comme le « traceur » par excellence ayant été transporté sur des distances parfois importantes (Pyrénées centrales, Quercy, Languedoc). Les études menées dans les Petites Pyrénées (travaux de R. Simonnet sur les types « Paillon » et « Montsaunès » : Simonnet 2002; 1998; 1981), en Chalosse (Bon *et al.* 1996; Normand 1986) et la découverte, en Quercy, de silex provenant du piémont pyrénéen au sens large, publié pour la première fois par M.-R. Séronie-Vivien (Séronie-Vivien *et al.* 1995; 53, 61, 199), sont venus démontrer l'existence d'une dynamique de circulation comparable. En effet, les silex à *Lepidorbitoides* sp. et *Orbitoides* sp. des Pyrénées centrales, et plus encore, ceux à *Lepidorbitoides* sp., caractéristiques de gîtes localisés dans certains anticlinaux de la Chalosse, devraient attirer l'attention des spécialistes. Les caractères distinctifs associés (coloration, texture et fonds micropaléontologiques) de ces matériaux, permettent également de les ranger parmi les traceurs lithologiques du Bassin aquitain. Il en est ainsi du type Chalosse à *Lepidorbitoides* sp., dont la reconnaissance dans les industries lithiques apporte des informations capitales sur la circulation des silex au Paléolithique supérieur.

La présente contribution s'inscrit dans une recherche à long terme sur cette matière première particulière. Elle prend en compte l'ensemble de l'étude d'un traceur lithologique, de la prospection des affleurements siliceux jusqu'à l'identification des silex prélevés par les artisans tailleurs qui les ont débités, transportés sur de longs parcours, et/ou échangés avec d'autres groupes ayant circulé dans des régions parfois très éloignées de la Chalosse. Il s'agit de présenter un premier bilan synthétique des résultats de nos recherches dans la perspective d'un développement plus systématique d'approches méthodologiques complémentaires (analyses micropaléontologiques et géochimiques) mais aussi thématiques relatives à l'étude des territoires d'exploitation. Par exemple, la mise en évidence des traceurs lithologiques nord-aquitains a permis de démontrer des circulations du Nord vers le Sud au cours du Paléolithique supérieur. Il est tout aussi important d'aboutir à une meilleure caractérisation de silex spécifiques pyrénéens afin d'étayer des hypothèses de diffusion de matières premières du Sud vers le Nord mais également en direction de la Corniche cantabrique.

La Chalosse : potentiel gitologique et indices archeologiques

Dans l'espace géographique qui intéresse notre étude (Fig. 2.1), quatre zones gîtologiques principales ont été identifiées : les anticlinaux de Tercis, de Saint-Lon-les-Mines, d'Audignon et le dôme-diapir de Bastennes-Gaujacq (Bon *et al.* 1996; Normand 1986). Les deux derniers contextes cités recèlent des silex présentant un cortège fossilifère caractéristique du Maastrichtien (Capdeville *et al.* 1997). En l'état actuel des recherches, seuls l'anticlinal d'Audignon et le Diapir de Bastennes-Gaujacq semblent contenir des silicifications dont les caractères micropaléontologiques permettent de les distinguer des autres silex du Maatrichtien du Bassin aquitain : absence d'*Orbitoides media* ; association de *Lepidorbitoides* sp., de *Siderolite* sp. et de *Clypeorbis mamillata*.

Des travaux anciens ont très tôt, dès la fin du XIXème et le début du XXème siècle, mis en évidence l'importance de la Chalosse en termes de potentiel pour l'archéologie paléolithique (voir notamment les travaux de Daguin, Dubalen et Mascaraux.). Mais il faut attendre le début des années 1970 et le magistral travail de synthèse de Claude Thibault (1970) pour que la richesse archéologique de cette région prenne toute sa dimension dans son cadre régional. Par la suite, au cours des vingt dernières années, on peut en particulier signaler les fouilles entreprises par Christian Normand dans le secteur de Tercis (Normand 1986; 1987; 1992–1993), celles de Jean-Claude Merlet à Benesse-les-Dax (Merlet 1992–1993) ou encore, en association avec Bernard Gellibert, sur le gisement Badegoulien de Cabannes à Brocas-les-Forges (Gellibert *et al.* 2001). Dans le même temps, on doit à de nombreux amateurs d'avoir complété la carte archéologique de la région et l'on peut notamment faire référence aux prospections menées par Michel Marsan et son équipe qui ont conduit à la découverte du site de Garet (Serreslous-et-Arribans), recelant en particulier une industrie attribuable à l'Aurignacien ancien (Klaric 1999). Il ne faut par ailleurs pas oublier que parallèlement, se poursuivaient les fouilles du site de référence pour le Paléolithique supérieur régional dans les grottes de Brassempouy, d'abord sous la direction d'Henri Delporte puis Dominique Buisson et enfin Dominique Henry-Gambier et François Bon (Buisson 1996; Bon *et al.* 1998; Henry-Gambier *et al.* 2004).

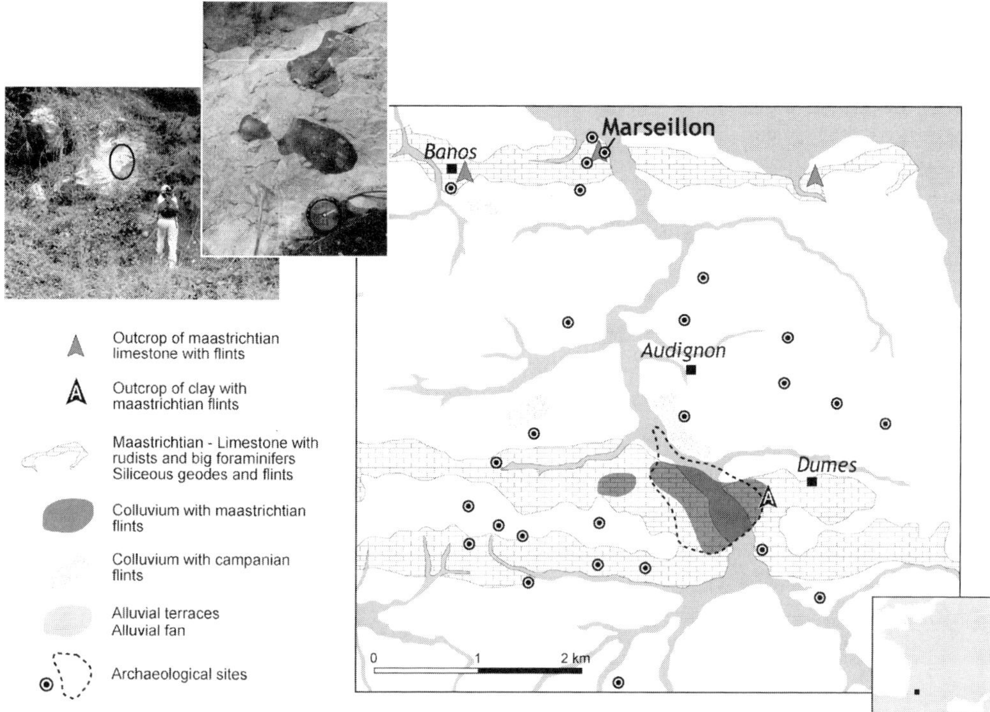

Figure 2.2. (lower) Location of the open air site of Marseillon (Proto-Solutrean) within the Audignon anticline (Chalosse). Localisation du site de plein air de Marseillon (Proto-Solutréen) au sein de l'anticlinal d'Audignon (Chalosse).

Parallèlement à ces travaux de fouilles archéologiques et à l'instar des recherches entreprises dans cette direction dans d'autres régions du sud-ouest de la France, des études se sont développées sur la localisation et la caractérisation des ressources minérales de Chalosse et plus particulièrement dans l'anticlinal d'Audignon. Des prospections initiées par C. Normand au cours des années 1980 puis par Dominique Buisson à partir de 1993, ont été poursuivies par F. Bon et de son équipe et enfin N. Teyssandier et ses collaborateurs. Ces investigations de terrain ont eu deux objectifs principaux : définir précisément la répartition des silicifications et leurs caractéristiques pétrographiques, et cartographier, par ailleurs, les gisements archéologiques tout en essayant d'en déterminer la chronologie. La possibilité d'observer dans les gîtes de Chalosse, constitués essentiellement d'argiles à silex, des rognons en place dans les calcaires, est demeurée très ponctuelle. Les travaux effectués depuis de nombreuses années au sein des affleurements de ce type de formations superficielles, ont révélé de très nombreux ateliers de taille associés à des gîtes à silex particulièrement abondants. Des découvertes récentes effectuées dans la vallée du Laudon viennent apporter des données inédites sur l'occupation de la Chalosse (Teyssandier *et al.* 2006). En effet, sur le site de plein air de Marseillon (Fig. 2.2), dans les Landes, une industrie lithique aux caractéristiques particulières a retenu l'attention des découvreurs. Parmi les 95 outils décomptés, se trouvent 18 éléments, éclats allongés le plus souvent, de morphologie triangulaire. Les aménagement affectant leurs parties proximales et les retouches ou endommagement latéraux identifiés sur une partie d'entre eux, permettent de considérer ces pièces comme des pointes de Vale Comprido (*op. cit.* 108; Zilhao and Aubry 1995). Si l'on prend en compte, par ailleurs, la présence d'un débitage à la percussion directe dure, de lames et de pointes, à partir de nucléus à lame sur face large et la découverte de deux fragments de pointes à face plane, l'attribution chronologique de cette série de surface se précise un peu plus. Il s'agit vraisemblablement d'un gisement du Proto-Solutréen (*op. cit.* 112), ce dernier venant combler une lacune chronologique au sein d'un vaste ensemble de stations de plein air dans l'anticlinal d'Audignon, comprenant des indices principalement aurignaciens et gravettiens. Ce nouveau jalon témoigne de la fréquentation régulière des gîtes à silex de Chalosse tout au long du Paléolithique supérieur. L'importance des silicifications maestrichtiennes chalossaises dans les stratégies d'exploitations des territoires par les chasseurs-cueilleurs, devait trouver un écho bien au-delà des Pyrénées occidentales. L'intensification des travaux sur les matières premières allochtones mises au jour dans des sites du Paléolithique supérieur du Bassin aquitain, voire de régions plus éloignées, vient confirmer cette hypothèse.

Diffusion et exploitation des silex a *lepidorbitoides* sp.

Diffusion

Les silex de Chalosse, et notamment les échantillons contenant les microfossiles du type *Lepidorbitoides* sp., ont, probablement grâce à leur grande aptitude à la taille, été largement exploités et diffusés au sein de l'aire Aquitano-pyrénéenne et de secteurs limitrophes. Il est dès lors possible de présenter un premier bilan des régions qui recèlent des gisements ayant livré ce type de traceur. Cependant, cette mise en perspective géographique et chronologique de la circulation de ce silex spécifique, établie à partir de nos observations directes ou de données publiées, doit être utilisée avec précaution et ne reflète qu'un état de la recherche (carte de la Fig. 2.3).

Comme cela a été déjà signalé, la Chalosse et ses marges sont riches en gisements paléolithiques (Normand 1991). Les silex à *Lepidorbitoides* sp. sont ainsi bien représentés dans les industries aurignaciennes et gravettiennes du site de Brassempouy (Bon 2002: Dartiguepeyrou 1995). À quelques dizaines de kilomètres au nord-ouest, dans les Landes, le gisement badegoulien de Cabannes a également livré des séries en silex de Chalosse (Gellibert *et al.* 2001). Le transport de ce traceur dans tout le piémont pyrénéen et particulièrement dans les Pyrénées centrales est aussi confirmé à l'Aurignacien ou au Gravettien dans la grotte de la Tuto de Camalhot (Bordes *et al.* 2005; Foucher and San Juan 2005), au Solutréen à l'abri des Harpons (Foucher and San Juan 2000) ou durant tout le Tardiglaciaire au sein des Petites Pyrénées (Simonnet 1998; 1996) dans la grotte d'Enlène ou en Barousse, à Troubat (Lacombe 2005; 1998). L'identification de silex de Chalosse exploités au Magdalénien moyen dans le gisement audois de Gazel (Langlais and Sacchi 2006), permet d'envisager la découverte prochaine de ce matériau allochtone dans d'autres sites du Languedoc.

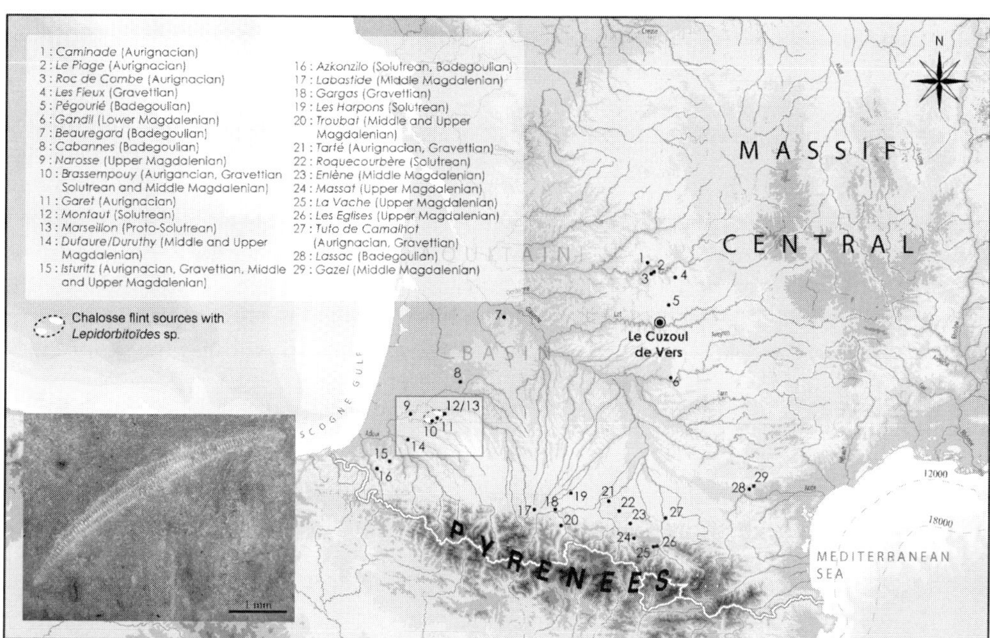

Figure 2.3. Distribution of Upper Palaeolithic sites with lithic industries that contain Chalosse-type flint with Lepidorbitoïdes *sp. Répartition des gisements du Paléolithique Supérieur dont les industries lithiques contiennent des silex à* Lepidorbitoïdes *sp. provenant de Chalosse.*

Dans le nord du Bassin aquitain, en Gironde, la station badegoulienne de plein air de Beauregard (Lenoir *et al.* 1997) pourrait constituer un jalon très intéressant de la diffusion du silex de Chalosse, entre ses points de prélèvements et le Périgord. Dans cette dernière région, ce sont les industries aurignaciennes du gisement de Caminade qui contiennent des silex à *Lepidorbitoides* sp. (Bordes *et al.* 2005). Plus à l'est, en Quercy, l'importation de matériaux depuis la Chalosse s'est faite au cours de différentes périodes du Paléolithique supérieur : à l'Aurignacien sur le site du Piage (Lebrun-Ricalens and Séronie-Vivien 2004; Séronie-Vivien 2003), au Gravettien dans la grotte des Fieux (travaux P. Chalard), au Badegoulien à Pégourié (Séronie-Vivien *et al.* 1995; Séronie-Vivien 2003) et à l'abri du Cuzoul de Vers (Chalard *et al.* à paraître; Ducasse and Lelouvier à paraître), enfin, au Magdalénien inférieur dans les gorges de l'Aveyron à Gandil (Chalard à paraître).

Ce tour d'horizon synthétique, de la diffusion du silex de type Chalosse au Paléolithique supérieur, démontre une circulation sur des centaines de kilomètres au sein du Bassin Aquitain et vraisemblablement du Languedoc. Les perspectives de découvertes dans des régions plus éloignées, les Charentes notamment ou le Massif Central, ne sont pas à écarter. Par ailleurs, la corniche vasco-cantabrique, située en dehors de notre zone d'étude, s'avère également un vaste champ d'investigations pour cette problématique relative à l'importation des silex de Chalosse (travaux de A. Tarriño et notamment Tarriño *et al.* 1998).

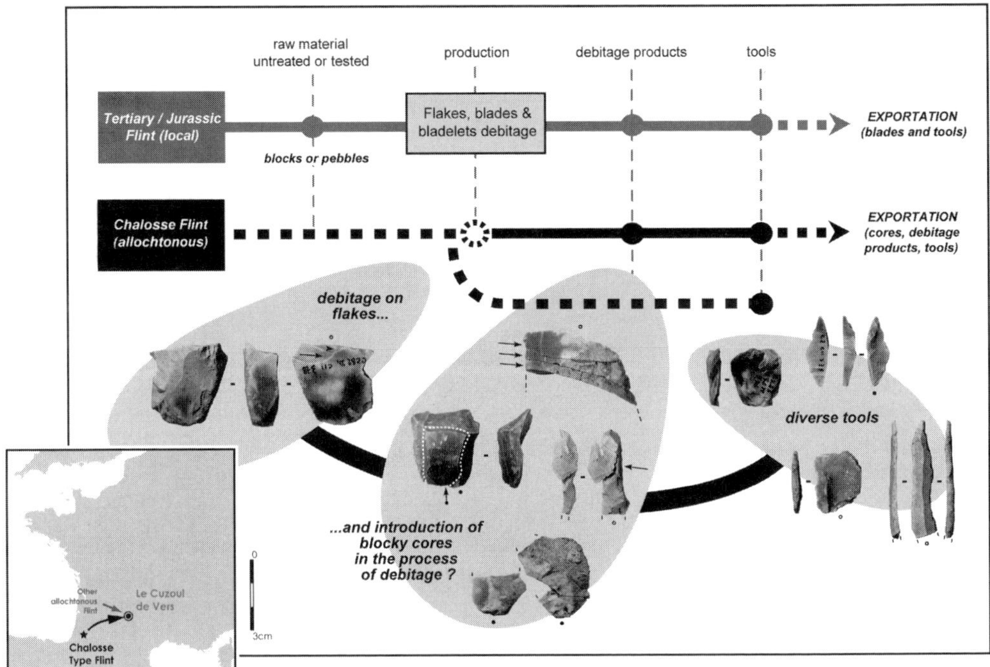

Figure 2.4. Example of Chalosse type flint exploitation during the Badegoulian as seen in the lithic industries of Cuzoul de Vers, Lot, France. Exemple d'exploitation du silex de type Chalosse à Lepidorbitoïdes *sp. au Badegoulien au sein des industries du Cuzoul de Vers (Lot, France).*

Exploitation

En ce qui concerne les stratégies d'exploitation de ce traceur lithologique, nous savons qu'elles ont pu varier avec le temps, illustrant certaines spécificités dans son traitement selon qu'il s'agisse d'Aurignacien, de Gravettien, de Solutréen, de Badegoulien ou de Magdalénien. Le manque actuel de données interdit donc d'effectuer ici une véritable synthèse diachronique. De ce fait, nous ne proposerons qu'un exemple d'exploitation au cours du Badegoulien.

C'est par l'étude des industries de l'abri du Cuzoul de Vers (Quercy) que nous avons pu documenter les modalités de gestion à longue distance du silex de Chalosse en contexte Badegoulien (Fig. 2.4). Ce gisement, à la stratigraphie développée, est caractérisé par une succession Solutréen/Badegoulien. L'existence d'un nombre de couches très important se situant au sein de l'intervalle chronologique 19.000–18.000 BP (nouvelles datations SMA), offre la possibilité d'effectuer des analyses couvrant les phases anciennes et récentes du Badegoulien. Contrairement à la plupart des techno-complexes du Paléolithique supérieur, le Badegoulien montre un approvisionnement en matières premières siliceuses essentiellement tourné vers les ressources locales, celles-ci étant exploitées en très grande partie lors de débitages visant à l'obtention d'éclats (Ducasse and Lelouvier à paraître). Ces derniers servaient ainsi à la confection d'outils (raclettes, perçoirs…) voire, dans une moindre mesure, de support de nucléus (à éclats, à lamelles…). Alors qu'un débitage laminaire a pu avoir lieu sur le gisement, il faut surtout remarquer la forte fragmentation spatio-temporelle de cette chaîne opératoire. Les silex à *Lepidorbitoides* sp. font donc partie des 10 à 15% de matières premières allochtones et sont introduits sous des formes diversifiées. Ainsi, la tendance générale montre l'introduction d'outils finis sur le site. Par ailleurs, si certains éléments pourraient signer le « passage » de nucléus sur bloc en cours de débitage, le silex de Chalosse marque aussi les industries par la présence de nucléus sur éclats pré-débités du type « burin transversal », exploités (nombreux déchets), abandonnés (nucléus), voire exportés par les hommes préhistoriques au cours de déplacements probablement saisonniers.

Conclusions

L'étude du silex de type Chalosse à *Lepidorbitoides* sp., engagée depuis de nombreuses années, demande encore un investissement important tant sur le terrain en terme de prospections, qu'en laboratoire. La Chalosse possède de nombreux affleurements siliceux dont la cartographie précise reste à établir. Bien que les caractéristiques principales de ce traceur soient connues, de nouvelles investigations en micropaléontologie, en pétrographie et vraisemblablement en géochimie, devront être effectuées pour obtenir une carte d'identité la plus pertinente possible, pour ce silex du Maestrichtien qui fait partie d'un ensemble plus vaste de matériaux attribuables au même étage géologique (silex du « Bergeracois » dans le nord du Bassin aquitain, silex de « Montsaunès » dans les Petites Pyrénées).

Par ailleurs, les résultats présentés dans cet article et publiés sur la diffusion du type Chalosse au cours du Paléolithique supérieur, témoignent du potentiel informatif de cette matière première particulière, quant à la définition des territoires d'approvisionnement et de circulation des peuples de chasseurs-cueilleurs. Les travaux sur l'exploitation de ce traceur par grandes périodes chronologiques du Paléolithique supérieur et sur l'ensemble de son espace de diffusion ne sont qu'embryonnaires et devraient être développés à l'avenir. La confrontation des données recueillies au terme de ces investigations avec les résultats obtenus pour d'autres traceurs bien connus des archéologues, mais dont les gîtes appartiennent à la sphère nord-aquitaine (silex du « Bergeracois », silex du « Fumélois »), offriront des perspectives de réflexions particulièrement prometteuses. Les premières synthèses publiées sur l'Aurignacien, s'appuyant entre autres sur cette problématique (Bon 2002; Bordes *et al.* 2005), nous confortent dans cette intention.

Enfin, les notions de mobilité et de territoire au cœur des recherches actuelles (Bressy *et al.* 2006; Jaubert and Barbaza 2005; Vialou *et al.* 2005), ne peuvent être appréhendées que dans l'interdisciplinarité. Les regards croisés des spécialistes de l'archéozoologie (Costamagno 2006) ou de l'art pariétal (Fritz and Tosello 2005) démontrent tout l'intérêt de mettre en œuvre une véritable intégration de ces approches complémentaires. La notion des traceurs lithologiques prend ici toute sa mesure pour contribuer aux comparaisons entre entités géomorphologiques riches en gîtes à silex, territoires de subsistance et espaces culturels. Le silex de type Chalosse à *Lepidorbitoides* sp., dont on retrouve des traces tout au long de la chaîne pyrénéenne et vraisemblablement jusqu'en

Espagne, mais aussi du Languedoc au Périgord en passant par le Quercy, est un des vecteurs de la compréhension des modalités d'exploitation du milieu et par voie de conséquence, des mode de vie au Paléolithique supérieur.

Remerciements/acknowledgments

Nous remercions chaleureusement Adrian Burke, professeur adjoint à l'Université de Montréal, qui nous a offert l'opportunité de présenter nos travaux dans le cadre de la session poster « Quarries : Where It All Began » organisée au cours du 71ème colloque de la SAA à Porto Rico en avril 2006 et de pouvoir en publier les résultats dans cet ouvrage

3 Neolithic Axe Quarries and Flint Mines: Towards an Ethnography of Prehistoric Extraction

Peter Topping

Summary

This paper attempts to draw contrasts between the Neolithic flint mines and stone-axe quarry sites (traditionally referred to as axe 'factories' in the UK) to explore similarities and differences between these two forms of extraction. Both site types emerged around 4000 BC at the beginning of the Neolithic period and faded from use when the first metal objects were being introduced c. *2300 BC. Geologically, the axe 'factories' are located in the uplands of the north and west of the UK, whereas the flint mines are largely restricted to the relatively low-lying chalk of southern England with a further two sites on secondary gravels in Aberdeenshire in north-east Scotland (cf. Saville 2005). The paper will build upon previous discussions (Barber* et al. *1999; Topping 1996, 2003, 2004, 2005, forthcoming; Topping and Lynott 2005) and review a number of pertinent themes:* e.g. *the role of ritualised journeys to stone and flint sources, locational preferences, the evidence for ritualised extraction, and the use-life and cultural role of artefacts of mined stone. It is hoped that the evidence presented here will move the debate forward towards a social contextualisation of extraction and explore the dichotomy and interplay between ritualised and functional procurement.*

Ritualised journeys

Ritualised journeys are a common theme in ethnography. In Australia, ethnography records journeys to important quarries of distances ranging between 500km (311 miles) (Taçon 2004, 34) to 1,000km (621 miles) (Brumm 2004, 153), demonstrating the deep cultural value sedimented into the participation in long-distance travel for mineral acquisition (Boivin 2004, 10). The lack of definitive settlement evidence for permanent habitation at any extraction site so far excavated in the UK, suggests that at least some of those exploiting these sites *may* have travelled from a distance, used temporary shelters *and* stayed for only a short period of time – not enough to generate significant quantities of cultural debris of a type which clearly defines domestic activity rather than quarrying, tool production or ritualised deposition. Alternatively, however, the record could be read as illustrating exploitation of stone resources from a local settlement, something which might have been accomplished during a short-stay visit – a scenario which would equally explain the paucity of cultural debris.

One of the few excavations to have revealed disturbed and ephemeral structural traces lay at Thunacar Knott, some 0.8km north of the Langdale axe quarries in Cumbria,

UK (cf. McK Clough 1973). This site is difficult to characterise, but may represent the remains of a temporary shelter at a knapping centre, with attendant hearth, knapping debris and broken rough-outs. Within the limits of the excavation, and considering the potential effects of the acid soils, little evidence for domestic activity survived, which might indicate that this site was nothing more than a temporary location for axe production. A similarly ambiguous picture is provided by excavations at the Harrow Hill flint mines in Sussex, where slight structural evidence was recorded around the mouth of Shaft 13 (see below).

Recent excavations have begun to reveal the scale of some Neolithic journeys. Analysis of trace-metal isotopes of a family group buried in the wall of a ceremonial pit at Monkton Up Wimborne, Dorset, revealed that they originated from a landscape of high lead-levels and had thus travelled eastwards at least 60km (37 miles) from the Mendip Hills, the nearest such location (Green 2000, 79). The Boscombe Bowmen, Wiltshire, originating from either Cumbria or south-west Wales had journeyed roughly 386km (240 miles) to Wessex (Fitzpatrick 2004), or perhaps even from northern France where identical isotope values can be obtained (Parker Pearson *et al.* 2007, 617–39). Finally, the Amesbury Archer discovered near Stonehenge had travelled some 1046km (650 miles) from the Alps to Wessex (Fitzpatrick 2003). At the flint mines at Grime's Graves, in Norfolk, there is some evidence to suggest exploitation by coastal inhabitants from the presence of the skull of a shore bird (phalarope) found in one of the galleries excavated by Canon Greenwell (Topping forthcoming) – a modest journey of at least 80km (50 miles).

The hypothesis for the seasonal use of extraction sites is lent weight by the often extreme locations of most extraction sites near mountain tops (*e.g.* Top Buttress, Langdale) or deep underground (*e.g.* some 12m deep in Greenwell's Pit), implying that they could only have been used safely during the warmer months with greater daylight hours, less precipitation and more settled weather conditions. Safety issues are survival-defining parameters at these extraction sites.

In the archaeological record lengthy journeys or extensive exchange networks are demonstrated by the widespread distribution of many types of stone axe, especially the abundant Group VI axes which were transported not only throughout the UK but a large number that crossed the Irish Sea to Ireland and the Isle of Man. In contrast the Group IX axes originating in Northern Ireland, travelled in the opposite direction eastwards over the Irish Sea and were transported throughout the UK (cf. McK Clough and Cummins 1988), illustrating the cultural importance of recognisable – and presumably iconic – tools. Also of interest in this respect are the Penrith henges in Cumbria, one of which, Mayburgh, has close structural parallels with henges in the Boyne Valley, Ireland (Topping 1992, 262–3). Conversely, the large stone circle at Ballynoe in County Down has many structural traits reminiscent of Cumbrian sites (Burl 1976, 237–240).

In Greenwell's Pit, a flint mine shaft at Grime's Graves, a stone axe was discovered in one of the galleries near the bird skull mentioned above, forming a placed deposit with a pair of antler picks (Topping 2003, 11; Fig. 3.1). Petrological analysis identified a Cornish origin for this axe and, while the journey need not have been achieved in a single attempt, it nevertheless demonstrates contact across a north-easterly distance of roughly 540km (335 miles). If reciprocity was practiced, then as with the movement of Group VI and IX stone axes, some Grime's Graves flint artefacts must also have

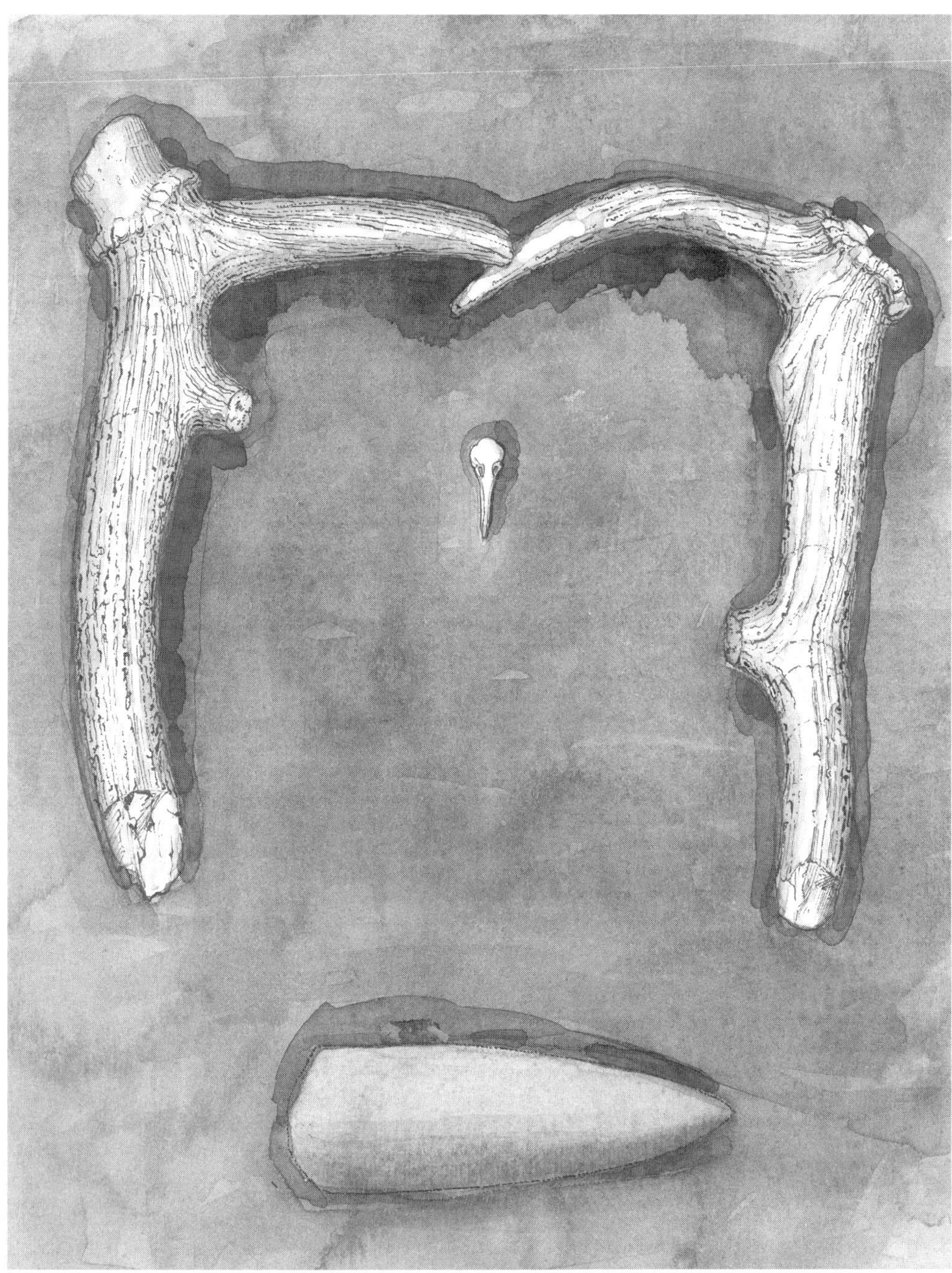

Figure 3.1. Red deer antlers frame the skull of a phalerope, a shore bird, and a ground stone axe that had been brought Grime's Graves from Cornwall and placed at the base of a shaft excavated by Canon W. Greenwell in 1870. © English heritage: painting Judith Dobie.

travelled equidistantly to the south-west. The archaeological record also illustrates the broader perspective – large numbers of Cornish axes were distributed throughout southern England and into East Anglia (particularly Essex), but rarely further north (McK Clough and Cummins 1988, 266–269, 279), demonstrating the presence of well-established exchange networks for particular types of prized artefacts.

The example of the Group VI stone-axe quarries at Langdale is also informative. The distribution of pre-forms and finished axes from the Cumbrian mountains suggests that transportation followed convenient valley routes eastwards to the Eden Valley and the cluster of henge monuments at Penrith: clearly this henge complex was constructed to monumentalise a key location in the cultural landscape. From Penrith, dispersal was widespread; one route led south-east through Yorkshire and would have funnelled people and their axes to another henge group at Thornborough, Yorkshire, an area also notable for its lack of workable flint (Frances Healy pers comm.). In contrast, axes from the two North Welsh quarry sites have distinctly different distributions: Group VII axes from Penmaenmawr (Graig Lwyd) are widely scattered throughout Wales and southern Britain, whereas conversely, the smaller numbers of Group XXI Mynydd Rhiw axes appear restricted to Wales (McKClough and Cummings 1988, 270, 282). This could demonstrate that the Penmaenmawr axes had a greater cultural value in Wales and beyond, whereas certain other quarries only produced material for more localised consumption – or for functional needs. Arguably, widespread distribution may be the defining characteristic for identifying those artefacts and extraction sites which had a deeper cultural value, produced iconic tools, and therefore had a symbolically embedded and ritualised extraction process. Alternatively, the sites with a more limited distribution may illustrate a different social context. Considering the movement of stone axes across the Irish Sea, it is curious why little evidence has been recognised so far for similar movements of stone or flint axes across the English Channel – in either direction – and this despite the obvious presence of Alpine jadeite axes in the UK demonstrating that cross-Channel movement did occur. The discovery of Scandinavian types of flint axe in Britain, may be further evidence of international trade – or population movements (see above).

The distribution of flint axes contrasts with that of stone axes, each inevitably reflecting the location of the parent material: flint has a predominantly southern British distribution and in certain areas such as Sussex, Norfolk and Kent 80% of axes are of flint (Pitts 1996, 322–5). North of Yorkshire, however, flint axes are far fewer, perhaps suggesting different cultural values in northern Britain where stone axes predominate. From the evidence of the extensive distribution patterns of certain stone axe types in the UK and Ireland, the same exchange or social mechanisms which transported these axes throughout northern Britain and beyond clearly had a lesser interest in those made from flint. Flint artefacts here must have had less social value than their stone counterparts, and may imply that communities had a stronger loyalty to their local or regional stone source as opposed to imported exotica. This has implications for the conceptualisation, symbolism and metaphysical association that might have been embedded in such loci. The comparatively restricted distribution of flint axes is illustrated by the evidence of caches of unfinished flint axes, which only occur in the south and east of the UK from Wessex to East Anglia (*ibid.* 326), emphasising the limitations of their distribution, paralleling their origins in the chalklands of the south, and demonstrating where their greatest social value lay.

Journeys and the process of experiencing a range of landscapes sedimented knowledge, as well as providing the resources necessary for the Neolithic lifeway. The artefacts obtained from some journeys must have been used to embed cultural narratives, reinforcing kinships, clans and alliances, and underpinning belief systems. Returning with an axe may also have satisfied rites of passage, as part of the initiation into the skills of quarrying and knapping, helping to define the newly-acquired social role of the initiate. Multiple meanings will have been embedded into these artefacts of mined or quarried stones; their iconic nature may have provided proof of an experienced 'close encounter' with the spirit world; they may have reinforced both social mechanisms and rites of renewal; and others will have simply been created for purely functional reasons.

Location

Australian ethnography often records that mine location and raw material choice are driven by supernatural associations, particularly in the selective acquisition of bright or colourful stones or minerals which are thought to be the fossilised body parts of powerful Ancestral Beings from the Dreaming (Brumm 2004, 147; Flood 1997, 114; Taçon 2004, 31). Gould (1977, 164) records that *'quarries occur at or near sacred sites – that is totemic "dreaming" places. People who believe themselves to be descended patrilineally from the particular totemic being at one of the sites will make special trips to the quarry to secure the stone there. A man places a high value on stone from a site of his dreamtime totem. Stone like this is often transported over long distances … and is given to distant kinsmen of the same totemic patrilineage … Because of his patrilineal relationship to the site, a man sees the stone as part of his own being …'*. Similar observations were recorded by Catlin amongst the plains tribes, particularly in relation to the use of 'Catlinite' or pipestone from Minnesota which was, and is, taken to symbolise Native Americans: *'You see (holding a red pipe to the side of his naked arm) that this pipe is part of our flesh. The red men are a part of the red stone'* (Matthiessen 1989, 432; cf. also Topping 2005, 86–89). The trade or exchange of recognisable types of stone to distant kin is thus used as a mechanism to create links between people and place, maintaining the cultural identity of individuals, clans or tribes (cf. Brumm 2004, 153). Many Aboriginal Australian quarries, and the Pipestone Quarries in Minnesota (cf. Scott and Thiessen 2005; Scott *et al.* 2006), were also used as backdrops for important ceremonies.

The geomorphology and topographic form of many extraction sites in the UK suggest that they may also have been mythologised, and it was cultural values which had led miners to these specific locations, prospecting for rare raw materials from mythologised loci which could carry cultural narratives. The prominent setting of many mines and quarries overlooking the surrounding landscape, positioned them in a doubly liminal zone, carefully placed on or near the horizon between the earth and the sky, and between the surface and the underworld. Contrary to practicality, many of these extraction sites were also located far from low-lying ground – isolation and visual prominence were clearly key factors. For example, the Penmaenmawr (Graig Lwyd) axe 'factory' is visible from a wide range of coastal areas and the Irish Sea – as is Mynydd Rhiw; the axe 'factory' at Le Pinacle on Jersey was located at the base of a massive, locally prominent granite outcrop on the north-western coastline. In addition, as Cooney (1998, 109) has observed, the fact that the axe-production sites visibly altered the landscape, gave them a monumentality that signposted their presence and located them conceptually into the cultural landscape.

At the Langdale axe 'factories' a study of the geology of the various outcrops discovered that some of the most useable tool stone was ignored, while near-inaccessible exposures of the same material *was* exploited – as Richard Bradley has suggested, it was the *'character of the place* [which] *seemed at least as important as the qualities of the material'* (Bradley 2000, 86–7). The Langdale extraction strategy is dramatically paralleled on the South Downs at both Harrow Hill and Blackpatch in Sussex, where the mines were deliberately positioned away from the better sources of flint (cf. Barber *et al.* 1999, 73), again suggesting that it was the importance of *place* rather than raw material quality which was paramount for these miners. Clearly cultural value was embedded into certain raw materials, but not others.

Topographically, the similarity in the profiles of the Pike O'Stickle in Cumbria and Tievebulliagh, Northern Ireland, axe 'factories' are notable (cf. also Cooney 1998), particularly as they lie on different sides of the Irish Sea. Such morphological similarities might help to explain the considerable movement of both Irish Group IX and Cumbrian group VI axes if they were considered to have originated from what were perceived as 'sacred' mountains lying beyond the horizon and over the sea, accessed by lengthy journeys and a potentially dangerous maritime crossing.

Overall, topographic location highlights the diametrically opposed differences between the axe 'factories' and the flint mines, perhaps suggesting other subtle cultural contrasts sedimented into their use and social context. The axe 'factories' as previously noted have a tendency for prominent, above ground, highly visible locations which are difficult and dangerous to access. In contrast, the flint mines by their very nature are subterranean and relatively hidden, but at times can still be sited on prominent landforms (*e.g.* Harrow Hill on the South Downs) and are equally dangerous workplaces. The prominent / hidden dichotomy is something which may have influenced the use-life of the resulting artefacts and explain the buried hoards of axes, particularly of flint, which might be paraphrasing their point of origin in the mines and be linked to renewal rituals.

Ritualised extraction

Evidence for ritualisation can be seen in most flint mines. The presence of hearths on shaft floors, or charcoal deposits in galleries, occurs at 10.7% of sites in the earlier Neolithic period (*e.g.* Cissbury; Harrow Hill) rising to 34.2% in the later Neolithic, suggesting that fire, heat, light and smoke played an increasingly important role in the extraction process (Topping forthcoming). Using ethnography as a guide, the ritualised purification of miners and their tools at a hearth may have been an integral part of the extraction process, particularly as many hearths were positioned at the base of the shafts and do not appear to have been located to provide light or heat to the galleries. The small deposits of unidentified charcoal in certain galleries in Greenwell's Pit and

Pit 15 at Grime's Graves (cf. Longworth and Varndell 1996, 12, 26–7, 55) may be further evidence of purification by smoke, particularly as these were too small to have been hearths and were clearly not used for lighting, as there is no smoke staining on the roofs of any gallery at Grime's Graves. In addition, the fact that these deposits remained intact and had not been smeared across the floors by the passage of miners, suggests that they may have been abandonment deposits set when the gallery was finally closed.

Ritualisation was further enhanced at flint mines by accompanying paraphernalia, such as graffiti (Cissbury, Grime's Graves, Harrow Hill), carved chalk objects (Blackpatch, Church Hill, Cissbury, Grime's Graves, Harrow Hill), pottery and the presence of chalk platforms with groups of antler picks, all recording a range of non-functional activities sedimented into the mining process. Human burials have also been recorded, particularly at Cissbury (cf. Topping 2005).

The presence of both flint and stone axes within some mine shafts bears consideration. Ethnographic records suggest such patterns of deposition may represent the return of tools to their place of origin as part of a process of symbolic renewal. This would explain the 300+ axe rough-outs recovered by excavation from Grime's Graves or the cache of axes at Harrow Hill, where 33 '*in various stages of manufacture*' were discovered in Shaft III (Holleyman 1937, 239). One of these was broken, the cutting edge discovered '*just beneath the turf and the butt end 8ft* [2.4m] *down* [the shaft]' (*ibid*. 242). The different provenances of these two parts of the same artefact suggests that the uppermost fragment may have remained in circulation longer, but had eventually been returned to the same mine as the first part – possibly to their place of origin.

Avifaunal remains are only rarely discovered in the flint mines. In Greenwell's Pit the skull of a phalarope, a shorebird, was placed between a pair of antler picks with tines facing inwards, and an imported Cornish greenstone axe positioned at the foot of the picks. Placing bird remains below ground could reference engendered sky and earth deities, creating a metaphor for fertility and renewal. The additional presence of carved chalk phalli in Greenwell's Pit and Pit 15 lend weight to this suggestion. Curiously, '*the skull of what appears to have been a mouse*' was discovered with an antler pick in Gallery III of Pit 21 at Harrow Hill (Curwen and Curwen 1926, 115), hinting at other forms of symbolism (the fact that only the skull was discovered again suggests careful curation).

Human burials provide another perspective. At Blackpatch, in Sussex, the contemporary Barrow 12 was placed amongst the mines (cf. Topping 2005, 67), clearly centring an ancestral presence at this extraction site. Less visible and equally rare are shaft burials such as Cissbury Shaft 27 where a female skeleton was discovered lying on her side and facing into the mines, deliberately referencing the source of the flint. Chalk carvings were found nearby alongside an unusual '*fossil like worm*' with curious phallic attributes. A formal male burial in Cissbury Shaft VI was surrounded by chalk blocks and accompanied by grave goods.

However, the treatment of human remains varied. Tindall's excavations at Cissbury discovered a human skull alongside that of a wild boar, two oxen and the bones of a goat, ox and pig (Willett 1875, 341). Although the contextual information regarding some of these pieces is not too firm, this juxtaposition of wild and domesticated animals with human remains created a specific cultural narrative. Disarticulated body parts have also been recovered from Blackpatch Shaft 4, Church Hill Shaft 6, Grime's Graves Pit 2 and Grime's Graves Pit 1; the latter a skull wedged between chalk blocks and lying above an ox bone midway up the shaft (Clarke 1915, 48–9, 69). Such selective body part use may have been associated with the wider excarnation continuum recorded at causewayed enclosures, long barrows and henges.

The female skeletal evidence raises questions about the association of women with the mines, particularly as a second female skeleton was discovered near the base of Shaft H at Cissbury. Ethnography is ambiguous, some cultures dictate taboos banning the presence of females, others prescribe a female only role in extraction. The slight evidence of children – a mandible from Blackpatch Shaft 4 – may be signposting taboos, paralleling Australian Aboriginal quarries which have age and gender restrictions *and* strict rules of conduct (*e.g.* Flood 1995, 271–3; 1997, 34–5).

An interesting feature is the episodic post-extraction deposits in shafts and galleries at all flint mines. For example at Cissbury Shaft 27, assemblages representing at least twelve depositional event horizons change significantly as the shaft filled, the lower deposits characterised by extraction, abandonment and human burial, whereas the upper fills record secondary activities which can be interpreted as relating to rites of renewal (cf. Topping 2005, 70–9). Such patterns of deposition illustrate that certain mines did remain open as a focus for post-extraction or abandonment events. The final deposit at Shaft 27 comprised three axe rough-outs placed on the backfilled Neolithic ground surface, a potent symbol of the mines' former location commemorated by its spoil dump encircling the axes. In contrast, a large fire was built over the backfilled shaft at Church Hill, Sussex, Shaft 5a, incorporating burnt flint, debitage, tools and axes, all alongside the bones of an ox, suggesting feasting, renewal and dedication rituals.

Little settlement evidence has been recorded amongst the flint mines, although this may reflect excavation bias. However, at Harrow Hill in Trench 2 lying to the north of Shaft 13 (McNabb *et al.* 1996, 28–30), a number of small 'depressions' and gulleys were discovered which could define a series of temporary structures such as a wind break or tent, with some form of scaffold or series of uprights set near to the mouth of the shaft. A small amount of knapping debris lay between the two structures, suggesting the definition of an activity area featuring the small-scale crafting of axes in this location. The fact that excavations did not recover evidence of large 'chipping floors' (*ibid.* 37), suggests that much of the raw material or pre-forms were transported off-site and reduction was not a major feature of mining when Shaft 13 was being exploited.

Unlike the mines, the axe 'factories' have little *overt* material record of ritualised activity beyond occasional hoards of axes, as at Penmaenmawr and Langdale. However, the disturbed nature of many axe-production sites and excavation bias may have obscured the true picture. A glimpse of what may have been a wider tradition of ritualisation is recorded at Graig Lwyd, where a rough-out axe was laid at the base of a quarry face and buried with debitage (Williams 1994, 36–8), suggesting an act of renewal. At the Eagle's Nest axe quarry on Lambay Island, extraction was accompanied initially by the digging of a sequence of pits, filled with extraction debris, tools and broken pottery. This phase was then followed by episodic surface deposition, comprising stone settings and a *'hearth-like feature … positioned centrally … with spreads of ashy sediment around it'*, then a larger deposit of stone sediment and artefacts. This phase was associated with a hoard consisting of a cushion macehead, a porphyry rough-out and axe; a further broken macehead was located elsewhere in the general spread alongside red jasper pendants which appear to have been worked on site from imported beach pebbles. The final episode was characterised by a *'cairn-like'* dump of quarry debris sealing the preceding stone settings (Cooney 2005, 19). Porphyry is a difficult rock to work, fractures prevent easy reduction, but despite this problem the raw material was still ground and polished to enhance the whiteness of the phenocrysts speckles against the green matrix. It may be that the cultural value of Lambay porphyry lay in the presence of the white speckling, creating a metaphoric link to *'life, power, fertility and the ancestors'*, which was enhanced by being crafted into axeheads (Cooney 2005, 25).

Hearths, other than for fire-setting are rare, grouped artefacts and deposits of animal- or human-skeletal remains equally so. If ritualised extraction did take place at axe 'factories', its nature may have been significantly different to that which occurred in the mines. Ritualisation at axe 'factories' may have been more subtle, relying upon the use of highly-charged, symbolic locations and not on an overtly ritualised extraction process. Nevertheless, certain stages of the extraction process do suggest ritualisation. For example, the hammerstones used at Langdale were off-site imports of granite and tuff, which had separate and distinct associations with individual quarries, even when they were on the same summit, leading Bradley and Edmonds (1993, 204) to speculate that *'Perhaps particular parts of the rock face, or even particular quarries, were the preserve of different communities'*. It may equally be possible that cultural taboos prescribed the rock types to be used in specific locations to appease aspects of the mythologised landscape.

As at the flint mines, little evidence of settlement has been recorded but again excavation bias may have distorted the picture. At Thunacar Knott, for example, one of a number of 'chipping sites' was discovered roughly a kilometre to the north-north-east of Pike O'Stickle. Excavation of this site revealed scattered stone spreads which might have defined temporary wind breaks, areas of recent disturbance, a post-hole and gulley alongside a large area of charcoal. The artefact assemblage suggested the primary reduction of raw material; a second small trench some 10m north-west of the first, recovered evidence for *'many thousands of small trimming flakes'* implying the final stages in crafting rough-outs (McK Clough 1973, 30–1). Taken together, this may characterise a production site which saw raw material processed into near-finished pre-forms ready for polishing. The post-hole, gulley, scattered stone and area of charcoal suggest that these features may have been some form of temporary structure, possibly roofed, to shelter the knappers. It would seem extremely unlikely that anyone would have chosen to live on these mountain tops during the winter months, so as with the flint mines, the suspicion is that these extraction sites were only used seasonally.

The fact that so many stone axes were widely distributed throughout the UK and Ireland and ended their use-life buried in hoards, implies they were culturally-significant, the end-products of ritualised extraction and imbued with a deep symbolic value.

The use-life and cultural role of artefacts of mined stone

Most of the flint mines and axe 'factories' provided raw materials primarily for axe making. Such iconic artefacts – if ethnographic analogy is an indicator – may have had a multiplicity of meanings ranging from *'a religious symbol, an item of exchange as well as a functional tool'* (Cooney 1998, 108) and, as Whittle (1995, 251) has pointed out, *'We should not be content to assume fixed or inherent values for things'*.

The South Downs mines conformed to this trend and produced flint largely for axe production. Analysis of the depositional patterns of axes from the adjacent coastal plain confirms that the majority were unused and carefully curated (cf. Gardiner 1990, 131; Holgate 1995, 157). Clearly here the source of the raw material was identified by the artefact type, which then followed a pre-determined trajectory and use-life. The Norfolk flint mines provide a similar picture (cf. Pitts 1996). The more extensive distribution of many types of stone axe demonstrates that they too had a deeply embedded cultural value, and a currency which arguably exceeded those of flint. The cultural value of axes made from special types of stone may thus have underpinned a greater number of social functions than those of flint, and transcended more social boundaries to become a universal in Neolithic lifeways.

Although it could not be easily proven that all extraction sites were special places in the cultural landscape, the degrees of ritualisation need to be considered. The ritualisation of mundane activities must have been an integral part of Neolithic lifeways, and taboos and social mores will have dictated the form and method of actions from food processing to rites of renewal. For more significant actions such as stone procurement from dangerous or difficult locations, the activity must have been bound up by more stringent restrictions to reflect and counter the inherent dangers, but also to arguably protect the social niche of those charged with extraction. In addition, the fact that many tools crafted from quarried stone clearly became culturally-important and were carefully curated – often in hoards – as a means of underpinning social renewal, demonstrates that the end-products of ritualised extraction were clearly bound up by strict rules for communal procedure, transaction and social performance.

The dangers of extraction were both physical and metaphysical, and would have heightened the cultural value of the raw materials, becoming as Bradley (2000, 85–90) has suggested *'pieces of places'*, embedded with a deeper symbolism than more easily obtained varieties of stone. This is graphically illustrated by the location of the dangerously exposed quarry sites on the near vertical faces of Top Buttress on Pike O'Stickle. It was the combination of difficult extraction strategies and the procurement of *recognisable* types of stone from culturally relevant sources that both visibly labelled the context of the raw material and thus created its value to the community. These identifiable types of stone – such as the banded flint from Krzemionki in Poland – sedimented biographies into an artefact, which then enabled them to transmit cultural narratives to society.

Acknowledgements

The author would like to thank Dave Field, as ever, for much helpful discussion and assistance in the formulation of these ideas. Dave McOmish likewise provided useful comment. The encouragement of English Heritage in the furtherance of this research is gratefully acknowledged. As always, errors, misrepresentations and unintended plagiarism are the sole responsibility of the author.

4 Systems of Raw Material Procurement and Supply in the Neolithic of Northern Thrace During the Seventh to Fifth Millennia BC

Ivan Gatsov

Summary

This essay outlines petrographic and geochemical analysis of flint from three sites in northern Thrace and suggests that two principle sources of flint were being utilized, one local, the other from a greater distance, probably from a source in north eastern Bulgaria.

The region

The stone assemblages, included in this report, have been recorded in the region of northern Thrace. This is the territory, which is located east of the town of Plovdiv and the eastern Rhodopes, south of Stara Planina and the Sredna Gora Mountains and reaching the Black Sea in the east. Northern Thrace is separated from eastern Thrace by the present political border (Fig. 4.1). The European part of Turkey, known as eastern or Turkish Thrace, is bounded by the Black Sea and in the south by the Aegean. The valley of the Maritsa (Meric or Evros) River marks the western border. Within these areas, three key sites have been investigated, all dated to the end of 7th and first half of 6th millennium BC. These are the settlements at Karanovo and Azmak in northern or Bulgarian Thrace and Hoca Çeşme in eastern or Turkish Thrace.

Raw material procurement and supply during the Neolithic Period in Northern Thrace

Until now the earliest evidence of Neolithic settlement in northern Thrace has been that associated with Tell Karanovo. The earliest Neolithic period in this area included Karanovo I and Karanovo II phases, which are dated to the first half of the 6th millennium BC as can the chipped stone assemblages from Early Neolithic layer at Azmak. About 60% of all artefacts from the Karanovo I and Karanovo II assemblages are made from raw material designated type A, of a yellow, or yellow – reddish brown color, not transparent, but with patterns of stripes or spots of various densities. More than 20 percent of specimens are made from raw material type B, the colour of which, in contrast, is highly variable, being dark grey, mid grey, beige grey, brown grey to red with irregular grey spots (Gatsov and Kurcatov 1997). It has been mineralogically analyzed by Dr. V. Kurcatov and the graphs (Figs 4.2 and 4.3) demonstrate similarity of raw material use between Karanovo I and Karanovo II.

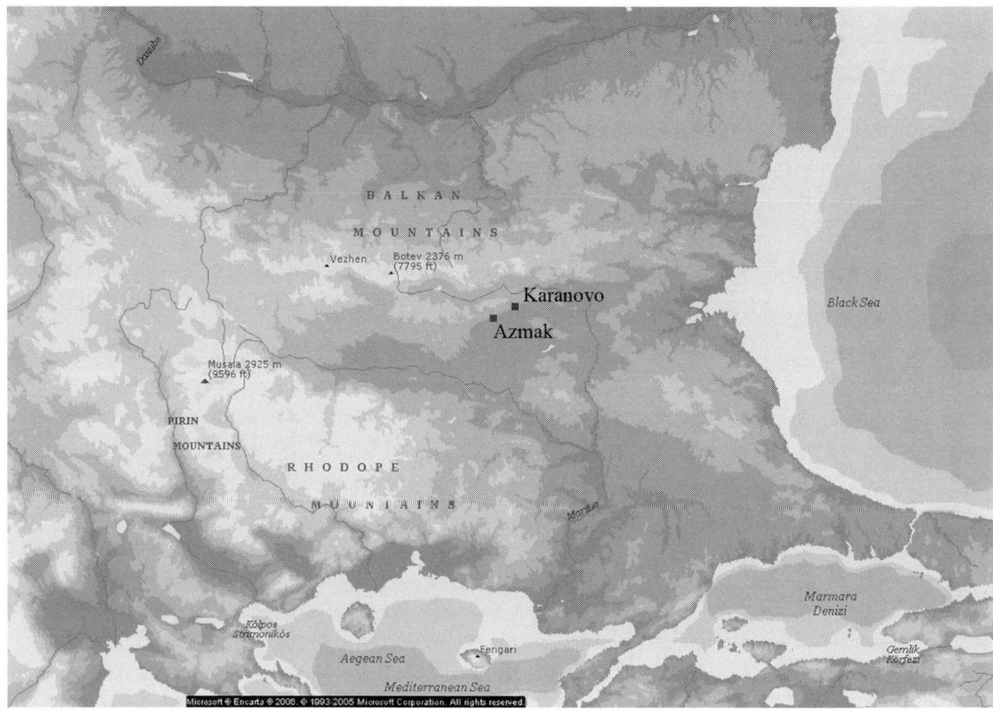

Figure 4.1. Location Map.

Chipped stone assemblages from Azmak: the Neolithic Layer

Recent investigations into the chipped stone assemblages from the early Neolithic layer, building levels V–I at Tell Azmak, using petrographic and geochemical methods produced interesting new results. Mineral composition, rock provenance, the origin and the probable source of the raw material were analysed and seen to correspond to the archeological data from Tell Karanovo, phases I and II (Gatsov *et al.* unpublished). Two thirds of specimens were made of raw material varieties 1 and 2, similar to the material used at Karanovo I and II – samples A and B. Analyses of the raw material samples were made by Dr. Vsevolod Kurčatov and his salient conclusions about the flint raw material from Karanovo I and II and the Neolithic layer at Tell Azmak are repeated here for convenience: first "the greater number of artifacts and raw material display a chalcedony-quartz composition (over 80%). Differing amounts of opal, clays, carbonate, ferric oxides and organic are also present as admixtures". Secondly "the elevated content of SiO_2 in the form of quartz, chalcedony and opal defines the basic raw material of the artifacts as chert". Thirdly "the colour of the samples varies greatly and depends on the admixture quantity, as for example the organic imparts black colors, the ferric oxides – yellow to red and dark brown colours (jaspers), the clayey components – grey to black. A lack of admixtures leaves a semi-transparent or transparent appearance". Fourth "the major part of heavily processed artifacts comprise opal, clays, carbonate, organic and ferric oxides, aside from frequently observed admixtures, chalcedony-quartz

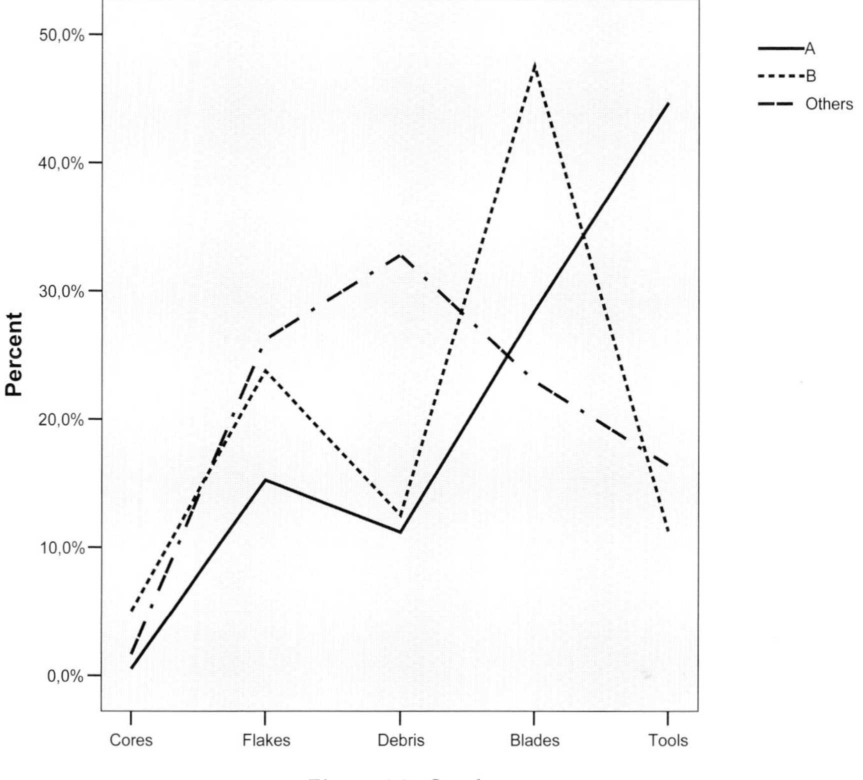

Figure 4.2. Graph.

groundmass of gel to cryptocrystalline texture. It results in a lower relative firmness that makes pieces easier to process, preserving at the same time their basic qualities of cleavage that result in sharp cutting edges". Fifth "the greater part of the artifact assemblage are of raw material varieties that have unrecognizable silicified detritus or preserved fossils which in turn provide evidence of their sedimentary origin". Sixth "part of the (mainly non-processed) samples have an igneous origin or are of quartzite. It implies that they have come together with the raw materials by chance". Seventh "the presence of many weatherworn crusts in the samples is evidence of the long duration of the weathering processes which are known to have taken place on the earth's surface as well as in the soil layer and consequently it can be suggested that the raw materials have derived from the surface of natural outcrops". Eighth "comparing the mineral composition and the characteristics of the stone assemblages with the rocks from the corresponding regions in Bulgaria (using geological data) it can be firmly suggested that the material is of regional origin, that is, they were obtained from southern Bulgaria". Ninth "in order to prove convincingly the local origin of the raw materials, a detailed geological study and mineralogical investigation of the corresponding rocks is necessary in the presumed areas of raw material sources" (Kurčatov, in press).

While no research related to the location of raw material sources has yet been

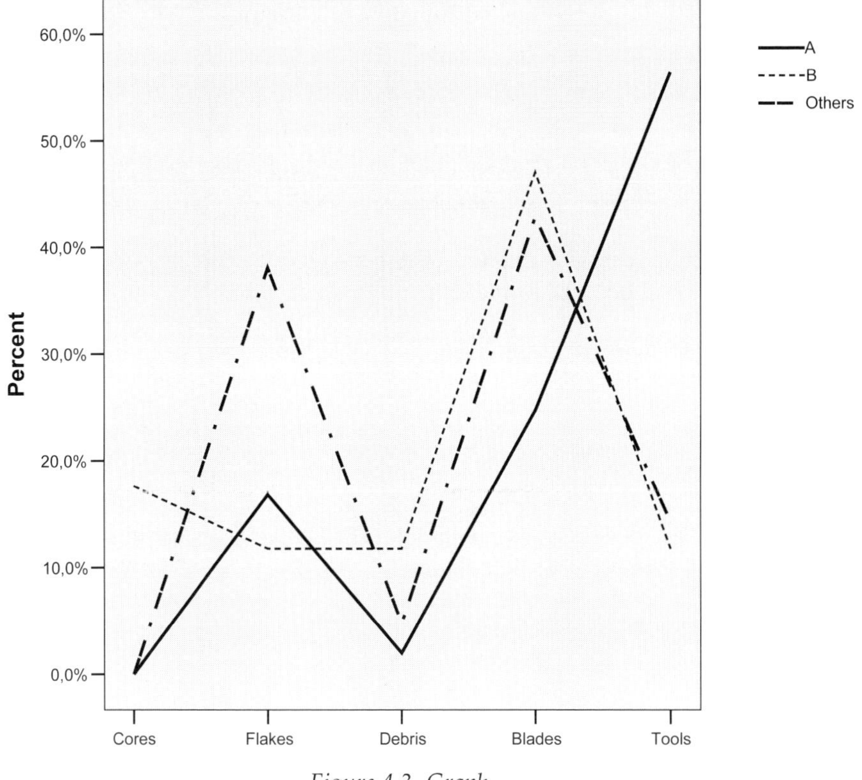

Figure 4.3. Graph.

undertaken, the presence of very high quality flint in all Early Neolithic assemblages in Northern Thrace is not in doubt. The flint is yellow, yellow-reddish to brown or grey in colour, opaque, with patterns of stripes or spots of varying density and it is not transparent. This type of flint has been found as relatively large blades in all sites dated to the first half of the 7th millennium in south and south west Bulgaria. Unfortunately, the precise location of flint outcrops or the locations of the workshops is still unknown. However, the idea that southern Bulgaria was a zone of supply during the early Neolithic period suggested by V. Kurčatov is not ruled out here. In this case, the existence of a relatively short and middle distance source of supply of the above mentioned high quality flint raw material can be suggested.

Raw material procurement and supply in Northern Thrace: an example from Azmak, the Chalcolithic layer, building levels I–VIII

Within the boundaries of the study all chipped stone artifacts can be attributed to one of eight raw material varieties, including a burnt one (Gatsov *et al.* unpublished). All artifacts from building levels I–VIII were processed and in both periods – early and late Chalcolithic (designated as Karanovo V and Karanovo VI) almost two thirds of all artifacts were made of raw material varieties 1, 4 and 7. Varieties 2 and 6 were of a very low frequency in both periods. All burnt pieces are of variety 3. The assemblages from both periods display similar typological features. More than half of all retouched specimens were made of raw material samples 1 and 4. The remainder is of a smaller number of retouched pieces. In both periods, the most representative tool types such as blade end scrapers, retouched blades, blades with denticulated retouch and blade truncations were made of raw material varieties 1 and 4.

It is also worth mentioning the possibility of contact between the Chalcolithic settlements at Tell Azmak and some regions in north eastern Bulgaria, first suggested by V. Kurcatov's analysis. This is based on raw material variety 7 from the Chalcolithic layer at Tell Azmak. Samples from the site alongside geological samples from the Razgrad region, north eastern Bulgaria were compared (Kurchatov in press) and the salient points repeated here: 'The identical mineral composition of the samples, the similarities in the trace element contents and the textural analogy of the raw material give us reason to assume that the initial raw material (type 7) was taken from one and the same region.

Most probably the raw material used in the Chalcolithic layers at Tell Azmak originates from the northern cretaceous carbonate province (present-day north eastern Bulgaria – the area situated to the north and northeast of the Razgrad town). This province extends further north into present day Romania (Hansen *et al.* 2005, 341–393). Undoubtedly, i) 'the raw material has a sedimentary origin – plant and animal silicified detritus is present'; ii) 'the presence of corroded carbonate in all artifacts gives reason to conclude that the chert rocks resulted from silicification of primary carbonate sediments (formation of chert cores)'; iii) 'the negligible variations in the Mn content is explained by its irregular distribution in the chert, whereas the elevated contents of Ca and Mn in sample No. 61 (quartz inclusion in the sample from Kamenovo) is explained by calcite relics and surface weathering enrichment of Mn-oxides. The latter explains the brownish color of the inclusion surface'; and iv) 'in order to find out the exact location of presumed source of raw material, it is necessary to analyze a higher number of artefacts, which have to be correlated with the sample from the Razgrad region, north eastern Bulgaria' (Kurčatov, in press).

On the basis of these points it can be suggested that blanks in the form of blade cores or/and blades were brought from present day northeastern Bulgaria to northern Thrace and notably to the area of Tell Azmak. Current analysis being carried out by LaPorta Associates should shed further light on this. In this case, it may be that two sources of raw material supply were utilized, one local the other from a greater distance. The longer distance supply derived from flint sources and flint workshops in north eastern Bulgaria where cores or/and blades were obtained and transported to northern Thrace. The local supply includes raw material extraction and core processing close to Tell Azmak or even on the spot.

5 Conservation of Ancient Stone Quarry Landscapes in Egypt

Per Storemyr, Elizabeth Bloxam, Tom Heldal and Adel Kelany

Summary

Ancient Stone Quarry Landscapes in Egypt are under immense pressure from urban, industrial agricultural and tourist development. This paper discusses the threats and possibilities for conservation using case studies from Widan el-Faras in the Northern Faiyum (3rd millenium BC), Chephren's Quarry in Lower Nubia (3rd millenium BC) and the Aswan quarry landscape (Palaeolithic to the Roman period).

Introduction

The archaeological record in ancient quarries comprises not only the evidence of stone extraction, but also a complex range of associated material culture, which can include roads, shelters, ceramics, object blanks and epigraphic data – all of which collectively constitute an "ancient quarry landscape". Such landscapes can not only enhance our understanding of stone working traditions and extraction technologies, but also give valuable insights into the social context of stone quarrying at both a micro and macro-level. In some instances ancient quarries have significantly contributed to physically and aesthetically shaping the landscape and may comprise significant landmarks, exemplified by the impressive Pharaonic gallery quarries along the Nile Valley. At the other end of the scale are prehistoric tool quarries and workshops, often invisible for the untrained eye, but certainly no less significant.

Regrettably, in Egypt and the Eastern Mediterranean, a region very rich in ancient quarries, such landscapes are disappearing at an alarming rate due to modern development projects (Storemyr and Heldal 2009). Many other archaeological landscapes are affected as well (*e.g.* Palumbo and Teutonico 2002), but quarry landscapes are particularly vulnerable because they often cover large tracts of land and are usually not listed as archaeological sites. In Egypt, for example, with the legal heritage system based on "antiquities" (Law 117/1983), non-monumental heritage and archaeological landscapes might be forgotten in terms of conservation; a situation not unfamiliar in Europe a few years ago, before "landscape" started to attract scholarly and public interest.

QuarryScapes (www.quarryscapes.no), an EU-funded 3-year international project (2005–2008), aims to remedy some of these problems in the Eastern Mediterranean. Focusing on the characteristics of ancient quarry landscapes, their significance, the threats facing them and possibilities for conservation, the project uses case study areas in Egypt, Turkey and Jordan. In addition to contributing to scholarly discussion, the project organises fieldwork and field courses, and in Egypt has a partnership with the Supreme Council of Antiquities (SCA) to specifically put ancient quarries on the conservation agenda.

Three case study areas in Egypt may serve to illustrate a range of problems facing globally significant ancient quarry landscapes and efforts undertaken in terms of their conservation. Comprising Widan el-Faras, Chephren's Quarry and the Aswan quarry landscape, the case studies are briefly presented below. Ancient mines are omitted from the presentation, but similar arguments related to significance, risks and conservation would also apply to many of them. Local involvement and promotion of quarry landscapes for visitors and tourists, keys to public awareness and thus sustainable conservation, are not part of the presentation (but see Storemyr 2006; Bloxam 2006).

Brief research history

The Predynastic (*c.* 4000–3000 BC), Pharaonic (*c.* 3000–332 BC) and Graeco-Roman (332 BC–AD 395) quarries of Egypt have since long attracted interest from scholars, but until recently mainly from the perspective of stone provenance to the grand architecture of the country. The technological feats represented by Pharaonic quarrying, stone transportation and stone working have also figured on the research agenda (*e.g.* overviews by Lucas and Harris 1999 (1962); Arnold 1991; De Putter and Karlshausen 1992; Klemm and Klemm 1993; Aston 1994; Aston *et al.* 2000; Stocks 2003; Goyon *et al.* 2004, and references to more specific works therein. See also references to specific quarries below). The long-term work and many publications of James Harrell (www.eeescience.utoledo.edu/faculty/harrell/Egypt/AGRG_Home.html) in particular have given a broad picture of the distribution of ancient quarries along the Nile and in the Eastern Desert (Fig. 5.1), their geoarchaeological characteristics and use. On the other hand, the important social context of quarrying in Ancient Egypt, the political and ideological mechanisms behind quarrying operations and conceptualisation of quarry sites within broader aspects of landscape studies is still in its infancy (but see *e.g.* Peacock 1992; Bloxam 2003; Bloxam *et al.* 2009; Heldal *et al.* 2007(a); Bloxam and Heldal in press).

Although there are more than 200 large ancient Egyptian quarries associated with acquisition of stone for monuments, statuary and vessels, few detailed surveys and excavations have been undertaken. The most important projects have been at Mons Claudianus (Peacock and Maxfield 1997) and Mons Porphyrites (Maxfield and Peacock 2001) in the Eastern Desert, but also at Chephren's Quarry and Widan el-Faras (see below). Moreover, the truly monumental Unfinished Obelisk Quarry in the Aswan granite quarries has been of long-term research interest (*e.g.* Engelbach 1922, 1923; Roeder 1965), with large-scale excavation recently carried out by the SCA. Unique to Egypt, a modern outdoor museum and a site management programme have been recently established (Fig. 5.2). A stone documentation centre is in the planning phase.

Prehistoric tool quarries have also attracted the interest of scholars for a long time, in particular during the 1960s when research of Palaeolithic quarries, in silicified and

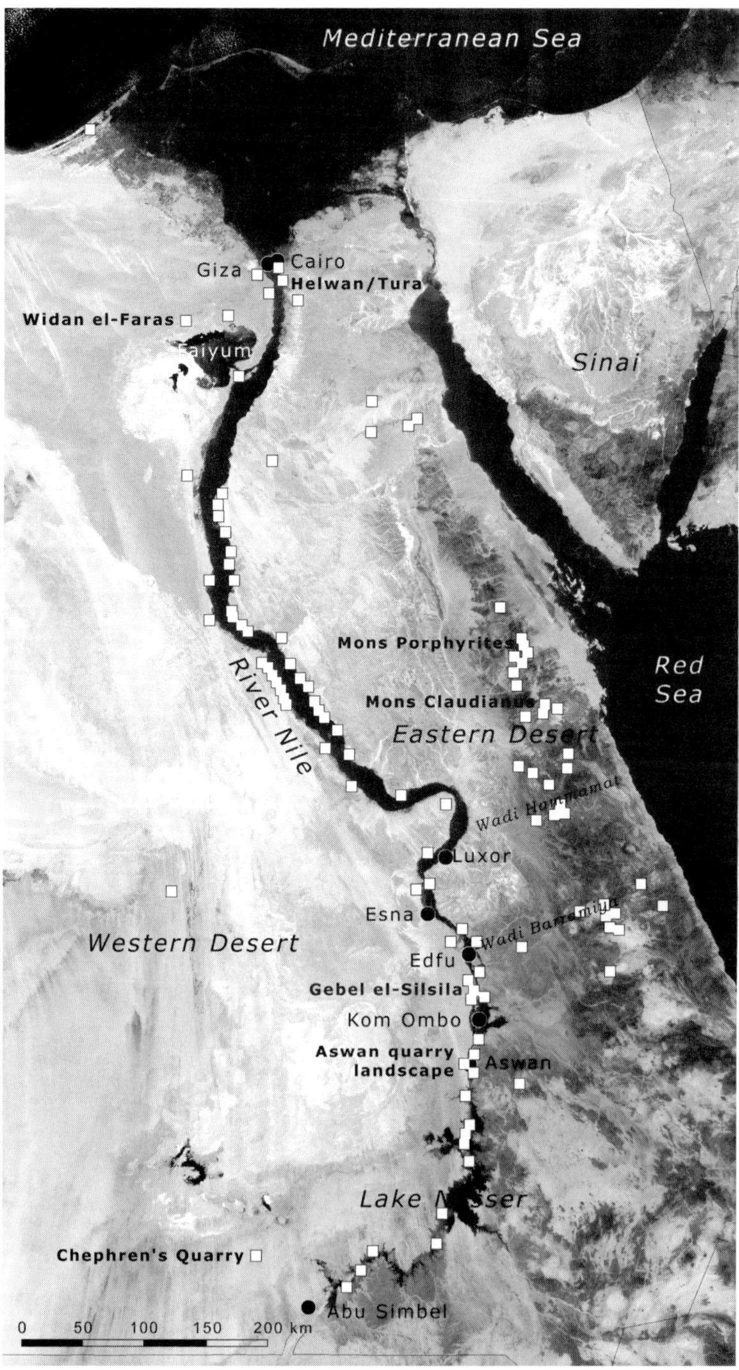

Figure 5.1. Distribution of major ancient quarries in Egypt. Source of location of quarry sites (white squares) provided by J. Harrell (see also www.eeescience.utoledo.edu/Faculty/Harrell/Egypt/AGRG_Home.html).

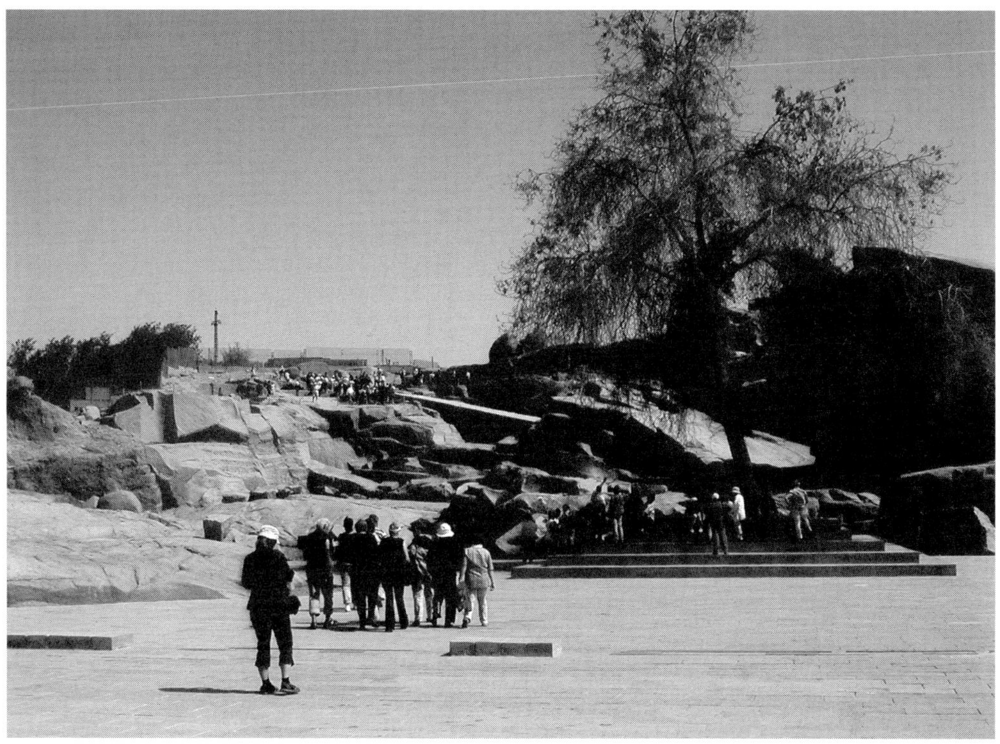

Figure 5.2. The Unfinished Obelisk quarry museum in Aswan. Photo by P. Storemyr.

ferruginous sandstone, was a part of the UNESCO archaeological rescue programme following the building of the High Dam at Aswan (*e.g.* Wendorf 1968). Later, Vermeersch (2002) and his colleagues have undertaken long-term research at Palaeolithic flint quarrying sites in Upper and Middle Egypt. The vast Eastern and Western Deserts are still virtually unknown in terms of prehistoric tool quarries, but surely many exist in these regions. Needless to say, such quarrying sites are extremely vulnerable to modern development activities, especially now that large-scale development of desert areas is high on the political agenda in Egypt.

Widan el-Faras: modern quarrying and pressure from greater Cairo

The Widan el-Faras basalt quarries are located in the Northern Faiyum Desert, about 60 km southwest of Giza (Fig. 5.3). They were primarily used for pyramid temple construction, especially temple floors at the pyramids of Khufu, Userkaf, Sahura and Nyuserra in the 4th and 5th dynasty (2575–2323 BC) (Hoffmeier 1993; Mallory-Greenough *et al.* 2000; Bloxam and Storemyr 2002), although one of the quarries was briefly reopened in the Early Roman period, probably for statuary (Bloxam and Storemyr 2002; Storemyr *et al.* 2009). The quarries have been known for more than a

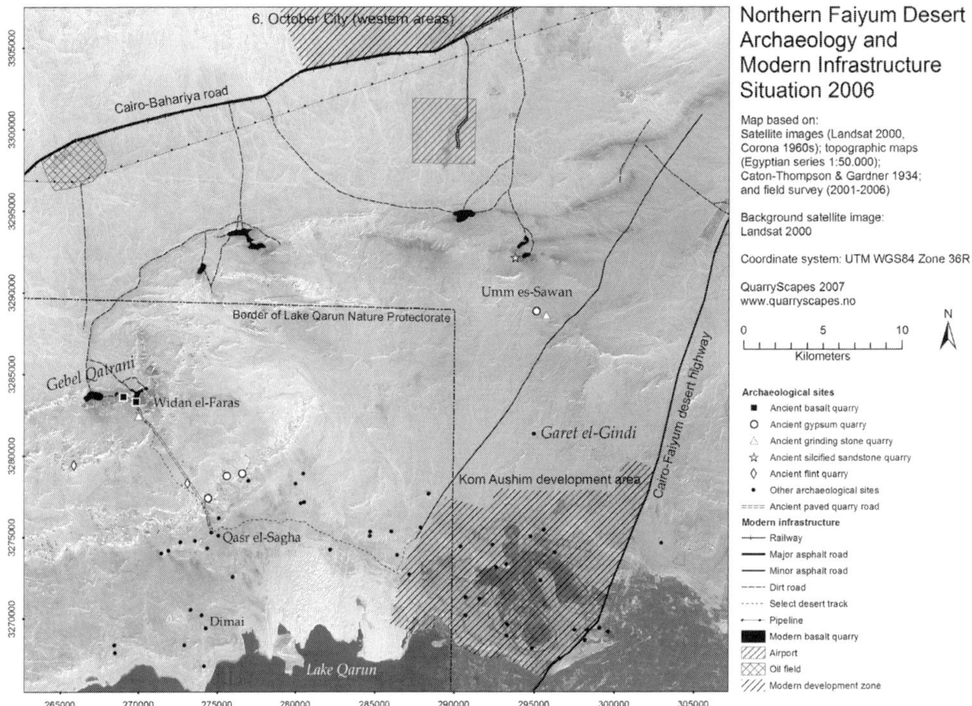

Figure 5.3. Archaeological sites and modern infrastructure in the Northern Faiyum. Map by QuarryScapes.

century (Beadnell 1905), but the actual extraction areas and parts of the infrastructure were discovered by Harrell and Bown (1995), their interpretations developed further with subsequent detailed surveys (Bloxam and Storemyr 2002; Bloxam 2003). Thus, a comprehensive picture has emerged, not only of the quarries themselves, but also of features related to transportation of the stone and organisation of the quarrying operations, such as roads, settlements, block storage areas and harbour facilities. Basalt blocks were taken from the quarries along an escarpment at 350 m above sea level to the plain immediately below, where they were collected for overland transport along an eleven kilometres long paved road to the Faiyum Depression, terminating at a quay by the ancient shore of Lake Moeris at some 20m above sea level (for a description of Lake Moeris, modern Lake Qarun, see *e.g.* Caton Thompson and Gardner 1934). The reasons why the use of basalt came to a halt by the end of the 5th Dynasty might have been due to a combination of political decentralization and declining Nile floods, leaving the harbour on dry land, thus complicating shipping across Lake Moeris to the Nile and eventually to the pyramid fields.

The uniqueness of the Widan el-Faras quarry landscape is neither related to the actual quarry traces, which are highly weathered, nor to its limited size. The most striking impression is given by its setting in a spectacular landscape and that it displays the whole organisation of an Old Kingdom remote quarrying operation, crowned by the transport system. Moreover, it represents a marker of important events in the development of technologies; the oldest preserved paved road in the world (Bown and Harrell 1995) was constructed for this exploitation, and the basalt floors in the pyramid complexes display one of the oldest known evidences of sawing large blocks of hard stone (Moores 1991).

Although Widan el-Faras is the most prominent quarry in the Northern Faiyum, this more than 1000 square kilometre large desert landscape features several other ancient quarries spread out across the area. The most well-known is Umm es-Sawan Old Kingdom gypsum quarries, 25km due east of Widan el-Faras, used mainly for small (funerary) vessels (Caton-Thompson and Gardner 1934; Heldal *et al.* 2006; Bloxam and Heldal 2007). By each of these quarries there are Old Kingdom grinding stone quarries and the area also holds a range of other gypsum quarries, sources for stone working tools such as basalt, silicified wood and silicified sandstone, as well as chert quarries. The products from the latter were presumably used at the rich prehistoric and later settlement areas along Lake Moeris. However, the Old Kingdom clearly was the period of the highest activity in the Northern Faiyum quarries; like Chephren's Quarry, described below, they form an outstandingly preserved industrial landscape that has hardly been overprinted by later operations, which is so typical at many other places. Hence, they give unique insights into a wealth of archaeological issues of a period when stone working reached proportions, in terms of quality and quantity, rarely later surpassed (Bloxam 2003; Bloxam and Heldal 2007).

Few, if any, of the archaeological sites in the Northern Faiyum Desert are under the supervision of SCA and there has been virtually no cultural heritage management of the area. However, a large part of the Northern Faiyum has, since 1989, enjoyed status as a nature protectorate, mainly due to its exceptionally rich tertiary fossil record (cf. Simons and Rasmussen 1991). Cultural heritage was apparently not part of the arguments leading to the establishment of the protectorate and its existence has had little impact on the conservation of the archaeological sites. For example, it did not prevent modern quarrying companies to start large-scale extraction of basalt for road building and construction at Widan el-Faras in 2001 – an activity previously confined to basalt outcrops closer to Cairo. Since then about one-third of the ancient basalt quarries have been destroyed (Fig. 5.4, cf. Storemyr *et al.* 2003).

The greatest danger to this largely undisturbed desert landscape is its proximity to Cairo which as one of the largest cities in the world is continually expanding. This landscape is thus attractive for development projects, notably road building, tourist facilities and development of residential areas, which are planned along the northern shores of Lake Qarun. Moreover, the Kom Aushim industrial and agricultural development zone is approaching from the east, and has already destroyed a range of archaeological sites in this area. Furthermore, industrial and residential areas of 6th October City, a part of Cairo developed from the 1970s, have already moved more than 40 km into the Western Desert and is now a mere 25km away from Widan el-Faras (Fig. 5.3). The proximity to a mega-city already leaves an imprint in form of uncontrolled tourist 4WD vehicle traffic directly on fragile sites (Fig. 5.5), as well as theft of artefacts such as stone tools and pottery.

Figure 5.4. Quarry site at Widan el-Faras in 2002 (above) and after destruction in 2006. Photos by P. Storemyr.

Clearly, in this situation, there is an urgent need for protection and management. However, official protection of single archaeological sites, not to mention a whole archaeological landscape, is a complex process in Egypt (generally, sites can be bought by SCA by Prime Ministerial Decree, or put under supervision by SCA by Decree of

Figure 5.5. The oldest paved road in the world leading from Widan el-Faras (hills in the background) to Qasr el-Sagha. Note modern vehicle tracks. Photo by Per Storemyr.

the Minister of Cultural Affairs; the latter option is usually the viable one in terms of ancient quarries). Moreover, there are limited financial resources at hand, for example, 4WD cars are normally not available for monitoring in desert areas; thus SCA depend on foreign missions for such work. In the QuarryScapes project, the Egyptian partners have concentrated on trying to halt the modern basalt quarrying. This strategy eventually led to a governorate decision on non-renewal of quarrying licences and since 2006 the most obvious destruction has stopped. However, until the site is under controlled supervision of SCA, it is likely that modern activities can resume at any time.

For the landscape at large the fortunate situation arose that the Egyptian branch of UNESCO and the national environmental authorities in 2006 decided to pursue nomination of parts of the Northern Faiyum as a World Heritage Site (WHS) on the basis of its fossil record and as an extension of Wadi Al-Hitan ("Whale Valley"), an already existing natural WHS to the west of the area (http://whc.unesco.org/en/list/1186). Much effort has been devoted by QuarryScapes to ensure that the ancient quarries and other archaeological sites were also used as arguments for inscription; as a combined natural and cultural WHS (cf. Storemyr *et al.* 2003; Bloxam and Heldal 2007). As of 2009 the situation remains unclear, but the Egyptian Authorities are still pursuing nomination and various conservation measures have been undertaken.

Generally, this work has revealed difficulties in nominating a combined natural and cultural WHS, as well as some shortcomings in the co-operation between cultural heritage and natural heritage/environmental authorities, issues probably not unique

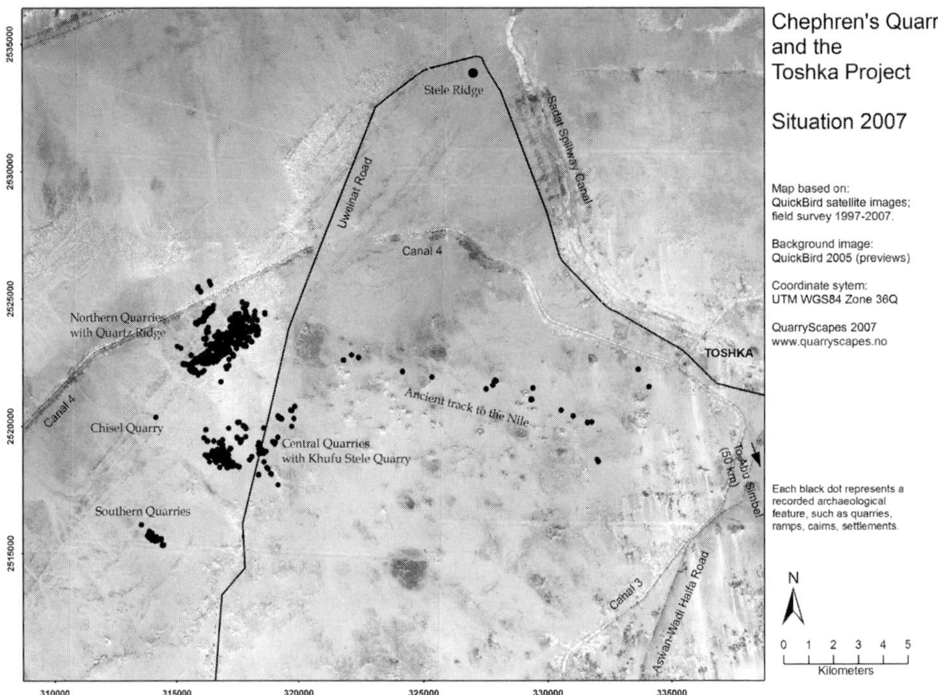

Figure 5.6. Archaeological sites in Chephren's Quarry and modern infrastructure related to the Toshka land reclamation project. Map by QuarryScapes.

to Egypt. Environmental authorities have experience in handling the protection and management of large tracts of land, and, clearly, the survival of archaeological landscapes can be ensured within nature protectorates. However, without the active involvement of cultural heritage authorities there is a risk that the archaeological resources are treated unprofessionally, are subject to mis-management, or are simply forgotten, like until recently in the Northern Faiyum. Whether or not the area will be inscribed as a World Heritage Site in the future, QuarryScapes aims at looking further into the relationships between cultural and natural heritage management in the conservation of ancient quarry landscapes (Storemyr 2006).

Chephren's quarry: mega-scale land reclamation

Hopefully, at least some parts of the Northern Faiyum quarry landscape will be preserved for the future. In the far south of Egypt other development projects might literally wipe out the 100 square kilometre large Chephren's Quarry in a few months. Located about 60km west of Abu Simbel, Chephren's Quarry (Fig. 5.6) was the source of stone for now world-famous sculptures and thousands of smaller funerary objects,

Figure 5.7. Part of Chephren's Quarry (Khufu Stele Quarry) with spoil heaps from quarrying (background) and loading ramp for transportation of blocks. Photo: P. Storemyr.

especially vessels, in the 3rd and 4th millennium BC. Engelbach (1938) and Murray (1939) made the first investigations in the 1930s, whereas recent research was carried out by Harrell and Brown (1994). Survey and excavation directed by Ian Shaw took place between 1997 and 2004 (Shaw and Bloxam 1999; Bloxam 2000, 2003; Storemyr *et al*. 2002; Heldal *et al*. 2009(b)).

Chephren's Quarry is situated within a complex of Precambrian, metamorphic igneous rocks, occurring as a window where younger Nubian sandstone has been removed by erosion. The rock type quarried is a light bluish, greyish to white gneiss with dark bands and spots – referred to as "Chephren Gneiss" (Harrell and Brown 1994). It occurs as large and small inclusions in granitic rocks, resulting in a highly irregular outcrop pattern of loose boulders formed by *in situ*, spheroidal weathering. Before quarrying commenced the flat desert landscape was covered with clusters of boulders, which were worked with stone hammers and axes from local sources. Fire-setting was also applied in the rough shaping of blocks. The quarrying process transformed the boulder landscape to clusters of sand-filled depressions surrounded by spoil heaps (Fig. 5.7). Almost all boulders of Chephren Gneiss were exploited and nearly 700 quarries of various sizes have been mapped. In addition to the extraction sites, the landscape displays roads, ramps, shelters and small camps, wells, cairns, inscribed stelae and other features related to the organisation of quarrying and maintenance of the labour force.

Presumably due to its aesthetic appearance, hardness and workability and, not least, the remoteness of the quarry site, Chephren Gneiss was a prestigious stone. The consumption record suggests that exploitation started in the Late Neolithic, but it peaked in the 3rd and 4th Dynasties of the Old Kingdom (Bloxam 2003). Since no evidence of permanent settlement has been found, it would seem that the quarrying was organised in the same manner as at Widan el-Faras – as short-lived campaigns for specific purposes (*e.g.* statues) involving relatively few highly skilled people (Bloxam 2003). One might wonder, though, whether there existed a more permanent presence associated with vessel-production. Semi-permanent settlement would presumably have been possible until the climate deteriorated in the 3rd millennium BC (Bloxam 2003; Nicoll 2004).

Paradoxically, in this currently driest of landscapes, one of the world's largest land-reclamation projects is now undertaken. Celebrated and highly criticised, the so-called Toshka or "New Valley" project ultimately aims to create a green zone through a corridor of the Eastern Sahara parallel to the Nile, from Lake Nasser to the Mediterranean. The first phase of the project, which started in the late 1990s, has involved the excavation of hundreds of kilometres of canals in the vicinity of Chephren's Quarry. These canals, of which two of four are in operation, are fed through a pumping station at Lake Nasser. Groundwater from the Nubian aquifer will be used in other regions of the vast project area to render the desert green (Wahby 2004; Ismail *et al.* undated).

According to original plans, the whole of Chephren's Quarry and the nearby Stele Ridge Middle Kingdom carnelian mining site should already have been bulldozed, covered with topsoil and now producing cash crops for the international market. Moreover, the planned Toshka city should have been the home for thousands of people having moved from the overpopulated Nile Valley. However, the project has apparently drained the Egyptian economy to such an extent that from 2003–4 it has come to a virtual standstill (*e.g.* El-Din 2006; Wahish 2006). The unfinished canal 4, which cuts through marginal areas of Chephren's Quarry, is left as a huge scar on the desert surface (Figs 5.6 and 5.8), but still most parts of the quarry landscape is reasonably well preserved, as observed in 2007. Destroyed areas mainly include those affected by initial road building in the region. Because of the new roads, the area is passed by desert tourists en route to Gilf Kebir and the Great Sand Sea. As at the famous nearby Nabta Playa Neolithic settlement sites, many of these tourists do not refrain from looting the sites for artefacts.

Although the quarry landscape has been designated for supervision by SCA after intervention by the authors in 2002, it will be severely threatened once the land-reclamation resumes. Thus, it should be of very high priority that protection regulations and monitoring are enforced. However, perhaps a more important issue is that the outline of the quarry landscape is not found on official maps of the Toshka project (cf. Ismail *et al.* undated). The failure to include archaeological sites and landscapes on development maps/plans is a general problem in Egypt: Many large development projects in desert areas and along the Nile were planned decades ago and are now carried out without reference to archaeological sites, long known by scholars and the

Figure 5.8. Mapping of Chephren's Quarry in 2003 while Canal 4 of the Toshka project is being constructed in the background. Photo by P. Storemyr.

SCA. This is not necessarily because of unwillingness from the side of the developers, but because they are often poorly informed about the archaeology; land has been sold, and it is understandably very difficult to change long-term, large-scale plans. In the case of Chephren's Quarry, the temporary halt of development activities might help in saving the site, and QuarryScapes is working on including the quarry landscape on development maps.

The Aswan quarry landscape: urban and industrial development

Unlike Widan el-Faras and Chephren's Quarry, which give unique glimpses into specifically Old Kingdom remote quarrying operations, the Aswan quarry landscape along a 15km stretch of the Nile in Upper Egypt is highly complex with a history of stone working that stretches back to the Palaeolithic. This quarry landscape is also immense, totalling more than 100 square kilometres, and includes three areas that are interconnected in various ways:

- Granite quarries within and to the south of Aswan City at the East Bank of the Nile
- Silicified sandstone quarries on the East Bank between Wadi Abu Agag and Wadi Abu Subeira
- Silicified and non-silicified sandstone quarries on the West Bank between the Old Aswan Dam and Wadi Kubbaniya

The well-known granite quarries have been on the research agenda since Napoleon's *savants* recorded the archaeology of Egypt around 1800. The use of the stone has a history back to the Early Dynastic Period for vessels, but consumption peaked in the Old Kingdom when the stone was used at a large scale for pyramid construction. Since then the quarries were in more or less continuous use until the Roman period (*e.g.* Röder 1965; Klemm and Klemm 1993, 305–53; Aston 1994, 15–8; Aston *et al.* 2000; Bloxam 2003, 142–4). Quarrying resumed in the late 19th century and is still a major industry in Aswan. In the early stages quarrying was undertaken like at Chephren's Quarry, using loose boulders for producing the desired products. Especially from the New Kingdom onwards there is evidence of true bedrock quarrying for the production of obelisks, statues and other items, with the New Kingdom Unfinished Obelisk quarry as the highlight for the modern visitor (see above).

The silicified sandstone quarries at the East Bank have only been subject of minor research (Harrell and Madbouly 2006), but it is clear that they are very extensive and showing multiple periods of use, probably much like similar quarries at the West Bank (Klemm and Klemm 1993, 289–303; Heldal *et al.* 2005; Bloxam and Storemyr 2005). These quarries have recently been surveyed in detail by the QuarryScapes project (Bloxam *et al.* 2007). They have been in use for production of tools in the Middle Palaeolithic or earlier (Heldal and Storemyr 2007), for grinding stone from the Late Palaeolithic to possibly the Roman period (*ibid.*; Roubet 1989), and for ornamental stone from probably the Old Kingdom to the Roman period (Heldal and Storemyr 2007). Although the grinding stone procurement was by far the most important quarrying activity that took place at the West Bank, the most pronounced quarries date to the New Kingdom (Heldal and Storemyr 2007) and is accompanied by a remarkable network of paved and cleared quarry roads, in total almost 20km long (Heldal *et al.* 2007). In addition to the silicified sandstone quarries there are numerous building stone quarries in non-silicified sandstone at the West Bank, mainly dating to the Graeco-Roman period (Heldal and Storemyr 2007).

Documentation of the material culture associated with the Aswan quarries is as of yet mainly available for the West Bank (Bloxam *et al.* 2007). This area incorporates features such as cemeteries, ancient desert tracks, a range of ephemeral stone structures, smithies, game drives and a vast body of Prehistoric to Roman period rock-art and inscriptions, some of which are associated with the quarries. Ancient ochre and iron production also took place within the quarry landscape.

With this extraordinary history of quarrying, Aswan must be regarded as one of the most varied and long-lived quarry landscapes in the world. A large amount of stone product types from nearly all prehistoric and historic periods is represented in the area. Although most of the quarry landscape looks far from monumental for the modern visitor, the significance of the landscape could perhaps best be described by this word: monumental. The landscape is a showcase of the history of quarrying hardly to be found elsewhere.

The landscape was well preserved until the 1960s and the building of the Aswan High Dam. In the wake of the construction of the High Dam, and influenced by large population growth from 50,000 in 1960 to a present 500,000 people, the quarry landscape has over the past 40 years been increasingly utilised for dwellings and industrial activities, including large-scale modern quarrying and mining. Also, small-scale but extensive artisan quarrying is taking place. This means that many quarries and associated archaeological features are now lost, especially in the granite quarry area. Recently, the construction of "New Aswan City" on the West Bank also commenced within the ancient quarry landscape (Figs 5.9 and 5.11). As at Chephren's Quarry, this huge development project, planned a long time ago, has until recently not incorporated archaeological sites on its official maps and plans. Due to the proximity to an urban area, looting and vandalism is another major threat in the Aswan quarries.

The conservation problems in Aswan are representative for the Nile Valley as a whole; they are as varied and complex as the quarry landscape itself. With the exception of the Unfinished Obelisk Quarry (see above), no quarries in Aswan are listed. QuarryScapes has developed a three-fold strategy for putting these quarries on the conservation agenda: First, rescue surveys are being carried out by the Egyptian partners working with the regional SCA office at sites which are immediately threatened. Such fieldwork and subsequent map-making are aided by other QuarryScapes partners. Second, cooperation between the heritage authorities and modern quarrying companies has been put forward and it has so far been a success in that several modern quarries have been relocated away from ancient extraction sites in the granite quarry landscape. A similar cooperation is underway with the New Aswan City authorities. Third, the less threatened parts, notably the West Bank south of New Aswan City, are used for in-depth studies of ancient quarrying activities as seen in a landscape perspective (Fig. 5.9). This strategy is based on the insight that, in practice, only small islands of archaeological remains can be saved in the "hottest" urban and industrial zones. However, in zones yet to be developed, the imperative is to articulate at local, national and international levels the significance, value and archaeological integrity of the landscape, in the hope that preservation of larger stretches of land can be enforced, hence considering the landscape context of the ancient quarrying operations.

Discussion and outlook

The conservation problems of ancient quarry landscapes in Egypt are linked largely to enormous pressure on land resources from rapid population growth and the physical threats arising from associated urban, industrial and agricultural development. Whereas two or three decades ago only ancient quarry landscapes in the Nile Valley were threatened; from now on desert areas will also be massively affected. Moreover, these conservation problems are compounded by a limited knowledge of ancient quarries, a cultural heritage legislation that does not account for archaeological landscapes, as well as difficulties in communication between different authorities and involved parties. There is also a fundamental lack of human and financial resources needed to undertake professional monitoring and management of sites and landscapes at risk. Generally, this situation is recognised by SCA, which established the Egyptian Antiquities Information System (EAIS, www.eais.org.eg), a nation-wide GIS for archaeological sites, some years ago. This programme is partially aimed at putting the enormous amount of archaeological sites on easily accessible official maps that should be consulted by developers before modern activities commence. However, it will certainly take time before this system will be in active use throughout Egypt.

In realising the complexity of the conservation problems and as the case studies

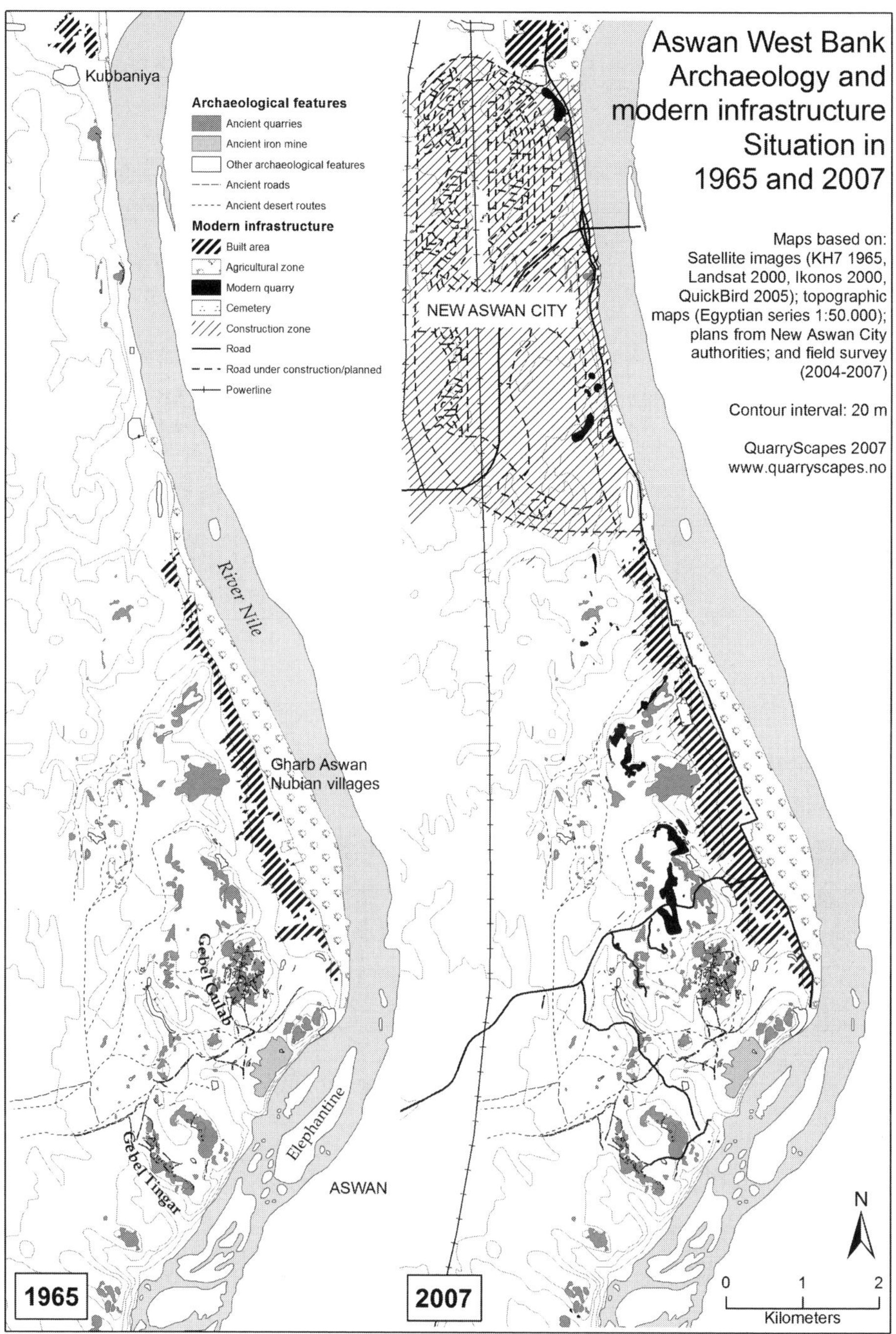

Figure 5.9. Example of the influence of modern infrastructure on archaeological sites in Aswan. Situation at the West Bank in 1965 and 2007. Map by QuarryScapes.

Figure 5.10. Part of the industrial landscape at Gebel Gulab with road leading from a block extraction place in the foreground. Photo by P. Storemyr.

Figure 5.11. Construction work at New Aswan city in 2005. In the background is a Nubian sandstone quarry from the Graeco-Roman period. Photo: P. Storemyr.

have shown, QuarryScapes has adopted an "opportunistic" strategy for promoting conservation. Not surprisingly, a key seems to be active co-operation with public and private developers and authorities in order to relocate or stop destructive activity. In the long term, this strategy is clearly not sufficient. It may help in protecting "islands" of archaeological remains in a strongly transformed, modern landscape, but it will hardly aid the prevention of new modern development within ancient quarry areas, which are not yet thoroughly overprinted by modern infrastructure. Thus, as the case studies have demonstrated, another key to protection is to put such archaeological landscapes on modern development maps and plans before land is sold or otherwise prepared for modern activities. Since only a tiny fraction of the ancient quarries in Egypt are as yet supervised or owned by the SCA, EAIS, as a QuarryScapes partner, is working on including all known quarries in their nation-wide GIS. This work is based on James Harrell's overviews of ancient quarries mentioned above, as well consulting a multitude of sources in order to reveal the actual legal status of the sites. Another key to long-term preventive conservation is improvement of knowledge of such landscapes within the cultural heritage authorities. Of great significance is the initiative from the SCA to establish a new department for conservation of ancient quarries and mines, in which the regional offices will assign two inspectors each for monitoring and management in their area of responsibility. In order to become an efficient unit, education of assigned inspectors is a high-priority task. A remaining problem is adequate funding.

More active co-operation between cultural heritage and environmental authorities is recommended. There are 27 nature protectorates in Egypt, covering more than 10% of the country's area (www.eeaa.gov.eg/English/main/Protectorates.asp). Few of these incorporate ancient quarries and mines, but several new protectorates are planned, especially in the Eastern Desert (Egypt State of the Environment Report 2004), encompassing very important quarry landscapes. If there is a failure to carry out active cultural resource management in these potential protectorates, prevention of destruction of ancient quarries might not be guaranteed, as demonstrated in the case of Widan el-Faras.

Concluding remarks

The work of QuarryScapes has demonstrated the urgent need for putting ancient quarry landscapes on the conservation agenda. Some results have already been obtained, but until the significance of such landscapes is recognised by broader parts of the scholarly community, the cultural resource management field and the public, it is difficult to envision a sustainable improvement. One way to obtain a greater interest for quarries is to promote such sites and landscapes for inclusion on the World Heritage List. Until now only one site is inscribed by virtue of its significance as a quarry (the Spiennes flint "mines" in Belgium), some others are coincidentally part of larger complexes, *e.g.* the Pyramid fields from Giza to Dashur. In contrast, there are more than 10 mining sites on the list, new ones frequently being added in the annual nomination process. The three Egyptian quarry landscapes described in this paper would all easily qualify for inclusion. There is certainly a wealth of other quarries in Egypt, the Eastern Mediterranean and worldwide that would qualify as well.

Acknowledgements

We would like to express our thanks to Secretary General Zahi Hawass and the Permanent Committee of the SCA as well as EAIS and the regional SCA offices in Faiyum, Aswan and Abu Simbel for partnership and co-operation. Thanks also to QuarryScapes partner North-South Consultants Exchange and Samir Ghabbour of UNESCO Egypt for aiding the work in Faiyum. We are very grateful to James Harrell for supplying us with a wealth of information on Egyptian quarries. QuarryScapes, Conservation of ancient stone quarry landscapes in the Eastern Mediterranean, is funded by the EC 6th Framework Programme for Research and Development (contract INCO-MED 015416).

This paper was originally written in 2007 and the QuarryScapes project was finalised with a workshop in Aswan in November 2008. In the meantime there have been various developments in the case study areas described above. Such developments and the general outcome of QuarryScapes are described in recent papers. Please visit http://www.quarryscapes.no for further information. See also Abu-Jaber, N., Bloxam, E., Degryse, P. and Heldal, T. (eds) 2009, *QuarryScapes. Ancient stone quarry landscapes in the Eastern Mediterranean*, Geological Survey of Norway Special Publication 12. Bloxam, E. and Heldal, T. 2008, *Identifying heritage values and character-defining elements of ancient quarry landscapes in the Eastern Mediterranean: an integrated analysis*, Geological Survey of Norway, QuarryScapes report, (downloadable from www.quarryscapes.no) and Storemyr, P., Bloxam, E. and Heldal, T. 2007, *Risk assessment and monitoring of ancient Egyptian quarry landscapes*. Geological Survey of Norway, QuarryScapes report, (downloadable from www.quarryscapes.no).

6 Dorset Palaeoeskimo Quarrying Techniques and the Production of Little Pots at Fleur de Lys, Newfoundland

John C. Erwin

Summary

Dorset Palaeoeskimo soapstone quarrying at Fleur de Lys can be described as a four stage process that includes quarry face preparation, pre-form isolation, pre-form extraction and vessel finishing. Evidence for quarrying methods and vessel finishing techniques demonstrate that the Dorset practiced a narrow range of techniques to produce a limited range of vessel types over time. On the basis of the relative size and shape of soapstone vessels and residue patterning, previous archaeological investigations of Dorset vessels only recognized two main vessel types: oil lamps, and cooking pots. The confirmation of another type of vessel, defined as a "little pot" found at the Fleur de Lys 1 (EaBa-1) soapstone quarry and the associated habitation/workshop site known as Shelley Garden (EaBa-10), suggests that Dorset soapstone quarrying was an activity which was socially more complex than previously believed. As such, it is argued that the production of little pots involved children who were likely imitating the work of their parents, and learning something of vessel production while at play.

Background

The prehistoric soapstone industry on the Island of Newfoundland is best known from the quarry site known as Fleur de Lys 1 (EaBa-1) located on the northern tip of the Baie Verte Peninsula (Fig. 6.1) (Erwin 1998; 1999; 2001; 2005a; Howley 1974 [1915]; Jenness 1932; Linnamae 1975; Nagle 1982; 1984; Thomson 1984; 1986; Wintemberg 1940). The quarry, which was in use from approximately AD 400 until AD 800 (Erwin 2005a, 125), provided the raw material for the production of cooking vessels and oil lamps used by the Dorset Palaeoeskimos. Fleur de Lys 1 is also the largest and best preserved Dorset quarry site yet discovered, and the only known prehistoric soapstone quarry on the Island of Newfoundland. While there is evidence that Fleur de Lys soapstone was used by earlier Maritime Archaic peoples for the production of plummets (Erwin 2001; 2005a), the vast majority of the quarrying activity is attributed to the Dorset Palaeoeskimos on the basis of the extraction scars (Wintemberg 1940, 310), the presence of broken vessel fragments (Nagle 1982, 105–106) and non-quarrying tools belonging to the Dorset (Erwin 1998, 13) that have been excavated from the site.

The soapstone carved from the exposed cliff faces of Fleur de Lys 1 is a relatively soft and easily workable material, visually distinctive owing to iron inclusions

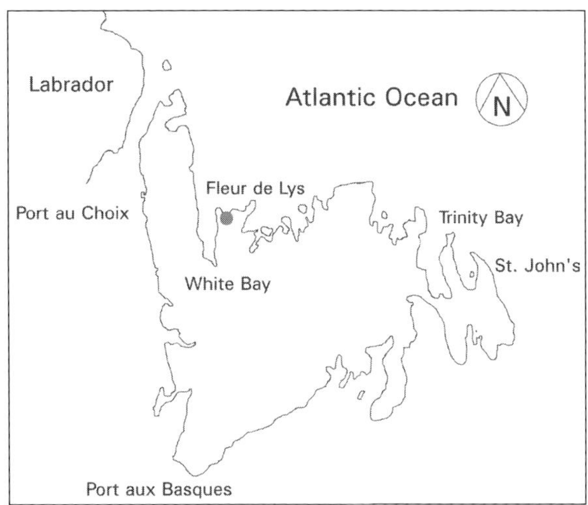

Figure 6.1. Location Plan.

which oxidize when exposed to the natural elements. As a result, vessels fashioned from Fleur de Lys soapstone have a characteristically pitted texture and are reddish-brown in colour. While rare earth element investigations (Allen *et al.* 1978; Allen *et al.* 1984) using neutron activation analysis have demonstrated that geological signatures can be recognized in soapstone, the wide range of signatures obtained from the Fleur de Lys outcrops make isolation of a Fleur de Lys signature problematic (Nagle 1984). In fact, the geological signatures from Fleur de Lys could account for most of the soapstone artifacts found throughout the entire province of Newfoundland and Labrador. In view of this geological variability, and lack of other known prehistoric soapstone quarries in the region, the Fleur de Lys quarry's place as the predominant source of soapstone in Newfoundland and Labrador has largely remained unquestioned (Erwin 2001, 49).

The quarry consists of six known soapstone outcrops situated along the north side of a well-protected harbour throughout the present-day town of Fleur de Lys. The quarry is also associated with a habitation/workshop site known as Shelley Garden (EaBa-10) (Erwin 2003; Thomson 1989). The total number of vessels produced from all six localities is estimated to be about 2000. This number is based upon estimates which take into account evidence for multiple courses of extraction scars buried below the present day ground surface (Erwin 2001, 154). The most heavily quarried area is designated Locality 1, which is an area comprised of a series of eleven discontinuous outcrops that measure 300m in length, and contain 654 visible pre-form scars (Erwin 2001, 58). Within this locality, an area identified as Group B (north), contains the greatest number (n=186) and many of the best preserved vessel removal scars (Fig. 6.2). This is also the area from which the little pots (see below) were recovered during excavations conducted by Erwin in 1997 and 1998 (Erwin 1998; 1999; 2001).

Dorset quarrying methods

With the exception of little pots, the evidence for Dorset quarrying methods at the Fleur de Lys quarry demonstrates a narrow range of techniques which do not significantly vary over time, or with vessel size or shape. These techniques are summarized as follows.

The first step in the quarrying process can be described as a preparation stage. This stage constitutes the removal of the naturally-weathered and brittle surface of the quarry

Figure 6.2. Potscar.

face, and/or the previously-worked areas of the outcrop. This was accomplished by battering the quarry face with heavy stone picks and mauls to achieve a fresh working surface. These tools were fashioned from local quartzite cobbles which were gathered by the Dorset from a now buried stream which once flowed alongside Locality 1. The recovery of hundreds of large and heavily battered quarry preparation tools, and the identification of weathered soapstone debris, including portions of pre-form removal scars, are indicative of this initial stage of the quarrying process. The presence of prepared, but un-worked areas of the quarry face, as indicated by the arrow in Fig. 6.3, provides additional evidence for this preparation stage.

Once a flat fresh surface was prepared, an outline of the intended pre-form vessel was pecked into the quarry face with angular-edged hand-held tabular picks fashioned from lithic materials which were derived from the local bedrock. This initial isolation process determined the maximum length and width of the intended vessel. Use-wear and breakage patterns on the corners of the quarrying tools are consistent with their use in this process. More specifically, the recovery of hundreds of broken tool ends from amongst the tailings is also evidence that some degree of percussion was involved in the use of these tools (Erwin 2001, 110–111; 2005a, 128).

The isolation process proceeded with longer and narrower picks as a means to deepen the excavation around the pre-form vessel (Erwin 2001, 99–100; 2005a, 128). This continued until the pre-form was excavated to a depth matching the desired height of the vessel. It is important to note that the angle and depth of the excavation determined the final size and shape of the finished vessel. In addition, this inward excavation also

Figure 6.3. Quarry Face (Locality 1).

served to reduce the amount of material which held the pre-form vessel to the quarry face, and would determine the size of the base of the finished vessel.

Once the desired depth of excavation was reached, the vessel pre-form was ready to be removed from the quarry face. Considering the relative mass of the pre-form, in comparison with the reduced surface area which held it to the quarry face, the removal was simply accomplished with a combination of wedge and hammerstone which were utilized to pry the vessel from the surrounding parent material. Use-wear on wedges such as distal abrasions and proximal battering provide strong evidence for their use in combination with battered hammerstones (Erwin 2001, 100–101; 2005a, 128). Dorset stone workers also quite likely recognized the usefulness of naturally occurring horizontal fractures in the quarry face which could facilitate the detachment process. Evidence for the utilization of these natural cleavages is shown in the vicinity of the arrow in Figure 6.3, where carvings can be seen in a fresh section of the quarry face situated behind an earlier course of pre-form removals. As illustrated, these naturally occurring horizontal fractures also provided a clean flat surface to repeat the removal process for production of multiple courses of pre-form removal.

Vessel finishing

The vessel finishing process was conducted in a similar fashion to the initial isolation of the intended pre-form on the quarry face. As with the initial isolation stage, the hollowing out of the interior of the detached pre-form began with carving of a groove which marked the size of the intended excavation. This step also determined the width of the rim and the wall thickness of the finished vessel (Fig. 6.4). While this hollowing procedure could have been accomplished by simply gouging out the middle of the pre-form until the desired depth was achieved, evidence from partially finished specimens

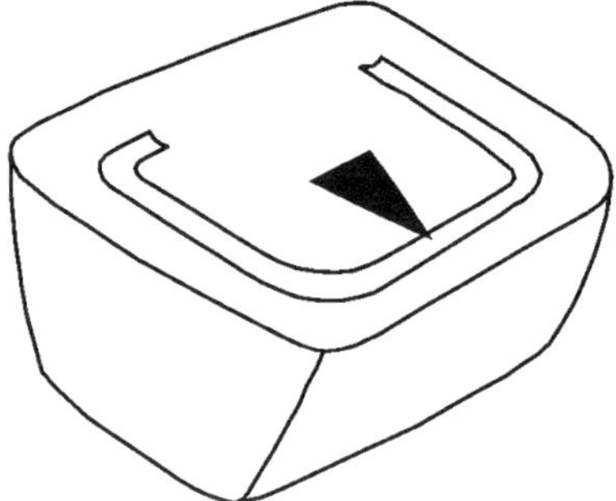

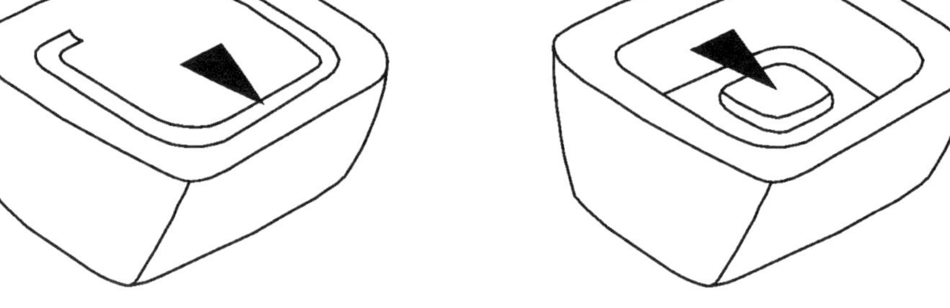

Figure 6.4. Vessel Finishing – Isolation. *Figure 6.5. Vessel Finishing – Removal.*

recovered from the quarry (Erwin 2001, 101–102) indicates that the preferred finishing technique was to first isolate the area of the intended removal by establishing the rim width, and then carving inward from the edges to the centre of the finished vessel.

This hollowing-out process continued with the widening of this groove toward the interior of the vessel using scraping and gouging tools. Evidence for this procedure is found in broken and abandoned pre-forms which contain a small mound of stone at the center of the interior of the unfinished vessel (Fig. 6.5). Upon the removal of this remaining material, the vessel was practically complete. Further finishing may have included abrading to remove gouge marks and to thin the vessel walls. In a few cases, there is evidence for carving of multiple horizontal grooves on the outside corners of the vessel (Erwin 2005a, 128; n.d.). While such grooves may have been decorative, it is speculated that they may have functioned as stays for the suspension of the pot over a lamp or other source of heat.

The completed vessel

Dorset vessels from this period on the Island of Newfoundland are characteristically rectangular in shape and functionally categorized as either lamps or cooking pots on the basis of their size and residue patterns. Lamp function is generally recognizable based upon relatively clean exterior surfaces, and burning residue on interior surfaces, particularly just below the rim of the vessel. Conversely, pot function is generally recognizable based upon burning and heavily encrusted charcoal residues on the exterior of vessels (Erwin n.d.). Vessel type can also be inferred from vessel size. Using base area as an indicator, measurements were made of every extraction scar at Locality 1 in Fleur de Lys, from which two discreet categories of vessels can be identified: (1) lamps: vessels with base areas less than 200cm^2 and, (2) cooking Pots: vessels with base areas greater than 200cm^2 (Erwin 2001, 75). While these categories represent maximum and minimum base areas, the average base area for lamps is 100cm^2 for lamps, and 500cm^2 for pots (see Fig. 6.6).

From the analysis of every available Dorset vessel and soapstone fragment from the collections of the Newfoundland Museum in 2004 (Erwin n.d.), it can be concluded that there is a limited range of vessel styles relative to geographic and temporal differences

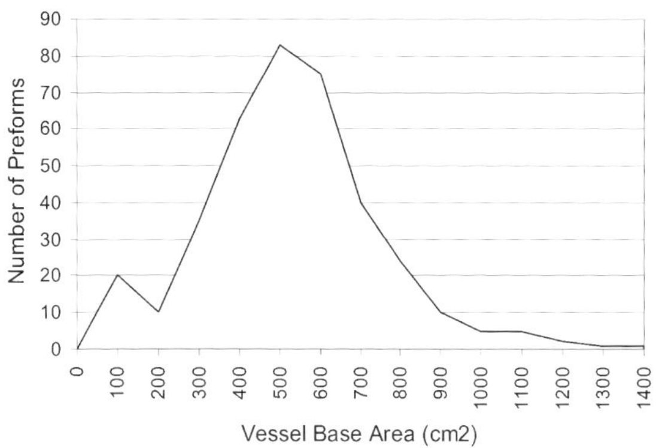

Figure 6.6. Preform Vessel Base Areas.

in Dorset culture. Notwithstanding such minor differences, there is a positive correlation between quality of soapstone and the level of craftsmanship. In this regard, vessel wall thickness is the single-most important attribute related to the quality of lithic material. Thicker-walled vessels are generally made of lower-grade soapstone, which can be characterized as being porous and containing numerous inclusions. Conversely, thinner-walled vessels tend to be made of higher-quality soapstone that can be described as homogeneous, fine-grained, and having fewer inclusions. Since Dorset lamps are often thin-walled exquisitely carved specimens, as illustrated in Figure 6.7, they must be fashioned from fine-grained materials that permit the carving of vessel walls which are only 2–3mm in thickness.

Figure 6.7. Dorset Hand Lamp.

In view of the varying grades of soapstone which are present in Fleur de Lys (Erwin 2001, 60), and the correlation between material quality and vessel wall thickness, it could be argued that lamp pre-form scars should be found in greater abundance in parts of the quarry where higher quality stone is found. In this regard, the "grotto", originally identified by Nagle (1982, 108–109), which contains the highest quality stone in Fleur de Lys (Erwin 2001, 60–61), should contain a greater proportion of smaller vessels. Upon the comparison of vessel base area measurements from the 13 discretely worked areas of Locality 1, there appears to be no such correlation. In fact, only one of 32 vessel pre-forms with a base area of less than 200cm^2 is carved into this location which contains the highest quality stone. While the Dorset did utilize the grotto extensively, it is uncertain why so few smaller vessels were carved. Speculatively, it might be argued that the Fleur de Lys quarry was a place known to the Dorset from which to fashion cooking pots, and that more suitable materials for the production of other items, such as lamps, and artistic miniatures (*e.g.* shamanistic art) were to be found elsewhere.

Evidence for Dorset miniature vessels

Notwithstanding the small size of Dorset hand lamps, a third category of vessel, namely, "little pots" was initially proposed by Christopher Nagle on the basis of small extraction scars which were "always located within a meter of the ground" at the Fleur de Lys quarry (Nagle 1982, 118). In reporting these smaller carvings, Nagle suggested that they were probably made by children who were emulating the work of their parents. A number of these so-called little pots were recovered from the 1997–98 excavations, and were compared to other Dorset vessels such as hand lamps. The little pots appeared to have some notable difference in relation to style, manufacture, and the fact that they were generally unbroken, yet discarded (Erwin 1999, 18–19). This initial assessment suggested that there may be sufficient evidence to test Nagle's hypothesis: that these little pots were made by children. Based upon the following comparison of physical attributes, including stylistic differences, and relative abundance, I propose that there is sufficient evidence to define a category of a miniature Dorset vessels (Fig. 6.8). The result of this evaluation is summarized in Table 6.1, and it suggests that there are two distinct groups of small vessels: (1) well-made rectangular specimens interpreted as lamps, and (2) crudely made little pots, which are the work of inexperienced hands.

Vessel Characteristics	*Little Pots*	*All Other Vessels*
Abundance at quarry	Many complete specimens	No complete specimens
General vessel shape	Round and oval	Square and rectangular
Breakage	Few broken	Mostly broken
Finishing technique	Outward from middle	Inward from rim
Location of preform scars	On boulders away from quarry face	On main quarry face
Height of scars	Within 1 meter of ground	Up to 3 meters from ground
Quality of manufacture	Crudely fashioned	Well made

Table 6.1. Comparison of Little Pots and Other Vessels from Fleur de Lys 1.

Figure 6.8. Dorset Little Pot.

Figure 6.9. Miniature Scars on Boulder Outcrop.

The most highly-visible evidence for the production of little pots are the four tiny, but clearly defined carvings which are located on a small boulder situated a few meters in front of the quarry face at Locality 1 (Fig. 6.9). There are an additional 10 comparable pre-form scars which are located across Locality 1. In addition to their small size, the most notable difference between these 14 carvings and the other 650 documented attempts is that only one of these 14 tiny scars appears to have resulted in the actual removal of a pre-form vessel. This stands in direct contrast to a removal success rate of 82% for the remainder of the 650 larger pre-form scars. While these 13 small and incomplete scars could represent abandoned attempts at lamp production, this seems unlikely considering that the extraction attempts were almost always made. In view of the lack of comparable small pre-form removals from the quarry face, the discovery of a number of small and crudely-fashioned small vessels from the 1997–98 excavations suggested that these vessels were made from scavenged quarry debris, and were not removed from the quarry face in the same manner as were the larger vessels.

Based upon a comparison of all excavated vessel fragments (n=56) recovered from the 1997–98 excavations, it was found that the only unbroken vessels were represented in a collection of small crudely-made vessels (n=6). Since no finished vessels were recovered from the quarry, it is arguable that all of the specimens which we recovered were discarded as a result of breakage and/or factors which made them unsuitable as functional vessels. As such, this small number of unfinished crudely-made specimens is an anomaly that could be explained in one of two ways: (1) they were intended as hand lamps, but subsequently discarded on the basis that they were too poorly made to be worth finishing, or (2) they were practice vessels, and/or expedient playthings made by children which were simply discarded.

The general shape and finishing technique of these crudely-fashioned examples also differentiates these specimens from all other vessels. More specifically, these little pots have rounded unstable bases, and lack the regular angular shape and standardized form which characterize other Dorset vessels. Little pots are also hollowed-out from the center outward, producing a shallow rounded central depression. Other Dorset vessels are finished from the rim, inwards, resulting in straight parallel walls and a regular rectangular interior. These differences are further illustrated in this comparison of a rounded little pot, and a rectangular hand lamp pre-form (Fig. 6.10). The crudeness of this specimen is suggestive of the inexperienced hand of an individual such as a child who has yet to develop the necessary skill and dexterity to produce a vessel in the typical Dorset fashion.

Quarry function

The Fleur de Lys quarry has long been interpreted as a resource collection site, where soapstone was procured for the manufacture of stone vessels (Howley 1974 [1915]; Jenness 1932; Linnamae 1975; Nagle 1982; Thomson 1984; 1986; Wintemberg 1940). However, it has been more recently demonstrated that the quarry also served as a workshop where vessels were actually finished (Erwin 1998; 1999; 2001; 2005a). Excavations by Thomson in 1985–1986 (Thomson 1986; 1989) of Shelley Garden (EaBa-10) also yielded some crudely-fashioned vessels that display some of the characteristics of little pots. While the function of Shelley Garden was initially interpreted as a habitation/workshop site associated with the quarry, further analysis indicates that it also probably served as a staging area and home base for hunting, fishing and collection forays (Erwin 2003, 10–11) which were undertaken at nearby sites such Cow Cove (Erwin 2005b) and Plat

Figure 6.10. Lamp Preform and Little Pot Comparison.

Bay (Erwin 1999). In this regard, it is suggested that the Dorset occupation of Fleur de Lys should not simply be characterized as a short-term specialized industrial activity, but one with a wider array of functions, and a corresponding number of individuals which likely included family groups with both adults and children.

If we take the view that Fleur de Lys 1 and Shelley Garden were simply places of resource extraction and vessel production, it is proposed that the only unutilized vessels which should be present at these sites are those which were abandoned during production due to breakage or other factors which would have made the vessel unusable. In the case of large vessels, this hypothesis stands, as not a single unbroken and unutilized vessel has been recovered from either of these sites. However, the presence of unbroken and unfinished miniature vessels suggest that the function of these smaller specimens might be related to some other activity. While it is possible that completion of these miniature vessels was planned for a future time, this strategy seems a more likely explanation for larger and heavier pre-form vessels which would have required considerably more effort to transport. As such, it is arguable that the presence of these crudely-fashioned and incomplete miniature vessels relates to practice carving and/or expedient playthings which are more likely to have been abandoned than a potentially functional vessel.

The function of miniatures

Dorset artistic practices are largely known from numerous tiny carvings in ivory, bone, wood and soapstone. These carvings generally depict a wide variety of animals, but also include human forms, all of which are recognized as part of adult Dorset behaviour, and most notably associated with shamanistic practices (*e.g.* McGhee 1976; 1987; 1996; Renouf 1999; Taçon 1983; Thomson 1985). Aside from the function of these types of Dorset carvings, this paper suggests that a class of Dorset miniatures relating to children's use and play does exist. This possibility was briefly mentioned by Park (1998) who explored the use of miniatures as children's toys in Inuit culture, noting that their use reflected the practice of treating children as "miniature adults". He also suggested that such concepts of childhood were visible in the archaeological record of their Thule ancestors, and that it would be interesting to investigate the extent to which they were visible in other cultures such as the Dorset. As with Inuit material culture there are numerous examples of miniatures in the Dorset archaeological record. However, unlike the Inuit examples, Dorset miniatures consist of animal and human representations which have largely been interpreted as items of ritual use by shamans (McGhee 1996). Notwithstanding this interpretation of Dorset art, Park questions whether "Dorset children have an equally extensive miniature material culture that is simply invisible within assemblages containing the many miniatures used by shamans?" (Park 1998, 280). The evidence from Fleur de Lys suggests that Dorset assemblages do indeed contain similar miniatures, such as the little pots, and that further exploration of this hypothesis is warranted.

Conclusions

In comparison to typical Dorset miniatures which are recognized for their artistic merit and their likely function as shamanistic accoutrements, there is a marked difference in quality of craftsmanship between well-made typical miniatures and the little pots. Other than their reduced size, the crudely fashioned and unfinished little pots share little in common with these other types of Dorset artifacts. Such differences suggest that less-skilled hands were at work, or at play, in the production of little pots. Owing to the fact that there is no evidence for other miniatures that might be considered as Dorset art from the Fleur de Lys quarry, the problem of recognizing little pots from those items normally associated with shamanistic practice is not an issue. As such, if we accept little pots as the work of children at play, we can begin to understand something more about the nature of the quarrying activities in Fleur de Lys, and lithic procurement in general. In this regard, it is proposed that the seemingly specialized task of soapstone quarrying is an activity which is socially more complex than previously believed. More specifically, the presence of children at the quarry, and their likely role as students in the process of soapstone vessel production, provide a glimpse of Dorset childhood experiences which may not have been so different than their Thule counterparts.

7 Geochemical Signature of Mistassini Quartzite and Ramah Chert Artefacts and Quarries, Québec/ Labrador, Canada

David LeBlanc, Isabelle Duval and Jean-François Moreau

Summary

Instrumental Neutron Activation Analysis (INAA) was used to geochemically characterize geological and archaeological lithic materials from northern Quebec and Labrador, Canada. One hundred and twenty seven geological samples of Mistassini quartzite from the colline Blanche quarry source were analyzed, along with eleven samples of Ramah chert from northern Labrador, twenty one archaeological samples identified by archaeologists as Mistassini quartzite or Ramah chert, and two geological standards. While there seems to be considerable overlap in the chemical element makeup of the Mistassini and Ramah sources, REE patterns and multivariate analyses point to ways of differentiating the two. Archaeological samples identified visually as Mistassini quartzite seem to fall within the geochemical range of the source material.

Introduction

Research which relies on chemical composition to establish the relation between sources of raw materials and artefacts, whether for ceramics, glass, metals, or lithic materials, has been increasing in archaeometry over the past three decades. Various chemical analysis techniques, such as Instrumental Neutron Activation Analysis (INAA), Inductively Coupled Plasma Mass Spectrometry (ICP-MS), and others, have now been applied to numerous types of lithic materials, including quartzite and chert (Edmonds 2001; Wilson and Pollard 2001).

In northeastern North America, intensive studies of quartz-rich stone are very limited, with the exception of research carried out on lithic materials from the Sheguiandah site (Julig 2002; Julig *et al.* 2002), and little has been done as regards determining the geochemical signature of Mistassini quartzite and Ramah chert, although these materials were among the most widely used in the manufacture of stone tools in western subarctic prehistory (Denton 1988; Loring, 2002).

Moreover, in the few studies carried out (Fitzhugh 1972; Gagnon 1988; Lazenby 1980; Rutherford and Stephens 1991), very few samples of each material were examined, and the authors remain cautious, agreeing that analysing additional samples would make it possible to define the geochemical signature and domain for the sources of these materials. Clear chemical variance of the sources and their signatures among artefacts from archaeological sites remains to be demonstrated.

Following exhaustive sampling of the Mistassini quartzite quarry (LeBlanc 2004), geochemical analyses helped to define its geochemical signature with a greater degree of confidence. This step completed, we now compare these data to a series of geochemical results from Ramah chert samples and a series of artefacts. Thus, the variance between the Mistassini quartzite geochemistry and that of Ramah chert needs to be established before the signatures of these materials among the artefacts can be determined.

The artefacts analysed were all classified by archaeologists beforehand, into one of two sources on the basis of visual comparison with reference samples, or according to lithic material descriptions found in the literature. However, the identifications are subjective since they rely on the experience and petrographical expertise of the analysts regarding the material they are identifying. Mistassini quartzite and Ramah chert are easily confused, especially when the samples are very small (Denton 1988). Geochemical analysis should resolve any discrepancies.

Lithic materials and their sources

Determining the geochemical signature of Mistassini quartzite and Ramah chert requires a basic understanding of source geology and the geologic unit dimensions to which they correspond.

Mistassini quartzite

The source of Mistassini quartzite, *colline Blanche* (latitude 51°04'07"N, longitude 72°54'05"W), overlooks the eastern shore of the Témiscamie River, located in central Quebec, Canada (Fig. 7.1). The hill has a surface area of 0.15km^2; it is on average 145 m wide and stretches along the river over a distance of 1.05km, in a NNE–SSW direction (Gagnon 1988). Prehistoric exploitation of lithic materials seems to have been concentrated mainly in an area called *"carrière de Rogers"* (Martijn and Rogers 1969), located on the western slope of the hill, which is made up of talus screes and steep embankments.

Colline Blanche as a whole is made up of various types of lithic materials with a great variety of textures and colours. The stone used for prehistoric tool-making thus only makes up a small part of the hill, where the material with the finest grain size is found. This aphanitic material is relatively opaque and has varying degrees of lustre, from waxy to matt. In archaeological artefacts, white is the dominant colour of Mistassini quartzite, while the source shows a clearly wider range of shades from very light grey darkening to almost black, or subtle colourings of pink, yellow, orange, red, and even shades of blue or green. The material is often striated with black venules. Figure 7.2 shows a few Mistassini quartzite samples, including the typical white variety. The terminology used to identify lithic material from *colline Blanche* varies from author to author: Mistassini quartzite, Albanel chert, conglomerite, *etc.* Denton (1998) clearly explains the issues concerning the nomenclature of this material. Herein, "Mistassini quartzite" will be used as it is the most widely used term among archaeologists.

As concerns the geological understanding of Mistassini quartzite, Gagnon (1988)

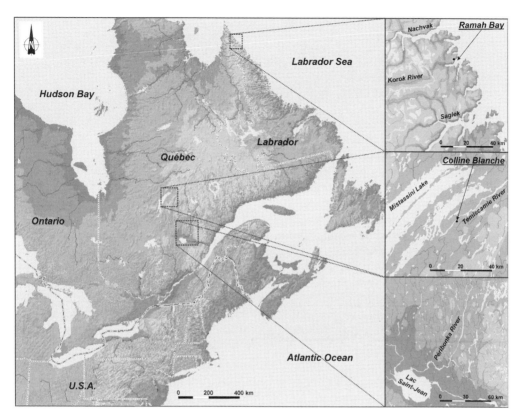

Figure 7.1. Geographic location of the regions mentioned in this article.

Figure 7.2. Mistassini quartzite samples.

suggests that the hill was formed by non-conformable clastic stacking stratigraphy followed by glacial erosion. The study identifies five stratigraphic units from bottom to top: conglomerite, metaquartzite, quartziferous sandstone, quartziferous conglomerate, and ferruginous sandstone. These units subdivide the Témiscamie formation, which belongs to the Mistassini group and dates back to the Proterozoic Era (Precambrian). According to Gagnon (1988), *colline Blanche* lithic material is an integral part of the conglomerite unit.

Walter (2003) for his part produced up with a new hypothesis concerning the origin and formation of *colline Blanche* stone; a chemical origin from spontaneous, low-amplitude hydrothermal activity. He identified three types of lithic materials, in particular, as a function of the degree of silicification. Type 1 resembles quartziferous sandstone as described by Gagnon (1988), while types 2 and 3 respectively correspond to metaquartzite and conglomerite. Walter maintains that the passage from lightly silicified to highly silicified units, as well as the presence of a combined joint system on *colline Blanche,* lead to a silicification model in which hydrothermal fluid flowed through quartz-rich sandstone. Acid and oxidising fluids circulating through fissures became silica-rich by causing the ambient silica to dissolve, and then flowed into an adjacent network of fissures in the form of orthochemical cement. "Towards the centre of the hill, type 2 gradually turns into type 3, the most highly altered unit and which corresponds to the chert-like material found by archaeologists. However, since this is not sandstone, but fine-grain siliceous rock, it is preferable to use the term silexite" (Walter 2003, 20).

Ramah chert

As with Mistassini quartzite, lithic material from Ramah Bay is referred to in various ways: quartzite, chert, metachert, Ramah chalcedony, smoky quartzite, Labrador quartzite. In this paper, we will adopt the most commonly used term: Ramah chert.

The translucent stone is found in shades varying from very light grey to black. It often has smoky bands or patches, different from those found in Mistassini quartzite, varying from dark grey to black (see Fig. 7.3). Small mineral inclusions are often found in the material, which, when they are at the surface of the stone, become oxidised to a rust colour in some places. Compared to Mistassini quartzite, Ramah chert samples are somewhat shinier with a slightly rougher texture, which makes them coarser to the touch, or "sugar-like".

According to Plumet (1981), prehistoric exploitation of Ramah chert was for the most part concentrated on either side of Ramah Bay (Fig. 7.1). Fitzugh (1972), Gramly (1978) and Lazenby (1980) described and documented the main exploitation area located near Hilda's Creek, which drains a cirque glacier where the material outcrops (latitude 58°53'40"N, longitude 63°08'04"W).

Geological studies by Knight and Morgan (1976; 1981) show that Ramah lithic material belongs to the Ramah group sedimentary formation of the Aphebian Era, which stretches from north to south from Nachvak Fjord to Saglek Fjord (Fig. 7.1). More precisely, the structure of stratified chert is identified as an integral part of the Nullataktok formation. Gramly (1978) and Lazenby (1980) showed that the geological

Figure 7.3. Ramah chert samples.

structure of the lithic material outcrops in beds of maximum 4.5m in thickness, and that this raw material is available in several areas over a distance of 40km.

Previous geochemical work

A certain amount of geochemical research has been undertaken in order to characterise these two lithic material types, and in some cases both Mistassini quartzite and Ramah chert were analysed together in an attempt to discern their respective geochemical natures.

Gagnon (1988) used the INAA method on 6 Mistassini quartzite samples. The results for 5 of them showed, for nearly all the chemical elements analysed, concentrations too low for quantification. In the same study, she dissolved a 38.48g sample into hydrofluoric acid and analysed the residue. A Rare Earth Elements (REE) pattern was then drawn up from this single Mistassini quartzite sample. Working on different lithic materials from Labrador, Lazenby (1980) documented the neutron activation analysis of Ramah chert geological samples. Twenty-five (25) chemical elements were detected and readings were taken on 15 of these, which showed very low concentrations. Variations in geochemical concentrations were observed and the heterogenous structure of the chert was also noted.

Fitzugh (1972) as well as Rutherford and Stephens (1991) compared the geochemical results from Mistassini quartzite and Ramah chert samples. Fitzugh published the sodium, manganese, and potassium concentrations from INAA results of 5 Ramah mineral samples. He also analysed archaeological samples visually attributed to Ramah and other sources, including Mistassini quartzite, for comparison. His results demonstrated that, overall, the geochemistry of Ramah chert showed large concentration differences for the 3 elements, making it difficult to clearly discern Ramah chert from Mistassini quartzite, solely based on those 3 elements. For their part, Rutherford and Stephens carried out atomic absorption and ICP-MS analyses on a total of 20 Ramah chert and 3 Mistassini quartzite samples. They observed differences between the materials and suggested that 4 chemical elements (Ba, Mo, Nb and Ta) could serve to distinguish Ramah chert from Mistassini quartzite. They however remained cautious in their conclusions due to the small sample size. Finally, INAA studies by CÉRANE (1984), mentioned in Denton (1988), give preliminary indications that the iron concentration detected in the two materials could be used to tell them apart.

Overall, these studies clearly demonstrate the difficulty in establishing the geochemical difference between Ramah chert and Mistassini quartzite. Element analyses showed that the two materials are silica-rich and have low concentrations of all other elements. The analyses described in those studies were made on small samples from each source and the authors remain cautious, agreeing that analysing additional samples would yield a better idea of the geochemical signature and domain for the sources of these materials. Therefore, the major difficulty arises from the fact that the geochemical variance of each of the sources has yet to be verified as a whole.

Before moving forward, it should be noted that reusing the geochemical results of previous studies can be tricky. Indeed, researchers use different analytical techniques and follow specific protocols, which can obviously lead to differing quantitative results. In the case of Mistassini and Ramah lithic materials, such variance could easily represent high amplitudes in relation to the low concentrations detected. In theory, even if this issue has a lower impact for minerals with higher geochemical concentrations, such as obsidian, it still concerns geochemical characterisation research as a whole. Publication of the results of a homogeneous geochemical reference standard, well known and widely available, and analysed conjointly with lithic samples could solve this problem. Thus, analysis of the mineral samples under study combined with the analysis of samples from a same reference standard would make it possible for future geochemical studies to rely on previous results, to make comparisons, and to progressively contribute to the development of databases for lithic sources.

A recent study (LeBlanc 2004) led to the analysis of numerous geological samples from *colline Blanche* using the INAA method. From the perspective of studies by Hughes (1994) and Shackley (1995), which state that complete and representative source samples are vital to any research, more than 150 samples were extracted from the Mistassini quartzite source. Two criteria had to be adhered to for sampling: first, the number of samples taken had to be sufficient to represent the macroscopic variability of the source, notably the various colour shades and grain sizes. Second, a certain number of samples had to be selected as a function of their being good knapping material, meaning that about one half of the stone samples needed to visually match the material found in archaeological sites. Of all of the samples taken from the source, 127 were prepared for INAA. They were subdivided into two sub-categories titled "A" and "B". The 63 samples of sub-category A visually resemble the material found in archaeological sites; they also correspond to the chert-textured silexite described in the Walter (2003) model. The other 64 samples, belonging sub-category B, seem to correspond to what Walter described as the original matrix of *colline Blanche,* and to the units least altered by silicification process. The properties (texture and grain size) of the B sub-category samples seem to make them less likely to be used in tool making, as opposed to the A samples. Figure 7.4 shows three samples from each group.

Geochemical analysis of the 127 *colline Blanche* samples made it possible to confirm the low chemical concentrations observed in previous work on Mistassini quartzite.

Figure 7.4. Colline Blanche varieties, including Mistassini quartzite (A).

Division of the samples into two sub-categories and their geochemical comparison showed the most altered geological unit, sub-category A (Mistassini quartzite), to be chemically impoverished compared to the original *colline Blanche* matrix (LeBlanc 2004). Average element concentrations of sub-category A show lower concentrations than sub-category B, which supports the model proposed by Walter (2003). The progressive dissolution of a part of the ambient silica by hydrothermal fluids washed out the trace elements contained in the original *colline Blanche* matrix. Recrystallisation of the silica contained in the solution produced silexite (Mistassini quartzite) which is practically free of impurities (LeBlanc, 2004). The studies carried out on *colline Blanche* material clearly show the distinctive geochemical and physical characteristics of Mistassini quartzite (A) within its geological location. The geochemical comparison of the Mistassini quartzite quarry with other minerals, such as Ramah chert, should therefore be based on the results from sub-category A samples.

Samples analysed and compared

The artefacts analysed in this study were found in archaeological sites along the Péribonka River (Fig. 7.1), where a collection of lithic materials from different origins was unearthed. Visual analysis of the raw material revealed a large amount of Mistassini quartzite, the source of which is located more than 200km west of the Péribonka River. However, the discovery of lithic remains visually similar to Ramah chert was particularly notable. It is important to specify that the source of this stone is located more than 1000km northeast of the Péribonka River. The presence of Ramah chert along this river is however not exceptional in comparison with the totality of the archaeological sites in that part of subarctic Québec (cf. Langevin 1990; Moreau *et al.* 1987; Moreau 1998).

The results of geochemical analysis of Mistassini quartzite from LeBlanc (2004), for a group of 63 sub-category A samples extracted from *colline Blanche,* are compared to the results from the Péribonka River artefacts and Ramah chert samples. For standardisation purposes, conjointly with those 63 samples, the geostandard geochemical results of 6 samples for the following two benchmarks are reported: JCh-1 (Ashio Chert) of the Geological Commission of Japan, and SpS (glass sand) of the Breitländer Institute, Czech Republic.

To these previous results are combined the analysis of 34 samples, 21 of which are artefacts from the Péribonka River collection, and 11 are considered to be from Ramah chert outcrops. The other 2 samples (one for each of the two geostandards JCh-1 and SpS) are used a reference for comparing results from Mistassini quartzite with those of the 32 stone samples of this project.

Of the 11 Ramah samples, 10 were supplied by *Institut Culturel Avataq,* and one by Patrick Plumet, which comes directly from the Ramah Bay outcrops. The Avataq samples are archaeological artefacts from sites IeDk-1 and IfDm-7 on the Korok River (Fig. 7.1). The nearness of the Korok River sites to Ramah Bay, combined with the identification expertise of the Avataq archaeologists, who are quite familiar with this material, strongly suggest that these samples are from the Ramah outcrops.

The Péribonka River artefacts were all visually associated to either Mistassini quartzite or Ramah chert by *Université du Québec à Chicoutimi* (UQAC) Archaeology Laboratory archaeologists. Among the 21 samples, 10 seem to visually correspond to Ramah chert, while 11 are linked to Mistassini quartzite.

Analyses and results

Geochemical analysis of all samples in this project was carried out using the INAA method. The samples were irradiated at the SLOWPOKE II nuclear reactor of *École Polytechnique de Montréal*. Measurements of the mid- and long-life elements were made at the UQAC Geochemical Laboratory. Details concerning the analysis technique, sample irradiation, and sample preparation and handling are described in detail in LeBlanc (2004).

Tables 7.1a, 7.1b, and 7.1c show the results obtained and compared for a total of 95 stone samples in this project, that is: 63 Mistassini quartzite samples, 11 Ramah chert samples, and 21 artefacts. Table 7.1b compiles the geochemical results of reference standards JCh-1 and SpS. Analysis of the results obtained from the geostandards and comparison with the values published by Govindaraju (1994) demonstrates the accuracy and precision of the INAA results. Finally, Table 7.1c shows compiled data for each of the lithic materials. Thus, the table shows the number of samples analyzed (n), the number of samples showing concentrations below the limit of determination (n <LOD, see below for definition of LOD), the average, the standard deviation, the median and the lowest and highest concentrations measured for Mistassini quartzite and Ramah chert.

As shown in Table 7.1 (a, b, and c), analysis of these practically impurity-free, high-silica-content materials leads to a high number of missing values, or values below the limit of determination (<LOD). The limit of determination corresponds to the lowest limit at which the analytical technique can obtain quantifiable results with an "acceptable" error ratio. In this project, the LOD for the acceptance or rejection of a result for a given chemical element was that established by LeBlanc (2004). Overall, the LOD corresponds to the low concentration average, with instrument uncertainty of 20% and above, plus two standard deviations, for a given chemical element. That limit, shown in Table 7.1a, is in the same order as that used by Flem and Bédard (2002) for the same analytical technique on geochemically similar materials.

Missing values (<LOD) are a problem in statistical calculation as the numerical void associated with them skews the results. For example, the lowest concentrations, that is to say those below the LOD, are not included in the calculation of the average, which is, as a result, erroneously high. According to Baxter (2003), this problem can be countered by replacing the missing values with a value equal to 55% of the limit of detection of the chemical element analysed. This substitution was therefore used to replace the missing values in the statistical calculations of this project.

The average chemical concentrations of Mistassini quartzite and Ramah chert are shown in Table 7.1c, and are in the same order as those presented in previous studies. The lowest and highest values for each material show that the geochemical domains for Ramah chert and Mistassini quartzite overlap for all chemical elements measured. This means that, for the 15 chemical elements analysed, there are no chemical markers specific to one or the other of the materials which would make it possible to clearly differentiate the two sources. However, certain tendencies can be noted, and these reveal a difference between the sources. Comparison of the 15 chemical elements in the two materials shows that, generally, Ramah chert has higher average element concentrations, except for sodium oxide, cesium, and thorium (Na_2O, Cs and Th). The standard deviations relative to average element concentrations show that the values are, for both materials, relatively spread out and heterogeneous.

Of the quantified chemical elements, 9 are Rare Earth Elements (RRE): La, Ce, Nd, Sm, Eu, Tb, Ho, Yb and Lu. Scandium (Sc), which has periodicity and chemical affinities similar to that group, is generally considered a rare earth element. The abundance of these elements, plotted on a graph, is frequently used to characterise and discern the geochemical affinity of different minerals. As concerns Mistassini quartzite, the total concentrations of rare earth elements (ΣREE), light rare earth elements (LREE, including Sc, La, Ce, Nd, Sm and Eu), and heavy rare earth elements (HREE, including Tb, Ho, Yb and Lu) are respectively within the ranges of 0.102–16.477; 0.092–16.454 and 0.010–0.093 ppm. Ramah chert shows ΣREE, LREE and HREE values of 0.391–7.280; 0.381–7.179

Chemical element		T-Fe2O3	Na2O	Ce	Cs	Eu	Ho	La	Lu	Nd	Sb	Sc	Sm	Tb	Th	Yb
		% (m/m)	% (m/m)	ug/g	ug/g	ug/g	ug/g	ug/g	ug/g	ug/g	ug/g	ug/g	ug/g	ug/g	ug/g	ug/g
Determination limit (LOD)		< 0,003	-	< 0,07	< 0,02	< 0,005	< 0,01	< 0,008	< 0,0007	< 0,08	< 0,005	< 0,002	< 0,003	< 0,004	< 0,006	< 0,003
# sample	type	**Mistassini quartzite (A)** - Geochemical contents (LeBlanc, 2004)														
mi-4	geological	0,039	0,0034	0,111	< 0,02	< 0,005	< 0,01	0,067	0,0010	< 0,08	0,086	0,039	0,011	< 0,004	0,041	< 0,003
mi-5	geological	0,015	0,0020	0,076	< 0,02	< 0,005	< 0,01	0,036	< 0,0007	< 0,08	0,010	0,021	0,006	< 0,004	0,019	< 0,003
mi-9	geological	0,009	0,0027	0,075	0,060	< 0,005	< 0,01	0,039	< 0,0007	< 0,08	0,007	0,019	0,004	< 0,004	0,025	< 0,003
mi-12	geological	< 0,003	0,0015	0,088	0,056	< 0,005	< 0,01	0,029	< 0,0007	< 0,08	0,006	0,016	0,004	< 0,004	0,022	< 0,003
mi-14	geological	0,003	0,0024	< 0,07	0,054	< 0,005	< 0,01	0,033	< 0,0007	< 0,08	0,008	0,018	0,005	< 0,004	0,026	< 0,003
mi-15	geological	0,017	0,0036	0,236	0,073	0,006	< 0,01	0,095	0,0009	< 0,08	0,011	0,028	0,017	< 0,004	0,031	0,003
mi-16	geological	< 0,003	0,0013	< 0,07	0,032	< 0,005	< 0,01	0,042	< 0,0007	< 0,08	0,007	0,014	0,004	< 0,004	0,017	< 0,003
mi-24	geological	0,010	0,0036	7,187	0,071	0,026	< 0,01	6,353	0,0018	2,711	0,021	0,029	0,148	0,008	0,026	0,007
mi-29	geological	< 0,003	0,0017	0,110	0,044	< 0,005	< 0,01	0,043	0,0011	< 0,08	0,008	0,017	0,007	< 0,004	0,030	< 0,003
mi-31	geological	< 0,003	0,0014	0,127	0,045	< 0,005	< 0,01	0,089	0,0009	< 0,08	0,008	0,009	0,013	< 0,004	0,017	< 0,003
mi-32	geological	0,006	0,0037	0,337	0,123	0,005	0,015	0,180	0,0071	< 0,08	0,010	0,044	0,027	< 0,004	0,090	< 0,003
mi-34	geological	0,004	0,0046	0,185	0,046	< 0,005	< 0,01	0,086	< 0,0007	< 0,08	0,007	0,033	0,010	< 0,004	0,035	0,004
mi-35	geological	0,010	0,0059	0,189	0,041	< 0,005	< 0,01	0,095	< 0,0007	< 0,08	0,011	0,071	0,015	0,005	0,066	0,013
mi-36	geological	0,005	0,0061	0,079	0,062	< 0,005	< 0,01	0,055	< 0,0007	< 0,08	0,013	0,026	0,008	0,005	0,040	0,004
mi-38	geological	0,005	0,0050	< 0,07	0,082	< 0,005	< 0,01	0,069	0,0017	< 0,08	0,010	0,030	0,008	< 0,004	0,028	0,004
mi-40	geological	0,011	0,0051	0,092	0,083	< 0,005	< 0,01	0,068	< 0,0007	< 0,08	0,011	0,033	0,011	< 0,004	0,038	< 0,003
mi-42	geological	0,005	0,0058	< 0,07	0,079	< 0,005	< 0,01	0,076	0,0008	< 0,08	0,008	0,031	0,007	< 0,004	0,024	0,005
mi-43	geological	0,005	0,0040	< 0,07	0,047	< 0,005	< 0,01	0,051	0,0008	< 0,08	0,009	0,025	0,006	< 0,004	0,027	0,005
mi-44	geological	0,003	0,0042	0,140	0,095	< 0,005	< 0,01	0,082	< 0,0007	< 0,08	0,008	0,039	0,009	< 0,004	0,043	0,003
mi-45	geological	0,005	0,0049	< 0,07	0,060	< 0,005	< 0,01	0,048	< 0,0007	< 0,08	0,008	0,027	0,005	< 0,004	0,026	< 0,003
mi-53	geological	0,005	0,0040	0,210	0,114	< 0,005	< 0,01	0,071	< 0,0007	< 0,08	0,037	0,063	0,015	< 0,004	0,050	< 0,003
mi-55	geological	0,006	0,0062	0,176	0,070	< 0,005	0,012	0,145	0,0013	< 0,08	0,033	0,043	0,017	< 0,004	0,050	0,005
mi-63	geological	0,014	0,0119	1,483	0,070	0,012	0,028	2,064	0,0089	0,563	0,025	0,070	0,088	0,009	0,210	0,047
mi-64	geological	0,006	0,0120	0,077	0,091	0,005	0,026	0,053	0,0034	< 0,08	0,108	0,069	0,015	< 0,004	0,042	0,022
mi-67	geological	< 0,003	0,0092	0,080	0,072	< 0,005	< 0,01	0,026	0,0011	< 0,08	0,061	0,029	0,008	< 0,004	0,021	0,005
mi-69	geological	< 0,003	0,0029	0,099	0,100	< 0,005	< 0,01	0,045	< 0,0007	< 0,08	0,009	0,034	0,009	< 0,004	0,051	< 0,003
mi-71	geological	0,003	0,0044	< 0,07	0,065	< 0,005	< 0,01	0,037	< 0,0007	< 0,08	0,011	0,022	0,006	< 0,004	0,029	< 0,003
mi-72	geological	0,004	0,0027	0,081	0,067	< 0,005	< 0,01	0,034	< 0,0007	< 0,08	0,010	0,023	0,006	< 0,004	0,030	< 0,003
mi-73	geological	< 0,003	0,0025	0,109	0,078	< 0,005	< 0,01	0,040	0,0007	< 0,08	0,050	0,030	0,008	< 0,004	0,035	< 0,003
mi-74	geological	< 0,003	0,0037	2,461	0,078	0,008	< 0,01	1,421	< 0,0007	0,631	0,008	0,029	0,052	< 0,004	0,052	< 0,003
mi-75	geological	0,008	0,0049	0,073	0,060	< 0,005	< 0,01	0,036	< 0,0007	< 0,08	0,010	0,038	0,008	< 0,004	0,034	< 0,003
mi-76	geological	0,004	0,0043	2,129	0,085	0,008	< 0,01	1,450	0,0010	0,338	0,011	0,030	0,025	< 0,004	0,071	0,004
mi-78	geological	0,003	0,0045	0,120	0,052	< 0,005	< 0,01	0,030	< 0,0007	< 0,08	0,010	0,022	0,005	< 0,004	0,026	< 0,003
mi-79	geological	< 0,003	0,0015	0,119	0,064	< 0,005	< 0,01	0,032	0,0008	< 0,08	0,005	0,026	0,007	< 0,004	0,036	< 0,003
mi-81	geological	< 0,003	0,0032	0,155	0,093	< 0,005	< 0,01	0,072	0,0010	< 0,08	0,009	0,051	0,013	< 0,004	0,071	0,006
mi-82	geological	< 0,003	0,0034	0,115	0,101	< 0,005	< 0,01	0,046	< 0,0007	< 0,08	0,008	0,032	0,007	< 0,004	0,038	< 0,003
mi-83	geological	0,004	0,0028	< 0,07	0,079	< 0,005	< 0,01	0,047	< 0,0007	< 0,08	0,009	0,022	0,006	< 0,004	0,039	< 0,003
mi-84	geological	< 0,003	0,0014	< 0,07	0,028	< 0,005	< 0,01	0,012	< 0,0007	< 0,08	0,006	0,008	< 0,003	< 0,004	0,009	< 0,003
mi-86	geological	0,005	0,0028	0,106	0,104	< 0,005	< 0,01	0,058	< 0,0007	< 0,08	0,011	0,039	0,010	< 0,004	0,051	0,003
mi-87	geological	0,004	0,0015	< 0,07	0,033	< 0,005	< 0,01	0,036	< 0,0007	< 0,08	0,008	0,020	0,006	< 0,004	0,025	< 0,003
mi-88	geological	< 0,003	0,0028	0,115	0,070	< 0,005	< 0,01	0,050	< 0,0007	< 0,08	0,010	0,033	0,010	< 0,004	0,047	< 0,003

Table 7.1a. Mistassini quartzite geochemical data.

Chemical element		T-Fe2O3	Na2O	Ce	Cs	Eu	Ho	La	Lu	Nd	Sb	Sc	Sm	Tb	Th	Yb
		% (m/m)	% (m/m)	ug/g	ug/g	ug/g	ug/g	ug/g	ug/g	ug/g	ug/g	ug/g	ug/g	ug/g	ug/g	ug/g
# sample	type	**Mistassini quartzite (A)** - Geochemical contents (LeBlanc, 2004)														
mi-89	geological	0,007	0,0027	0,123	0,063	< 0,005	< 0,01	0,039	0,0008	< 0,08	0,010	0,028	0,008	< 0,004	0,035	< 0,003
mi-90	geological	0,005	0,0057	0,198	0,119	< 0,005	< 0,01	0,080	0,0008	< 0,08	0,013	0,048	0,014	< 0,004	0,073	< 0,003
mi-91	geological	< 0,003	0,0018	0,096	0,079	< 0,005	< 0,01	0,049	0,0008	< 0,08	0,006	0,034	0,009	< 0,004	0,043	< 0,003
mi-93	geological	< 0,003	0,0020	0,121	0,083	< 0,005	< 0,01	0,056	0,0009	< 0,08	0,007	0,037	0,010	< 0,004	0,051	< 0,003
mi-94	geological	< 0,003	0,0029	< 0,07	0,053	< 0,005	< 0,01	0,035	< 0,0007	< 0,08	0,009	0,025	0,007	< 0,004	0,031	< 0,003
mi-95	geological	0,003	0,0048	0,092	0,084	< 0,005	< 0,01	0,043	0,0007	< 0,08	0,009	0,031	0,009	< 0,004	0,039	< 0,003
mi-96	geological	< 0,003	0,0022	0,074	< 0,02	< 0,005	< 0,01	0,044	< 0,0007	< 0,08	0,010	0,023	0,007	< 0,004	0,026	< 0,003
mi-97	geological	0,006	0,0031	0,224	0,118	0,006	< 0,01	0,099	< 0,0007	< 0,08	0,012	0,064	0,015	< 0,004	0,085	0,004
mi-98	geological	0,004	0,0023	0,160	0,108	< 0,005	< 0,01	0,077	< 0,0007	< 0,08	0,010	0,048	0,012	< 0,004	0,063	0,004
mi-100	geological	0,005	0,0045	0,580	0,076	0,005	< 0,01	0,351	< 0,0007	< 0,08	0,011	0,040	0,014	< 0,004	0,114	< 0,003
mi-103	geological	0,005	0,0029	0,090	0,024	< 0,005	< 0,01	0,049	< 0,0007	< 0,08	0,008	0,032	0,008	< 0,004	0,033	< 0,003
mi-104	geological	0,010	0,0024	< 0,07	0,023	< 0,005	< 0,01	0,033	< 0,0007	< 0,08	0,006	0,021	0,006	< 0,004	0,022	< 0,003
mi-106	geological	0,004	0,0027	0,074	0,053	< 0,005	< 0,01	0,034	< 0,0007	< 0,08	0,012	0,019	0,007	< 0,004	0,024	< 0,003
mi-115	geological	< 0,003	0,0039	< 0,07	0,027	< 0,005	< 0,01	0,008	< 0,0007	< 0,08	0,013	0,007	0,003	< 0,004	0,008	< 0,003
mi-116	geological	< 0,003	0,0031	< 0,07	0,027	< 0,005	< 0,01	0,023	< 0,0007	< 0,08	0,008	0,014	0,004	< 0,004	0,019	< 0,003
mi-117	geological	< 0,003	0,0044	< 0,07	< 0,02	< 0,005	< 0,01	0,012	< 0,0007	< 0,08	0,007	0,008	< 0,003	< 0,004	0,010	< 0,003
mi-118	geological	< 0,003	0,0037	< 0,07	0,050	< 0,005	< 0,01	0,027	0,0009	< 0,08	< 0,005	0,010	< 0,003	< 0,004	0,008	< 0,003
mi-119	geological	< 0,003	0,0032	< 0,07	0,054	< 0,005	< 0,01	0,019	< 0,0007	< 0,08	0,008	0,014	0,004	< 0,004	0,017	< 0,003
mi-120	geological	< 0,003	0,0001	< 0,07	0,028	< 0,005	< 0,01	< 0,008	< 0,0007	< 0,08	< 0,005	< 0,002	< 0,003	< 0,004	< 0,006	< 0,003
mi-121	geological	0,006	0,0036	< 0,07	0,067	< 0,005	< 0,01	0,026	< 0,0007	0,090	0,006	0,008	0,003	< 0,004	0,017	< 0,003
mi-122	geological	0,005	0,0041	< 0,07	0,074	< 0,005	< 0,01	0,036	< 0,0007	< 0,08	0,011	0,023	0,005	< 0,004	0,027	< 0,003
mi-128	geological	0,091	0,0020	0,525	0,062	0,008	< 0,01	0,472	0,0041	0,162	0,073	0,037	0,039	0,004	0,079	0,025
# sample	type	**Ramah chert** - Geochemical contents														
IeDk-1-1	archaeological	0,270	0,0027	0,166	0,020	0,009	< 0,01	0,072	< 0,0007	< 0,08	0,084	0,043	0,048	< 0,004	0,015	< 0,003
IeDk-1-2	archaeological	0,237	0,0020	3,722	< 0,02	0,045	< 0,01	1,422	0,0122	1,096	0,031	0,289	0,220	0,012	0,057	0,035
IeDk-1-3	archaeological	0,031	0,0016	0,651	< 0,02	0,010	< 0,01	0,222	0,0009	0,121	0,016	0,046	0,032	< 0,004	0,025	0,005
IeDk-1-4	archaeological	0,038	0,0019	1,180	< 0,02	0,014	< 0,01	0,357	0,0016	0,263	0,024	0,062	0,047	< 0,004	0,026	0,010
IeDk-1-5	archaeological	0,014	0,0016	1,960	< 0,02	0,020	< 0,01	0,952	0,0018	0,637	0,009	0,034	0,103	< 0,004	0,022	0,008
IfDm-7-1	archaeological	0,129	0,0021	1,536	< 0,02	0,017	< 0,01	0,560	0,0028	0,338	0,012	0,080	0,076	0,004	0,052	0,015
IfDm-7-2	archaeological	0,047	0,0021	0,884	< 0,02	0,022	< 0,01	0,305	0,0029	0,298	0,021	0,043	0,097	0,009	0,015	0,024
IfDm-7-3	archaeological	0,046	0,0022	0,623	< 0,02	0,011	< 0,01	0,205	0,0012	0,156	0,017	0,050	0,031	< 0,004	0,036	0,007
IfDm-7-4	archaeological	0,872	0,0034	4,479	0,025	0,059	< 0,01	1,220	0,0106	0,868	0,027	0,363	0,190	0,021	0,029	0,064
IfDm-7-5	archaeological	0,015	0,0025	0,374	< 0,02	0,008	< 0,01	0,173	0,0008	< 0,08	0,011	0,041	0,031	< 0,004	0,038	0,004
Rh (Plumet)	geological	0,489	0,0013	1,496	< 0,02	0,016	< 0,01	0,372	0,0010	0,307	0,095	0,016	0,063	< 0,004	0,007	< 0,003
		Compilation for the geostandard SpS (glass sand), n = 7														
(Govindaraju, 1994)		0,037	0,044	5,9	0,12	0,06	-	2,5	0,06	-	0,74	0,29	0,61	0,1	1,08	0,32
Average		0,037	0,04719	7,552	0,098	0,059	0,078	3,012	0,04878	2,424	0,099	0,273	0,531	0,075	1,279	0,288
Standard deviation		0,011	0,00309	0,620	0,030	0,005	0,050	0,133	0,00583	0,254	0,005	0,010	0,021	0,007	0,052	0,046
		Compilation for the geostandard JCh-1 (Ashio chert), n = 7														
(Govindaraju, 1994)		0,356	0,0305	5,21	0,243	0,0594	0,112	1,52	0,0344	2,05	-	0,979	0,359	0,0385	0,735	0,182
Average		0,345	0,03062	4,808	0,279	0,062	0,098	1,472	0,02353	1,219	0,085	0,981	0,348	0,045	0,642	0,144
Standard deviation		0,010	0,00167	0,270	0,063	0,013	0,037	0,066	0,00293	0,175	0,006	0,022	0,013	0,012	0,018	0,045

Table 7.1b. Mistassini quartzite (continued) and Ramah chert geochemical data, and compilation of geostandards.

Chemical element		T-Fe2O3	Na2O	Ce	Cs	Eu	Ho	La	Lu	Nd	Sb	Sc	Sm	Tb	Th	Yb
		% (m/m)	% (m/m)	ug/g	ug/g	ug/g	ug/g	ug/g	ug/g	ug/g	ug/g	ug/g	ug/g	ug/g	ug/g	ug/g
# sample	**visual id.**	**Péribonka river artefacts** - Geochemical contents														
DjEt-1-1	Ramah	0,053	0,0056	0,689	< 0,02	0,033	< 0,01	0,486	< 0,0007	< 0,08	0,025	0,160	0,058	< 0,004	< 0,006	< 0,003
DjEt-1-2	Ramah	0,016	0,0030	0,131	< 0,02	0,015	< 0,01	0,064	0,0008	< 0,08	0,050	0,057	0,053	0,006	0,027	< 0,003
DjEt-1-3	Ramah	0,037	0,0047	< 0,07	< 0,02	0,014	< 0,01	0,082	< 0,0007	< 0,08	0,061	0,100	0,051	< 0,004	0,031	< 0,003
DjEt-1-4	Ramah	0,020	0,0044	< 0,07	< 0,02	0,014	< 0,01	0,097	< 0,0007	< 0,08	0,016	0,084	0,014	< 0,004	0,052	< 0,003
DjEt-1-5	Ramah	0,110	0,0032	0,560	< 0,02	0,034	< 0,01	0,283	< 0,0007	< 0,08	0,033	0,091	0,038	< 0,004	< 0,006	< 0,003
DjEt-1-6	Ramah	0,073	0,0034	0,303	0,030	0,009	< 0,01	0,138	0,0035	< 0,08	0,059	0,115	0,028	< 0,004	0,070	0,017
DjEt-1-7	Ramah	0,015	0,0026	1,366	0,042	0,021	< 0,01	0,521	0,0013	0,334	0,018	0,079	0,080	< 0,004	0,052	0,007
DjEt-1-8	Ramah	0,414	0,0041	0,920	0,052	0,027	< 0,01	0,295	< 0,0007	< 0,08	0,127	0,126	0,063	< 0,004	0,062	0,007
DfEu-3-1	Ramah	0,145	0,0039	2,538	< 0,02	0,047	< 0,01	0,815	0,0029	0,505	0,022	0,093	0,111	0,010	< 0,006	0,021
DfEu-3-2	Ramah	0,040	0,0043	0,368	< 0,02	0,032	< 0,01	0,124	< 0,0007	< 0,08	0,010	0,127	0,013	< 0,004	< 0,006	< 0,003
DfEu-2-45	Mistassini	< 0,003	0,0027	0,165	0,111	< 0,005	< 0,01	0,071	0,0011	< 0,08	0,014	0,044	0,013	< 0,004	0,058	0,006
DfEu-2-54	Mistassini	0,089	0,0031	0,129	0,070	0,005	< 0,01	0,059	0,0022	< 0,08	0,024	0,038	0,014	< 0,004	0,038	0,006
DfEu-2-58	Mistassini	0,039	0,0036	0,187	0,113	0,006	< 0,01	0,080	0,0009	< 0,08	0,014	0,049	0,013	< 0,004	0,059	0,004
DfEu-3-16	Mistassini	< 0,003	0,0050	0,262	0,137	0,005	< 0,01	0,135	0,0007	0,084	0,017	0,071	0,016	< 0,004	0,086	0,004
DfEu-3-19	Mistassini	< 0,003	0,0031	0,179	0,118	< 0,005	< 0,01	0,076	0,0008	< 0,08	0,020	0,043	0,012	< 0,004	0,055	0,004
DfEu-3-37	Mistassini	< 0,003	0,0025	0,090	0,075	< 0,005	< 0,01	0,043	< 0,0007	< 0,08	0,010	0,027	0,007	< 0,004	0,031	< 0,003
DfEu-3-41	Mistassini	< 0,003	0,0023	0,146	0,066	< 0,005	< 0,01	0,059	0,0007	< 0,08	0,009	0,033	0,009	< 0,004	0,046	0,004
DfEu-3-48	Mistassini	0,034	0,0022	0,138	0,115	< 0,005	< 0,01	0,079	0,0009	< 0,08	0,011	0,043	0,014	< 0,004	0,064	0,006
DfEu-3-57	Mistassini	0,035	0,0040	1,107	0,158	0,011	< 0,01	0,740	0,0049	0,437	0,028	0,117	0,057	< 0,004	0,147	0,024
DfEu-3-68	Mistassini	0,031	0,0024	0,141	0,112	0,007	< 0,01	0,085	0,0007	< 0,08	0,012	0,052	0,014	< 0,004	0,062	0,005
DfEu-5-56	Mistassini	0,041	0,0061	0,074	0,089	0,007	< 0,01	0,059	0,0022	< 0,08	0,010	0,044	0,010	< 0,004	0,042	0,008
		Compilation for the Mistasini quartzite, n = 63														
n < LOD *(missing values)*		23	0	20	4	53	59	1	39	57	2	1	4	58	1	44
Average		0,006	0,0037	0,315	0,064	0,004	0,006	0,239	0,0009	0,111	0,015	0,030	0,013	0,003	0,040	0,004
Standard deviation		0,012	0,0021	0,980	0,028	0,003	0,004	0,858	0,0015	0,349	0,020	0,016	0,022	0,001	0,031	0,007
Median		0,004	0,0034	0,092	0,065	0,003	0,006	0,047	0,0004	0,044	0,010	0,029	0,008	0,002	0,033	0,002
Min		< 0,003	0,0001	< 0,07	< 0,02	< 0,005	< 0,01	< 0,008	< 0,0007	< 0,08	< 0,005	< 0,002	< 0,003	< 0,004	< 0,006	< 0,003
Max		0,091	0,0120	7,187	0,123	0,026	0,028	6,353	0,0089	2,711	0,108	0,071	0,148	0,009	0,210	0,047
		Compilation for the Ramah chert, n = 11														
n < LOD *(missing values)*		0	0	0	9	0	11	0	1	2	0	0	0	7	0	2
Average		0,199	0,0021	1,552	0,013	0,021	0,006	0,533	0,0033	0,379	0,032	0,097	0,085	0,006	0,029	0,016
Standard deviation		0,268	0,0006	1,379	0,005	0,016	0,000	0,458	0,0041	0,345	0,030	0,116	0,065	0,006	0,015	0,019
Median		0,047	0,0021	1,180	0,011	0,016	0,006	0,35735	0,0016	0,298	0,021	0,046	0,063	0,002	0,026	0,008
Min		0,014	0,0013	0,166	< 0,02	0,008	< 0,01	0,072	< 0,0007	< 0,08	0,009	0,016	0,031	< 0,004	0,007	< 0,003
Max		0,872	0,0034	4,479	0,025	0,059	0,006	1,422	0,0122	1,096	0,095	0,363	0,220	0,021	0,057	0,064

Table 7.1c. Artefact geochemical data and Mistassini quartzite and Ramah chert compilations.

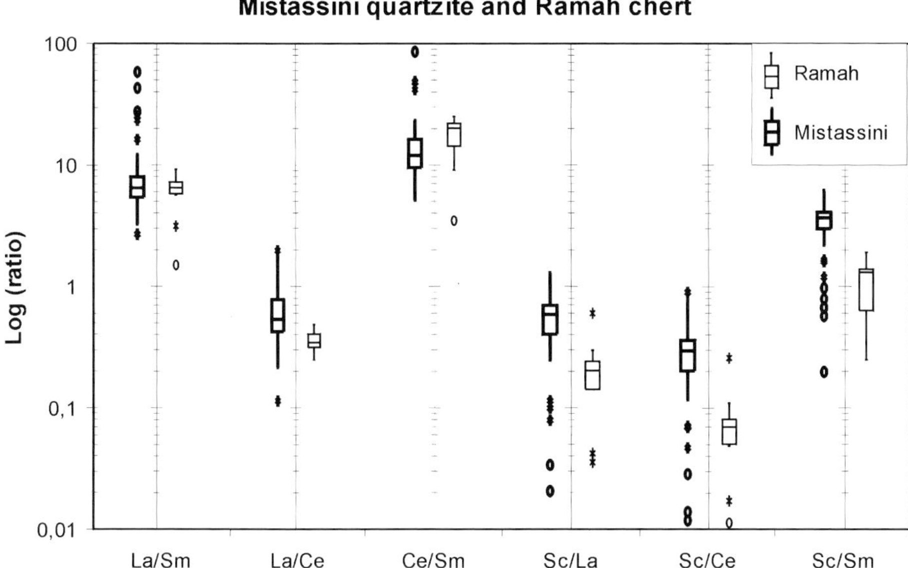

Figure 7.5. Variance of the REE ratios for Mistassini and Ramah.

and 0.010–0.101ppm, respectively. The LREE/HREE ratios are, for Mistassini and Ramah respectively, 4.985–721.680 and 39.142–219.280. The LREE/ΣREE ratio averages at 0.951 with a standard deviation of 0.833–0.999 for Mistassini samples. This ratio (LREE/ ΣREE) is similar for Ramah samples, with an average value of 0.987 and low deviation of 0.975–0.995. The HREE/ ΣREE ratio for Mistassini varies between 0.001 and 0.167 with an average of 0.049, while, for this ratio, Ramah shows an average of 0.013 with a deviation of 0.005–0.25. These data clearly show that the geochemical domains for the two materials overlap.

Of the REEs analysed, lanthanum (La), samarium (Sm), cerium (Ce), and scandium (Sc) least frequently fall below the limit of determination. Consequently, ratio-type relations (La/Sm, La/Ce, Ce/Sm, Sc/La, Sc/Ce and Sc/Sm) were calculated for the totality of Mistassini and Ramah specimens. Figure 7.5 shows, using box-and-whisker diagrams, the distribution of these ratios. Thus, the horizontal line inside the boxes represents the median value obtained for each ratio. The length of each box corresponds to the spread of the values from the first to third quartiles. The whiskers correspond to 1.5 times the quartile range and their limits neighbour the first and 99th percentiles. The asterisks indicate the values that are close but outside the limits of the whiskers, while the distant values are represented by circles. Despite a few instances of overlap between Mistassini and Ramah, it can be noted that the spreads of ratios Sc/La, Sc/Ce and Sc/Sm show considerable differences. The Sc/Sm ratio relation is shown in greater detail in Fig. 7.6. Essentially, the figure shows a distinction between the specimens from the two

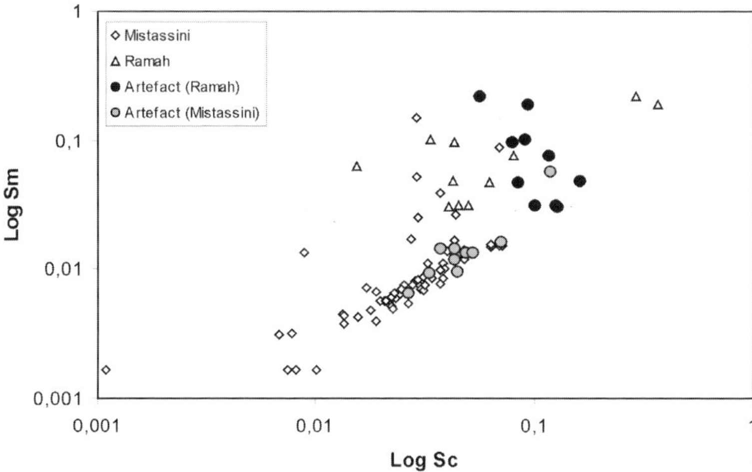

Figure 7.6. Sm and Sc concentrations for Mistassini, Ramah and archaeological artefacts.

quarries, and the generally accurate classification of the lithic material artefacts within the variance of the two sources, for Sc/Sm.

Figure 7.7 shows different REE patterns for Mistassini quartzite and Ramah chert. The differences in REE concentrations are graphically expressed by the different curve shapes for each source. For each pattern shown, the average element concentration is normalised using the chondrite values in Anders and Grevesse (1989). As mentioned earlier, Figure 7.7 first shows the REE pattern as drawn up by LeBlanc (2004) from the *colline Blanche* A and B sub-categories. These two patterns practically have the same curve shape, but show lower concentrations for the area of *colline Blanche* where Mistassini quartzite (A) is found. The REE concentrations obtained here for Ramah chert are shown graphically in Figure 7.7. The Ramah chert pattern, compared to Mistassini quartzite (A), shows higher trace element concentrations, and the shapes of the two curves are different. It is interesting to note that the REE concentrations for Ramah chert are highly similar to those of the original *colline Blanche* matrix (B), but the curve shapes are different. For comparison, the results obtained by Rutherford and Stephens (1991) from ICP-MS analysis of 2 Mistassini quartzite samples and 10 Ramah chert samples were normalised and are shown in Figure 7.7.

Multivariate statistical analyses allow comparison of overall results for Mistassini quartzite and Ramah chert sources with the Péribonka River artefacts. The chemical elements selected for multivariate analyses are those which, first of all, show the fewest missing values for Ramah and Mistassini materials: Na_2O, La, Sb, Sc, Sm and Th. Secondly, to obtain the best statistical separation, the chemical elements which appear to be the most discriminant between the two sources were retained. From this perspective, analysis of the data compiled from each source shows that certain chemical

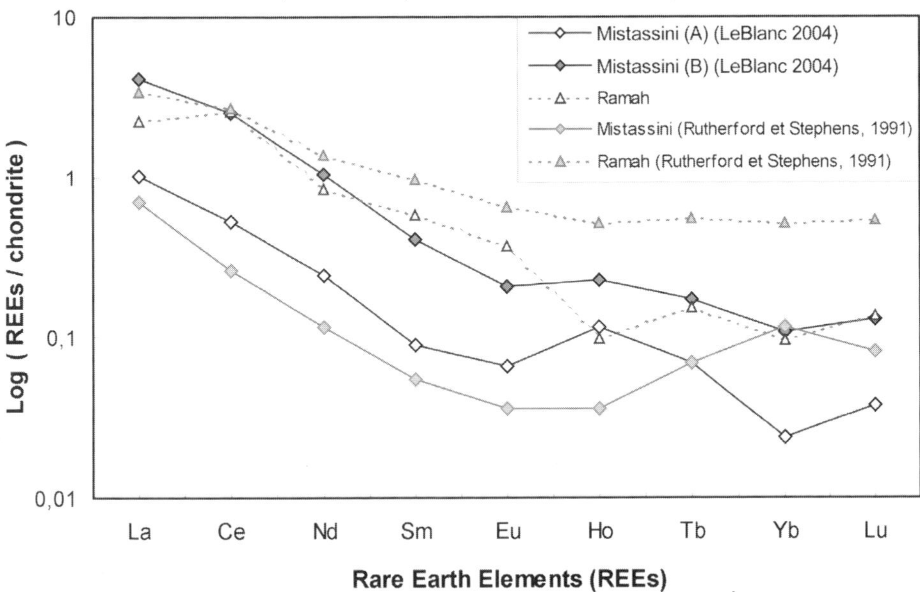

Figure 7.7. Rare Earth Element pattern for the Mistassini and Ramah geologic materials.

elements could be quantified for the majority of samples of one source, while the other source has many missing values. These observations can be translated into absence or presence of a chemical element, which can help to differentiate the two sources. For example, europium (Eu) concentrations were determined for each of the Ramah chert samples, while the levels 53 of the 63 Mistassini quartzite samples were too low for quantification (see Table 7.1c). The opposite is true for cesium (Cs), 9 of the 11 Ramah samples were undetermined, while only 4 of the 63 Mistassini samples had missing values.

The first Principal Components Analysis (PCA) is shown in Figure 7.8 and takes into account the following eight variables: Na_2O, Cs, Eu, La, Sb, Sc, Sm and Th. The total variance of the statistical analysis for Factors 1 and 2 is 62.3%. Factor 1 accounts for 39.0% of the variance, and elements Eu, Sc and Sm make the largest contribution to this factor. Elements Cs and Th heavily contribute to Factor 2, which accounts for 23.3% of the variance. Figure 7.8 shows a tight grouping of the majority of Mistassini samples compared with the totality of samples, even though some samples (Mi-24, Mi-63 and Mi-64) stray from the group. All of the Ramah chert samples have a tendency, as per Factor 1, to statistically differ from Mistassini quartzite. Most Ramah samples seem to group together, except for IfDm-7-4 and IeDk-1-2, which stray from the group. All artefacts visually identified as Ramah chert are distant from the Mistassini grouping and statistically closer to the Ramah samples. The majority of the artefacts identified as

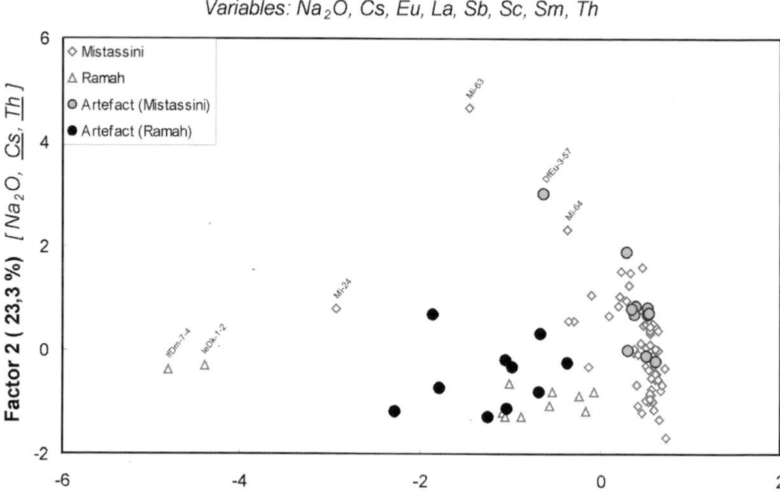

Figure 7.8. First multivariate analysis comparing sources and artefacts.

Mistassini quartzite fall within the variance of the Mistassini quarry grouping, although one artefact is outside the group (DfEu-3-57).

A second Principal Components Analysis is shown in Figure 7.9 and takes into account the chemical elements which showed the greatest relative contribution in the previous statistical analysis: Cs, Eu, Sc, Sm and Th. The total of the two axes of variance for this analysis is 85.7%. Factor 1, which accounts for 54.9% of the variance, tightly groups the Mistassini samples and dissociates Ramah chert from the Mistassini quartzite. Two confidence ellipses circumscribe the Mistassini quartzite sample population, one at 68.3% and the other at 95.0%. It can be noted that two Mistassini samples (Mi-24 and Mi-63) are outside the ellipses. One Ramah chert sample (IfDm-7-5) is perceptibly included in the Mistassini 95% confidence ellipse. One can observe in Figure 7.9 the nearness to the Ramah chert samples of many artefacts determined to be of Ramah origin. None of the artefacts identified as Ramah are found inside the Mistassini ellipses. Ten of the eleven artefacts visually identified as Mistassini are included in the Mistassini ellipses, while one sample (DfEu-3-57) lies outside the ellipses.

Discussion and conclusion

Analysis of a few samples supplied by *Institut Culturel Avataq* and Patrick Plumet has yielded new geochemical data concerning Ramah chert. Despite the small sample size, comparison with the concentrations measured from a large number of Mistassini quartzite samples leads to the observation that the geochemical signatures of these two lithic materials are very similar. However, statistical analyses made it possible

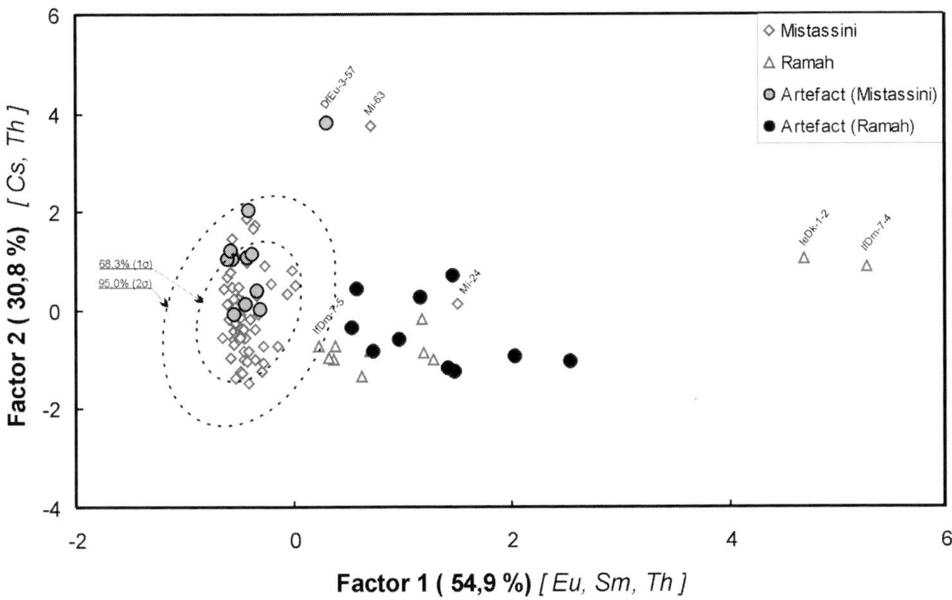

Figure 7.9. Second multivariate analysis comparing sources and artefacts.

to circumscribe the Mistassini quartzite geochemical domain with a high level of confidence, and to dissociate it from Ramah chert. Despite the geochemical distinction between Ramah chert and Mistassini quartzite, analysis of a greater number of geological specimens from the different outcrops of Ramah material is necessary, not only to confirm the difference between the materials, but primarily to firmly establish the range of variance in Ramah chert, as previously done for Mistassini quartzite. Figures 7.8 and 7.9 show that samples IfDm-7-4 and IeDk-1-2 are statistically different from the Ramah grouping. If, in fact, the Avataq samples, which are from archaeological sites, originate from the Ramah outcrops, then their geochemistry is heterogeneous and determining its range becomes important.

Comparison between the data from the Péribonka River artefacts and the Ramah chert and Mistassini quartzite samples shows the possibility of establishing a geochemical relation or distinction between the artefacts and the two source materials. Statistical analyses demonstrate that 10 of the 21 artefacts are clearly within the geochemical domain of Mistassini quartzite, while 11 are excluded. Analysis of 63 Mistassini quartzite samples extracted from the source made it possible to establish geochemical concordance with a high level of confidence. Of the 11 artefacts which are statistically excluded from the Mistassini geochemical domain, 10 tend towards Ramah chert geochemistry. However, correspondence of those artefacts with the Ramah source is fragile since the geochemical nature of the source is still largely unknown. The geochemistry of one artefact (DfEu-

3-57), visually identified as Mistassini quartzite, does not seem to correspond to either Mistassini quartzite or Ramah chert. In addition, Figures 7.8 and 7.9 show that within the Mistassini quarry group, two samples (Mi-24 and Mi-63) stand apart from the rest. A macroscopic examination of these specimens shows that their statistical distance with the main grouping formed by Mistassini seems attributable to their classification. As illustrated by Figure 7.10, the specimen Mi-63 was first associated to the subgroup A while it has partly the physical characteristics of the subgroup B. The geochemical contents of the Mi-63 specimen are higher than those observed for the subgroup A and correspond more to the contents of the subgroup B.

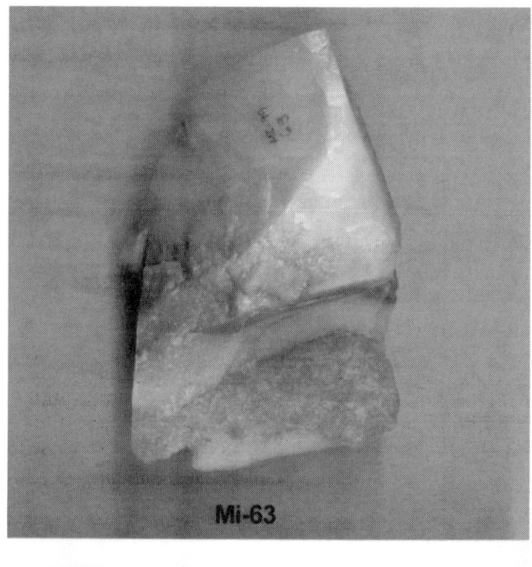

CM

Figure 7.10. Macroscopic characteristics of the Mi-63 specimen.

As concerns the artefacts associated with Mistassini quartzite, excepting one (DfEu-3-57), it can be maintained that visual identification by archaeologists are supported by geochemistry and, therefore, seems to be accurate. Concerning the 10 artefacts visually associated with Ramah chert, their geochemistry does not correspond to Mistassini quartzite, and statistical analysis shows nearness to Ramah chert. However, the current state of knowledge regarding the geochemical domain of Ramah chert does not allow for establishing with confidence artefacts-to-source relations. No data however dissociates those artefacts from the Ramah outcrops. For all intents and purposes, the origin of the artefacts as visually determined by archaeologists still stands.

All in all, trace element concentrations of these lithic materials are very close to the INAA limits of detection. Consequently, other analytical methods (ICP-MS or TIMS, for example) need to be called upon as other avenues and means to circumscribe the low-concentration issues encountered in this INAA analysis.

Acknowledgements

Erik Langevin, Joane Girard and Marie-Josée Fortin, Archaeology Laboratory (UQAC); Jacques Carignan, Pierre Cousineau, Paul Bédard and Dany Savard, Earth Sciences (UQAC); David Denton and the Cree Regional Administration; Daniel Gendron and Institut Culturel Avataq; Charles Martijn; Patrick Plumet; Adrian Burke; Roland Tremblay; André Burroughs; Julien Walter; Philip LaPorta; Margaret C. Brewer-Laporta; Jean Talbot; Joseph Tarabulsy; The archaeometry project directed by R. Auger at Laval University (co-researcher at UQAC: J.-F. Moreau) covered some of the neutron activation analysis costs for this paper. Hydro-Québec within the framework of the Péribonka-4 project covered some of the neutron activation analysis costs for this paper.

8 Extraction, Reduction, and Production at a Late Paleoindian Chert Quarry in Eastern Québec

Adrian L. Burke

Summary

Late Paleoindian bifacial technology is best understood within the context of local geology and the constraints posed by the raw material. Geological characteristics of the material influence fracture and thus not only methods of extraction but also of artefact reduction. Theses natural constraints completely eliminate certain technological choices and oblige the flintknapper to apply certain gestures (gestes). Understanding the geological context present at the raw material source thus becomes a critical factor in understanding the organization of Late Paleoindian lithic technology.

Introduction

This paper describes how the geological characteristics of a chert member or outcrop articulate with the reduction sequence or chaîne opératoire at two prehistoric chert quarries. It demonstrates that the formal aspects of Late Paleoindian stone tool technology are best understood within the context of local geology and the constraints posed by the raw material that control most, but not all, dimensions of extraction and initial reduction. The quarry and habitation/workshop sites described are located in the small village of La Martre on the north shore of the Gaspé Peninsula, Quebec, Canada (Fig. 8.1). All of the sites date to the Late Paleoindian period, which corresponds roughly to 10,000 to 8000 BP (uncalibrated) for this part of far northeast North America. These dates are based solely on stone tool morphology and flaking styles referred to as parallel flaked or "Plano" (Chalifoux 1999a and b; Chapdelaine 1994; Dumais *et al.* 1996). Understanding the lithic extraction and production process at these quarries is important at a regional level because the Gaspé region contains the largest concentration of Late Paleoindian sites in Quebec, and the presence of chert outcrops at La Martre is undoubtedly one of the main reasons for this considerable Paleoindian presence. Studying the raw material economy of Late Paleoindians in Gaspé is also significant at a continental level given the central role that high quality lithic materials seem to have played in North American Paleoindian adaptations (Goodyear 1989; Meltzer 1989).

Two quarries have been discovered to date in La Martre. The Suroît quarry (Borden site code DhDn-8) is located on a high plateau above the village. This quarry overlooks the La Martre river valley to the east and the Saint Lawrence river estuary to the north. The quarry is between 270–300m (900 and 1000 feet) above sea-level and covers at least 200,000m^2. The second quarry, Montagne Bleue (DhDn-9 and 10), is located below in the La Martre River valley along the west branch of the river at 105m (350 feet) altitude. The

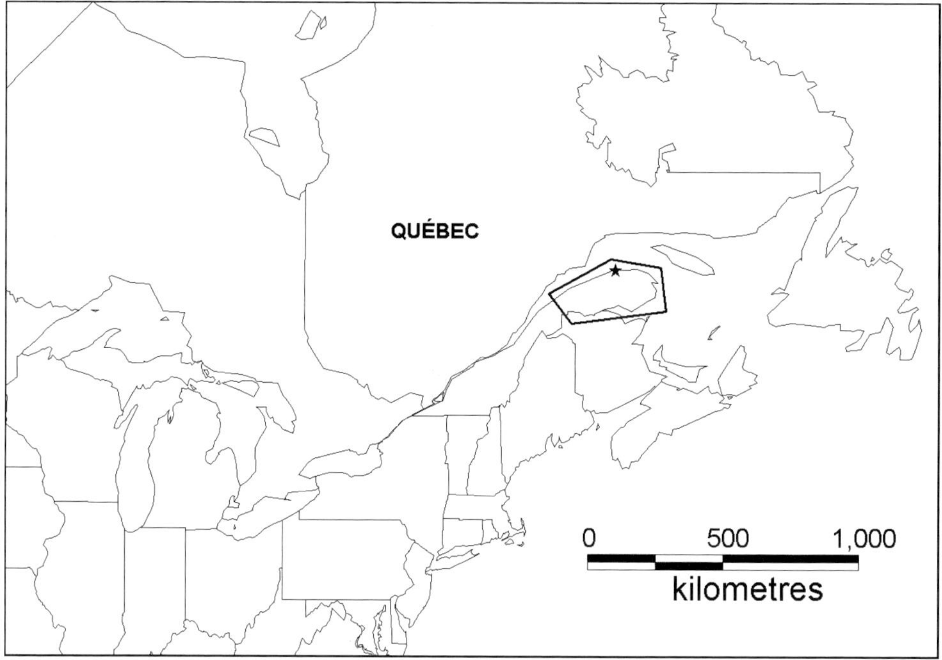

Figure 8.1. Location of the village of La Martre where the quarries are located (indicated by a star), and the Gaspé Peninsula, Quebec (polygon).

Montagne Bleue quarry has not been as extensively explored but its extent is estimated to be at least 80,000m^2. Systematic surface collections were carried out at both quarries, and extensive excavations have been carried out at thirteen related Late Paleoindian habitation/workshop sites in the village of La Martre, within 3km distance of the quarries (Chalifoux 1999a and b; Chalifoux and Tremblay 1998). Tools and debitage recovered at the quarries are described here with particular attention to the bifacial reduction sequence.

Geology

The quarries are located within the Ordovician aged Cap Chat mélange (*Occ*). This geological unit is a chaotic mix of shale, claystone, chert and other lithologies that were combined during the Taconic orogen. The allochtonous chert within the mélange is originally from the related Ordovician Des Landes formation (*Ode*) immediately to the south and east of La Martre. The chert blocks that have been included into the mélange can be quite large – up to 1km in maximum dimension in some cases (Slivitzky et al 1991). While the Cap Chat chert is not strictly speaking bedded since it is no longer in situ, some larger blocks measuring several meters will exhibit the original bedding of the chert as it was deposited and formed in the Des Landes formation (Fig 8.2). This fact makes Cap Chat chert attractive to flintknappers since the chert blocks that can be extracted are not necessarily limited in size as they might otherwise be in a mélange.

Figure 8.2. Photograph of an outcrop of chert at the Montagne Bleue quarry (DhDn-9 and 10) showing the original sedimentary bedding in the chert blocks that have been incorporated into the Cap Chat mélange.

As we will see below, the chert is in fact extracted in a tabular form that often follows the original bedrock bedding. In addition, thin section petrography of the chert shows that it has not undergone significant deformation or recrystallization due to later metamorphism which means that the chert is relatively "fresh" and good to knap (Burke 2002; Slivitzky *et al.* 1991). However, not all of the Cap Chat chert is highly siliceous or "cherty" and it often has the appearance of a dull, conchoidally fracturing, siliceous mudstone. The geological context of the chert, as well as its visual characteristics, are presented in greater detail in another paper by the author (Burke 2002).

Bifacial reduction and production at the quarries

Seventy-nine bifacial tools were analyzed from the Suroît quarry (DhDn-8) (Fig 8.3). Callahan's classification scheme for biface production was used (Callahan 2000, vii, 36–37), which was expressly developed for the Eastern Paleoindian fluted point tradition and is an excellent analogue for the early stages of our Late Paleoindian reduction sequence. The results of the classification are presented in Table 8.1. The range of dimensions for the bifaces using only complete pieces or dimensions is as follows: length, 97mm to 226mm, width, 34mm to 148mm, and thickness, 11mm to 52mm.

Bifacial tools from the Surôit quarry are clearly dominated by Callahan's (2000) stage 3 "primary pre-forms". There are also many earlier stage 2 and 2–3 "rough outs", but few of the later stages 4 and 5 "secondary pre-forms" and "final pre-forms". Finished tools equivalent to Callahan's stages 6+ or "flaked implements" (*e.g.*, broken projectile points) are occasionally found at the quarry site, which suggests that the lower number of stage

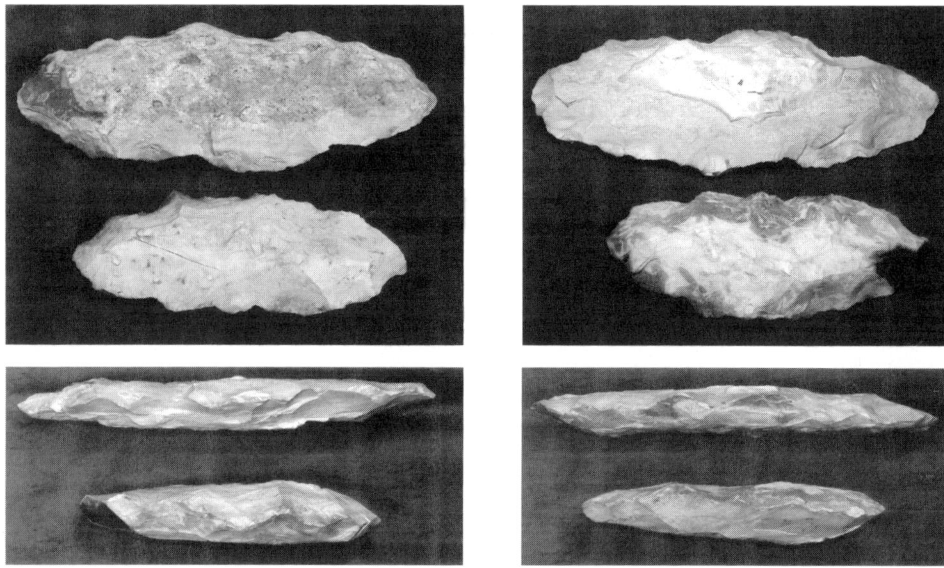

Figure 8.3. Plan and side views of two complete Callahan Stage 2 bifacial preforms (top DhDn-8.43, bottom DhDn-8.26). Note the sinuous edge on these early stage bifaces as well as the original sedimentary layer still visible on parts of the preform faces. The longer bifacial preform, no. 43, pictured at top is 265mm long by 97mm wide, 29mm in thickness and 898.8g in weight. The shorter example, no. 26, depicted beneath is 188mm long by 76mm wide, 38mm in thickness and 532.8g in weight.

Stage	Count
Stage 1 *(Blank)*	3
Stage 2 *(Rough Out)*	9
Stage 2–3	13
Stage 3 *(Primary Pre-form)*	35
Stage 3–4	7
Stage 4 *(Secondary Pre-form)*	9
Stage 5 *(Final Pre-form)*	3

Table 8.1. Classification of bifaces recovered from the Suroît Late Paleoindian quarry using Callahan's (2000) biface stages.

4 or 5 pre-forms could be an artifact of our sampling. Stage 3 bifacial pre-forms should have a width-thickness ratio of between 3.0 and 4.0 according to Callahan (2000, 30–31). All of the 79 bifaces together have an average width-thickness ratio of 3.3, and the 35 Stage 3 bifaces average only 3.0. This is an indication that, in fact, many of the pre-forms from the quarry are quite early in the reduction sequence which is corroborated by the large number (22) of Stage 2 and 2–3 "rough outs". As a comparison, the biface pre-forms recovered at the Early Paleoindian quarry of West Athens Hill in the Hudson River Valley of New York have similar width to thickness dimensions: ratio of 2.7 for stage 2 equivalents, and 3.4 for stage 3 equivalents (Funk 2004). This is noteworthy because the chert at West Athens Hill is also an Ordovician chert making up part of a mélange dominated by shales. Nodules or chunks extracted at West Athens Hill are similar in dimension as well as form to the La Martre quarries, but less often tabular (personal observation at the quarry). Edge angles on the biface pre-forms provide additional

information. They range from 30° to 65° for Stage 3 pre-forms, and all but 4 fall into the 40°–60° range predicted by Callahan for stage 3 primary pre-forms.

Judging from what was left on the surface of the quarry, the majority of production appears to be dedicated to the production of stage 2–3–4 pre-forms for transport to the habitation/workshop sites in the valley below. In particular, production at the quarry is dominated by the production of "primary pre-forms" (Stage 3) defined by Callahan as having a "symmetrical handaxe-like outline with a generous lenticular cross-section and a straight and centered, bi-convex edge. Principal flakes should generally just contact or overlap in the middle zone… and be without such concavities, convexities, steps, or other irregularities as would hinder successful execution in the next stage" (Callahan 2000, vii). This description corresponds well to our Stage 3 bifacial pre-forms (Fig. 8.3). It also suggests that the majority of production failures at the quarry occurred at this stage of production.

The initial steps of the reduction process or the chaîne opératoire

In analyzing the bifacial production at the La Martre Paleoindian quarries I was intrigued both as a lithic analyst and as a flintknapper as to how the raw material, once extracted, could constrain the initial steps of the reduction process. Would the form of the raw material as it was created geologically, and then extracted and selected at the quarry, set the initial critical parameters, in part or in whole, for the chaîne opératoire? How did prehistoric flintknappers use the tabular chunks to their advantage and how did they tackle problems such as blocks with rectangular cross sections and 90° angles? Of those pre-forms that still retain enough information for analysis, the large majority is knapped parallel to the sedimentary layers in the chert: 52 parallel to the sedimentary layers, and 9 parallel to a joint set (Fig. 8.3). This means that the two faces of the bifacial pre-form and its center plane are parallel to the original sedimentary layers in the tabular chert block. On the early stage bifaces that still contain two layers of sedimentary chert 'cortex' the average thickness of the original tabular piece appears to have been rather thin; about 30mm (measured on 10 artifacts). Half of the earlier stage bifaces (Stages 1 to 3) still retain some sedimentary 'cortex' on at least one face. This is not cobble or nodular cortex but rather the coarser and less cherty sedimentary layer found between chert layers. Many bifaces (36 in total) show evidence of joint surfaces, and half of these (18) show two or more joints at obtuse angles to each other. Joint surfaces are roughly perpendicular to the sedimentary layers.

The choices that the flintknappers at La Martre have made are in part constrained by the form in which the material is extracted. At the same time, the tabular form also benefits the flintknapper in the production of the bifacial forms by producing a starting point that already has an excellent, or high, width to thickness ratio. Moreover, if the joint surfaces or sets that also help define the shape and size of the tabular chert blocks provide useful angles to begin the reduction process, then the raw material constraints can prove to be an advantage rather than a hindrance for specific reduction sequences or chaînes opératoires. We can use Waldorf's (1993, 33) models for the initial stages of biface pre-form manufacture to look at how Late Paleoindian flintknappers exploited the combination of sedimentary layers and joint surfaces present in the chert at La Martre (Fig. 8.4).

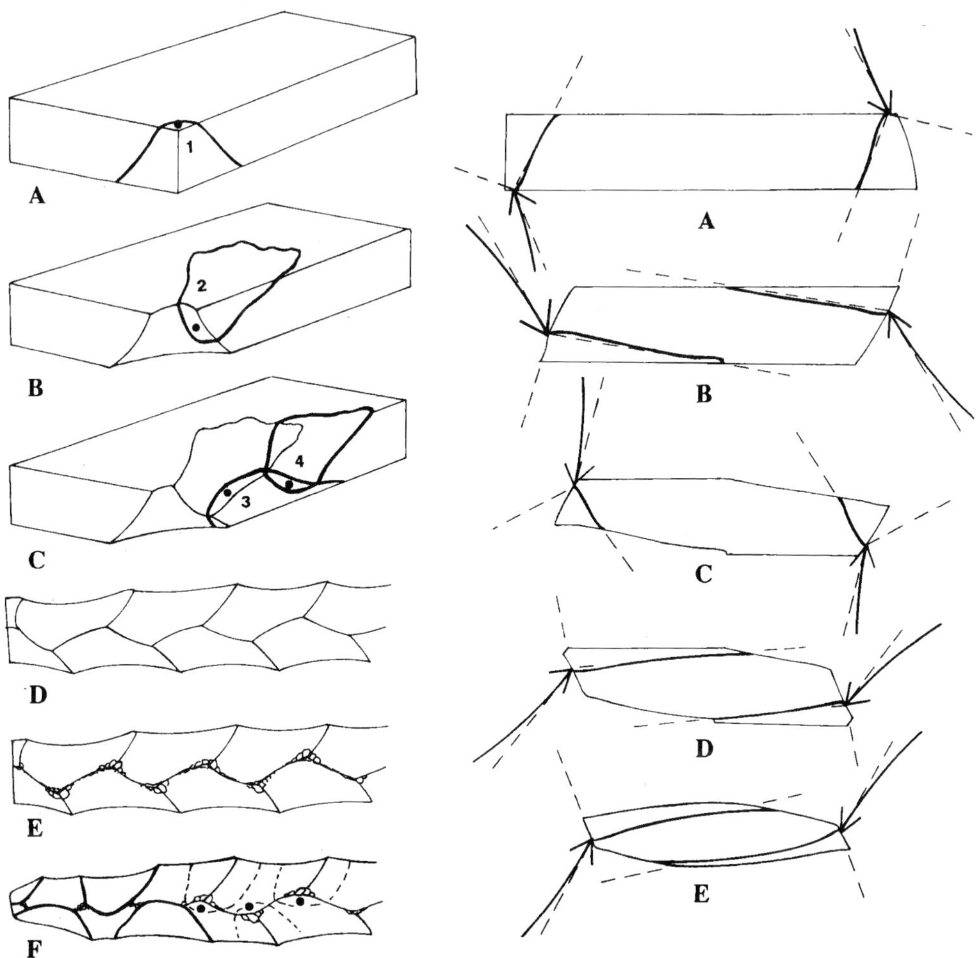

Figure 8.4. Two approaches to reducing a tabular block with a rectangular or trapezoidal cross section as proposed by Waldorf (1993, 33). Drawings by Val Waldorf. Reproduced with kind permission of the author, D.C. Waldorf, and the publisher, Mound Builder Books.

The majority of bifacial pre-forms analyzed show alternate flaking along each of the long edges of the tabular block. Figure 8.5 presents the *schéma diacritique* or diacritical schema for two complete biface pre-forms recovered from the Suroît quarry (see also Fig. 8.3). Each edge removal is carried out relatively independent of the other, that is, it does not proceed in a continuous circumferential manner. Some pre-forms show a second technique referred to by Waldorf (1993, 33) as "platform reversal" (Fig. 8.4). This technique produces a characteristic beveled cross-section in which the original sedimentary layers are no longer parallel to the center plane of the biface (Fig. 8.6). This reduction strategy will be favoured when the edges of the tabular block are not at right angles, but rather are formed by joint surfaces at acute angles thus facilitating the initial flaking of the tabular block.

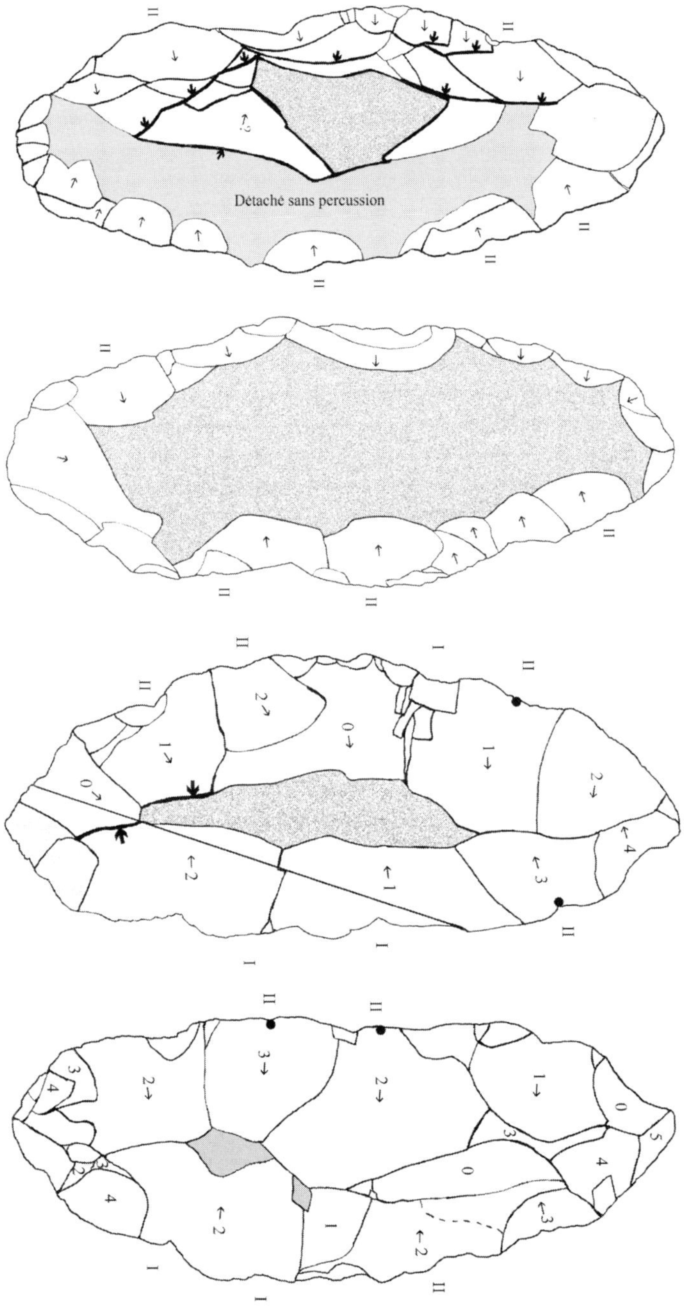

Figure 8.5. Schéma diacritique or diacritical schema showing the sequence of flake removals (sequential Arabic numerals) on each face of the stage 2 bifacial preforms shown in Figure 8.3. In the cases where the sequence of removals alternates between faces and can be clearly distinguished, these are indicated in order of removal by Roman numerals. Grey stippling represents original sedimentary layer 'cortex'. Drawing and analysis by Manek Kolhatkar.

Figure 8.6. Cross section of two bifacial preform fragments broken during manufacture. Note the opposing beveled edges.

This analysis was not geared specifically towards trying to evaluate or measure the rate of manufacturing errors or failures (cf. Brumbach and Weinstein 1999). It was possible to identify a few end thinning and lateral thinning fractures. Only three overshot (outrepassé) flakes led to failure and rejection. Failure may not be an accurate descriptor since the bifaces could be salvaged, but these three biface pre-forms were abandoned. Many of the production failures show snaps and can be related to bend or perverse fractures as defined by Whittaker (1994, 212–217, see also Waldorf 1993, 50–53; Callahan 2000, 108–113). These would seem to occur on a regular basis in the manufacture of larger bifaces. Only five of the biface pre-forms had visible stacks which probably led the flintknapper to stop the thinning process and abandon the biface pre-form. Raw material flaws do not seem to be a major factor in the failure to complete the chaîne opératoire. I have identified only one biface which seems to have failed along a joint surface. The chert is in fact surprisingly homogeneous, and even the laminations that reflect the original sedimentary layers do not have any incidence on flaking. There are no vugs or clasts that interfere with the knapping quality either.

Debitage

A sub-sample of 50 complete flakes that were surface collected at the Suroît quarry was analyzed. These flakes are short and wide, average length to width ratio is 1.1, and they are relatively thick (13.5mm). Only 20 have cortex on the dorsal surface (covering 25% to 75% of the dorsal surface) (Fig. 8.7). Those flakes without cortex often have several

Figure 8.7. Debitage recovered from the Suroît quarry (DhDn-8). Top row: flakes from the initial series of removals along the edge of the tabular block with remnant sedimentary layer on dorsal side, large platforms, and large platform angles. Middle row: second series of flakes removed showing multiple flake scars on the dorsal side originating from various directions, small platforms, and acute platform angles. All flake platforms are towards the top. Bottom row: biface abandoned due to an overshot flake, and overshot flake with remnant biface edge at the top.

prior flake scars on the dorsal surface, with an average of 5 flake scars and a range of 3 to 10. Previous flake scars almost invariably originate from opposing directions (Fig. 8.7). Platform angles range from 45° to 80° degrees, with an average of 62.5°. 24 flakes have one flake scar on the striking platform, 15 flakes have two, 3 flakes have three or more scars. Surprisingly, none of the flakes analyzed have cortex on the platform. This lack of cortex on platforms may be a sampling artifact. Conversely, it may be due to the fact that most tabular pieces will not exhibit "cortex" on their sides since that is where the chert block has fractured or separated along a joint surface.

Thirty-three flakes have evidence of platform grinding for preparation, only 4 do not. Platform preparation by grinding is also apparent on the bifacial pre-forms. A large number of flakes (18) have bulbar scars (éraillures) and one fifth (10) have strongly lipped platforms. The dimensions of the flakes and the bulb scars, combined with the fact that many biface pre-forms have deeply plunging and indented flake scars (Fig. 8.3), suggests that most early reduction work at the quarry was done by hard hammer

Figure 8.8. Utilized hard hammers found at the Suroît quarry (DhDn-8) showing crushing along the edges. Materials are quartzite and various types of arkose, quartz-arenite, or sandstone based on visual inspection.

percussion. This is confirmed by the discovery of several hammerstones made of rounded cobbles that may have originated in the river valley below or in the surface tills at the quarry itself (Fig. 8.8). The hard hammers are made of quartzite, and an arkose/quartz-arenite/sandstone rock with similar knapping characteristics to quartzite. Soft hammers (caribou antler billets?) most likely were used at the quarry as well since there is ample evidence of thinning of pre-forms to produce finished bifaces (Stage 5+). Most of this thinning would have been difficult with the hard hammers found at the quarry. A substantial proportion, if not the majority, of the finishing of bifaces took place at the nearby habitation/workshop sites. This is based on the many late stage bifaces broken during thinning and the tens of thousands of flakes recovered during excavations at these habitation/workshop sites (Fig. 8.9).

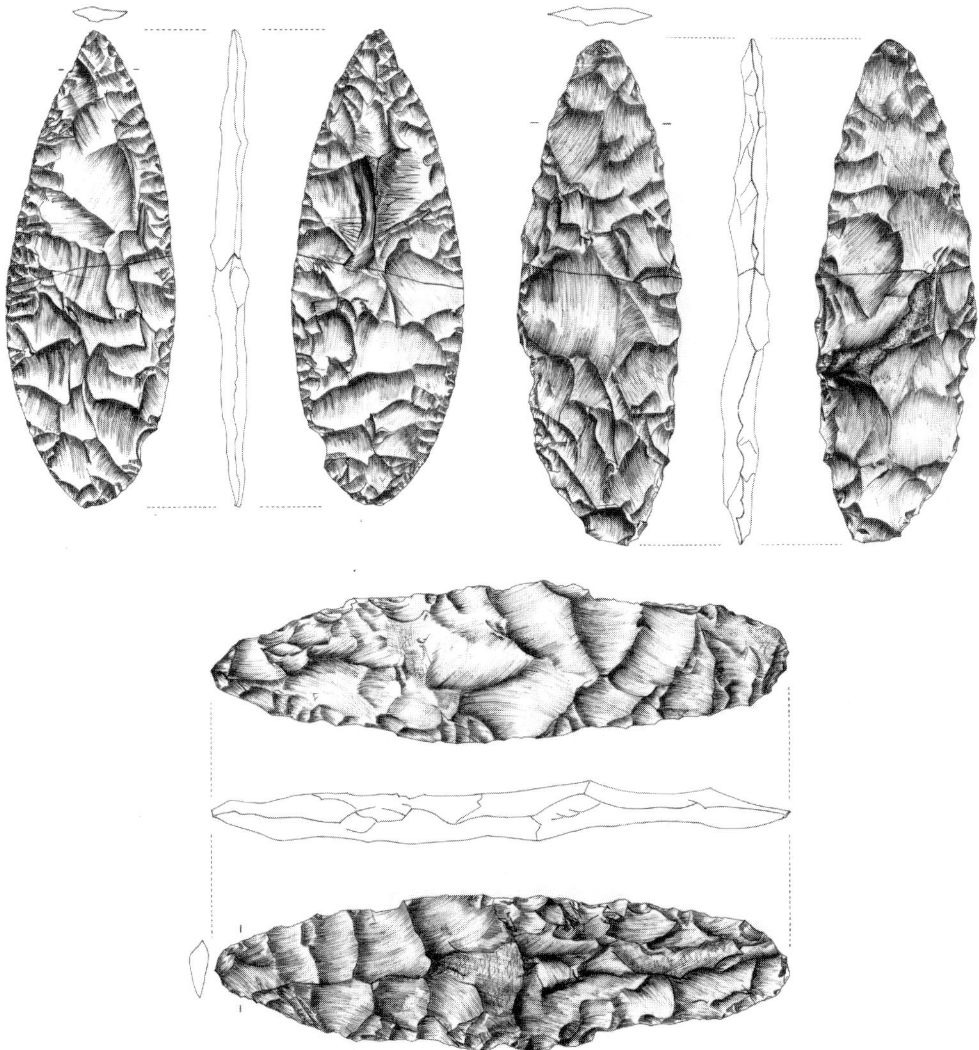

Figure 8.9. Late stage bifaces broken during thinning recovered at Late Paleoindian habitation/ workshop sites around La Martre village (DhDm-1). Drawings by Sophie Limoges.

Conclusion

The aim of this paper is to describe how the geological characteristics of a chert source articulate with the reduction sequence or chaîne opératoire of chipped stone tools. Two Late Paleoindian chert quarries were used to explore this concept. Our analysis demonstrates that the highly formalized aspects of Late Paleoindian bifacial technology are best understood within the context of local geology and the constraints posed by the raw material. These constraints control most aspects of the extraction of the raw material and therefore the forms of raw material made available to the flintknapper. In this case the raw material takes the form of rectangular tabular blocks bounded by sedimentary layers and joint sets. These geological raw material dimensional characteristics consequently place natural constraints on the initial reduction of the raw material. The natural constraints, in turn, completely eliminate certain technological choices and oblige the flintknapper to apply certain gestures (*gestes*). This can be seen in those segments of the chaîne opératoire that are visible at the La Martre quarries.

Raw material constraints therefore control most, but not necessarily all aspects of lithic reduction. The related Late Paleoindian habitation/workshop sites in the valley below have in fact produced smaller tools (*e.g.* scrapers) that are made from flake blanks but these are rare. Most, if not all, formal tool production at the quarries and the habitation/workshop sites follows a bifacial reduction sequence leading to the production of knives, projectile points, drills, and possibly large sidescrapers. Consequently, the geological constraints described above should not be seen exclusively as limitations. The sedimentary layers within the chert that lead to large tabular blocks being extracted provide an excellent starting point for the production of large bifaces given their high width to thickness ratio. In addition, the joint sets often present ideal angles for the initiation of bifacial thinning thus providing opportunities for technological choices rather than simply imposing constraints. As a comparison, the Témiscouata quarries of eastern Quebec also provide a medium to high quality chert that is very similar to the La Martre chert (Burke and Chalifoux 1998). Chert from Témiscouata is also sedimentary, and blocks extracted from the quarry are usually bounded by joint sets. However, in this case the joint sets are more closely spaced than at La Martre and therefore it is impossible to make the large bifaces we see at La Martre. Understanding the geological context present at the raw material source thus becomes a critical factor in understanding the organization of Late Paleoindian lithic technology. In this paper we have only addressed the first steps taken by flintknappers at the quarry, but it seems clear that without a better sense of these initial steps it will be difficult to accurately reconstruct the rest of the chaîne opératoire and the choices made by these people at their campsites in the valley below.

Acknowledgments

I wish to thank Manek Kolhatkar who helped me to do the analysis for this paper and who produced the schémas diacritiques presented in Figure 8.5. Thank you to Sophie Limoges and Éric Chalifoux for allowing me to use the drawings of bifaces in Figure 8.3. My thanks also to D. C. Waldorf for allowing me to reproduce Figure 8.4 from his book. Thank you to the two reviewers who improved this paper. Thank you especially to Éric Chalifoux for inviting me to participate in the research on Late Paleoindians in the Gaspé Peninsula; it was a lot of fun!

9 Why did Paleo-Indians Select the Sheguiandah Site? An Evaluation of Quarrying and Quartzite Material Selection Based on Petrographic Analysis of Core Artifacts

Patrick J. Julig and Darrel Long

Summary

Petrographic analysis of samples of Bar River Formation quartzite (quartz-arenite) from the Sheguiandah Paleo-Indian and surrounding sites on Manitoulin Island, Ontario, Canada, indicates that the preferred facies quarried for tool manufacture was glassier and more extensively recrystallized than other typical strained and fractured Bar River and Lorrain Formation outcrops in the immediate area. The quarrying methods and reduction strategies employed by the Paleo-Indians to obtain cores for large biface pre-forms and blade-like flakes may have led to the preference for a particular facies at the Sheguiandah site over other surrounding sites situated on these formations. Quarrying the massive, extensively recrystallized glassy facies at Sheguiandah may have been facilitated by the presence of well-developed joints at spacings of 10 to 15cm, which allowed extraction of material of adequate size and quality for production of cores and subsequent biface and blade manufacture. Regionally, Paleo-Indian quarry and workshop site location appears to be strongly correlated to strain recrystallized glassy facies in the Bar River and Lorrain Formations. Paleo-Indian artisans appear to have favoured sites on or adjacent to protected beaches of the early Holocene Great Lake, where joint spacing in the preferred lithofacies was regular, and closely spaced.

Introduction

One of the most noted characteristics of Paleo-Indian cultures across North America is their use of high quality, often non-local or exotic cherts, and the similarities of their lithic assemblages across broad regions (Mason 1981; 1986; Goodyear 1989). However in the upper Great Lakes region of North America, particularly on the ancient rocks of the Pre-Cambrian shield, cherts are uncommon and other quartz rich lithic materials were widely used in the manufacture of stone artifacts. The Late Paleo-Indian Plano culture in the central and northern regions (*c.* 10,000–7,500 YBP) commonly used coarser grained lithic materials, including quartzite (crystalline material), silicious quartz arenite (sandstone), taconite (banded iron formation and ferruginous chert) and siltstone from bedrock quarry sources (Clark 1989; Julig 1994; 2002; Julig and McAndrews 1993; Julig *et al.* 1998). At many Late Paleo-Indian sites non-cryptocrystalline lithics form over

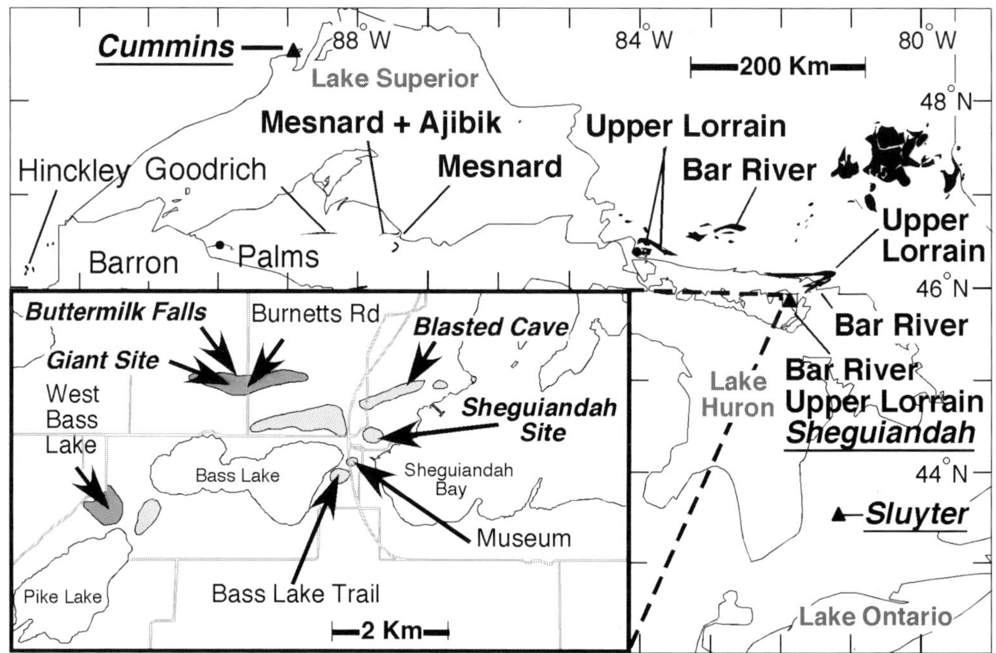

Figure 9:1. Quartz arenite (black) in the Upper Great Lakes region of Canada and United States. Triangles represent sites from which Late Palaeo-Indian artifacts were examined for this study (Archaeological site names in italics).

95% of artifact assemblages (Clark 1989; Buckmaster 1989; Julig 1994). The formal and curated tools and assemblages appear to be more commonly made from higher quality recrystallized glassy facies lithic materials, such as those found in localized bands at Sheguiandah (Bar River Formation) and to a lesser extent in some of the adjacent sites where exposures of the Bar River Formation and upper Lorrain Formation are exposed (Fig. 9.1 insert). Expedient tools may also be made from lower quality local materials (Julig *et al.* 1998; Long *et al.* 2002), especially in areas of superficially similar, white, fine grained, silicified quartz arenite.

In areas of eastern Manitoulin Island, immediately west of Sheguiandah Bay (Fig. 9.1), white quartzite outcrops are common. Despite this fact, prehistoric quarry workshop sites are restricted to just a few locations, including around the Sheguiandah site, with numerous workshop sites. At Sheguiandah only the south side of the quartz knoll has been extensively quarried, while the north side, which has more extensively fractured quartzite, has almost no worked quarry pits (Julig 2002). In this paper we discuss possible factors that determined selection of the outcrops quarried. During the Paleo-Indian cultural interval higher water levels would have prevented access to low lying sites; however for topographically higher sites it appears that specific characteristics of the raw materials must have attracted the inhabitants. Previous research (Julig *et al.* 1998; Long *et al.* 2002) examined the petrographic characteristics of geological samples

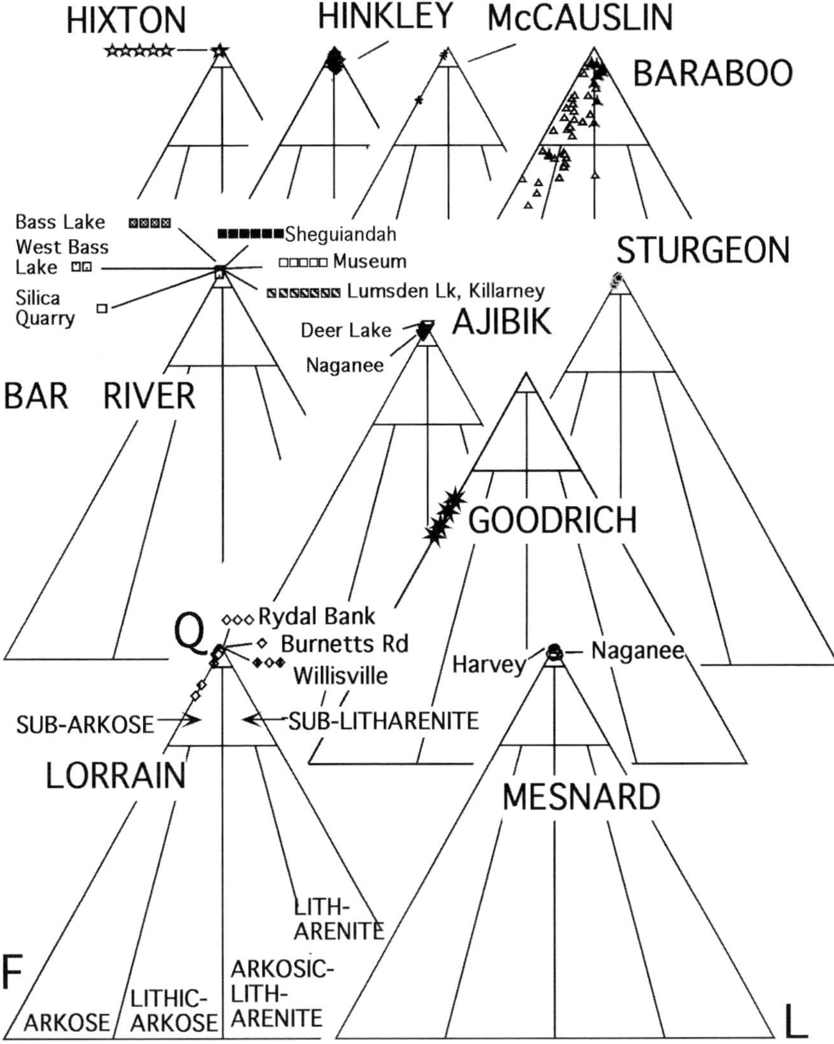

Figure 9.2. Petrographic analysis of potential lithic sources in the Great Lakes region (from Long et al. 2002). These plots represent the relative percentage of quartz (Q), feldspar (F) and lithic fragments (L) in the framework component of representative samples (cements are not included in this type of analysis – only primary detrital grains). Note the abundance of samples that fall into the small triangular field at the top of the QFL diagrams representing sandstones (quartz arenites) with more than 95% quartz grains.

of quartzite (quartz-arenite) from the Bar River and Lorrain Formations, as well as other quartzite bearing formations across the Great Lakes Region and found that in most cases only lithic material with a very high percentage of detrital quartz grains was used (Figs 9.1 and 9.2).

Objectives

In this study we compare petrographic analysis of artifacts (cores) from the Sheguiandah Paleo-Indian and other local quarry sites (Fig. 9.1 inset), with local geological sources. This work confirms that the preferred facies quarried for tool manufacture was both glassier and more extensively recrystallized than other typical Bar River and Lorrain Formation outcrops in the immediate area, which are also strained and fractured. Our primary objectives in this research was to A) determine if petrographic characteristics of artifacts could be matched to local bedrock; B) determine if desirable facies exist in other sites underlain by the Bar River and Lorrain Formations in the Sheguiandah area (Fig. 9.1). In addition we attempted to determine if grain size and sorting is useful in distinguish sources, and if recrystallization features are distinctive at different sites.

Geological background of early Proterozoic Bar River Formation quartzites

Paleo-Indians extensively quarried lithic material from the Paleoproterozoic Bar River Formation at and around Sheguiandah (Fig. 9.3) and to a lesser extent at the George Lake sites near Lumsden Lake, 50km to the northeast (Fig. 9.1; Card 1978). Strata of the Early Paleoproterozoic Bar River Formation underlie a prominent 33km long range of hills in this area of Killarney Provincial Park and are exposed in a belt of Lake Huron islands, which extend 40km SSW of Killarney towards Sheguiandah on Manitoulin Island (Fig. 9.1). The crests of these hills would have been exposed, and probably surrounded by water at 10,000 BP, and would certainly have been accessible by 9,500 BP. Much further to the NE minor exposures of the Bar River Formation are present in the Cobalt Plane between Smoothwater, Lady Evelyn and Welcome Lakes (Long *et al.* 2002). These may have been covered by ice during Late Paleo-Indian times. Low relief exposures of the formation are also present 180km to the WNW in three small areas near Sault Ste Marie, and in the Flack Lake area ~100km NW of Sheguiandah (Fig. 9.1).

The Bar River Formation is up to 900m thick; it is dominated by white, and to a lesser extent pink, well sorted fine to medium grained, quartz-cemented, sandstone (quartzite) with >98% quartz (Fig. 9.2). The strata are superficially similar to the upper part of the Lorrain Formation (see below). Most sand grains in the Bar River Formation samples are rounded to well rounded. In northern areas the siliceous cements, where present, show little to no sign of post burial strain (uneven extinction), while those in the south have been more severely deformed, and show abundant evidence of strain, as will be discussed later. Minor components include muscovite and hematite (Julig *et al.*1998; Long *et al.* 2002).

Samples of the Bar River Formation were collected from the Sheguiandah archaeological site, (Latitude 45°53'51"N, Longitude 81°55'19"W), where the quartzite has a pronounced cleavage and an excellent conchoidal fracture (Fig. 9.3 lower left). Other samples were collected from outcrops 1 to 5km north and west of the Sheguiandah quarry site and other locations (see inset on Fig. 9.1), where strata break into rhombs along joints at spacings of 5 to 45cm, with a sub-conchoidal fracture. Additional moderately strained samples were collected from the Lumsden Lake (George Lake) archeological site in Killarney Park

Figure 9.3. Exposures of the Bar River Formation at the Sheguiandah archaeological site. Top: Exposure of the Bar River Formation showing closely spaced joints which may have facilitated extraction of core material. Lower left: Detail of quarry showing contrast between irregular conchoidal fracture surfaces, which would have been an asset in artifact production, and planar fractures (joints) which would have facilitated removal of blocks of workable material. Lower Right: Worked quarry face at Sheguiandah, showing extensive quarried blocks, of similar size to the joint spacing.

(46°01'35"N, 81°26'05"W) and included one feldspathic sample (a sub-arkose). Unstrained samples of the formation were collected in the vicinity of Mississagi Provincial Park (46°32'N, 82°48"W). These samples were analyzed previously (Julig *et al.* 1998; Long *et al.* 2002), and the data presented here (Figs 9.2, 9.4) for comparison to the artifacts.

Early-Paleoproterozoic Lorrain Formation quartzites

Strata of the Early Paleoproterozoic Lorrain Formation are exposed in a 250km long series of hills between Sault St. Marie and Killarney Provincial Park, along the northern margin of Lake Huron, Ontario, as well as in numerous ridges across the Cobalt Plain, 25–100km north of Lake Huron (Fig. 9.1). The Formation, which is between 1.5 and 2.4km thick, was metamorphosed during the Penokean Orogeny (Young *et al.* 2001), and includes silicified quartz arenite, subarkose and arkose (Folk 1980). Quartz arenite samples that are superficially similar too, and have been confused with, sandstones of the Bar River Formation at Sheguiandah are most common in the upper third of the formation.

Samples collected from the Willisville area (46°07'41"N, 81°44'08"W), in the LaCloche Mountains, south of Espanola Ontario, are from the upper member of the formation, which is dominated by sheared, white, well-sorted, medium to very fine sandstones with >98% quartz (Fig. 9.2). At this locality the formation is dominated by massive and through cross stratified medium to fine sandstones, which break with a sub-conchoidal fracture. Major joints (planar fractures) are spaced at 1 to 1.5m, hence weathered blocks may have been too large for transport over extended distances. Local field area samples are from the upper member of the Lorrain Formation along Burnetts Side Road (Fig. 9.1 inset) near Sheguiandah (45°54'27"N, 81°56'53"W), which is adjacent to the Giant Site (BlHl-1). Samples were predominantly medium to coarse sand grade, and break, with an irregular hackley fracture into irregular polygonal blocks along master joints at 20 to 40cm apart. Additional samples were collected from the upper member at Rydal Bank (46°22'06"N, 83°43'38"W) and Gordon Lake (46°24'14"N, 83°49'27"W) near Sault St. Marie, where the formation is significantly less deformed. At both these localities (Fig. 9.1) the strata broke with a hackley, rather than conchoidal fracture and the majority of samples would not have been suitable for artifact production. Major sub-vertical joints were 5–10cm apart, with bedding plane joints at 30 to 120cm. This stone is similar to the geological material at the north side of the Sheguiandah site, which is Bar River Formation, and was not quarried to any extent.

Archaeological samples

Quarry workshop sites occur along both the Bar River and upper Lorrain Formation outcrops, and examples sampled are shown in italics on Figure 9.1 (inset). Several quarry workshops located along the strike have been surveyed in addition to Sheguiandah (Julig 2002) and museum collections from the Canadian Museum of Civilization were made available from several sites, including the Giant site (BlHl-1), Blasted Cave, and Northwest Sheguiandah, (BlHl-4). We obtained permission to analyze the main color varieties and textures of selected cores, as depicted in a later section. Thin sections were made from representative sub-samples of core artifacts. These were examined petrographically and the grain size, nature of grain contacts and relative abundance of quartz and other types were quantified using point counts (Table 9.1). These were then plotted on ternary plots along with previously analyzed Bar River and Lorrain Formation geological samples (Figs 9.4 and 9.5).

Sample	n =	Q m	Q p	Q s	%M	Mode	Grade
Giant 224	300	10	14	75	19	0.11	vfS
GIANT 73	257	12	12	77	7	0.18	fS
Giant 1626	254	16	4	80	2	0.44	mS
Giant May5-15	251	0	27	72	1	0.17	fS
Giant 1684	250	1	29	70	4	0.24	fS
Giant OMAV5	255	0	69	31	5	0.14	vfS
Giant 1860	250	18	11	71	2	0.28	mS
Giant 1627	258	17	3	80	5	0.16	fS
Giant 1628	275	12	4	84	9	0.18	fS
Giant 81	289	24	10	66	13	0.22	fS
Blasted 1	263	20	3	76	5	0.65	mS
Blasted 2	282	8	27	64	11	0.14	vfS
Blasted 3	265	2	40	57	6	0.21	fS
Blasted 4	252	1	40	58	1	0.38	mS
BIHI 4:2	271	21	5	74	8	0.30	mS
BIHI 4:3	278	8	24	68	10	0.30	mS
BIHI 4:4	275	7	18	75	9	0.21	fS

Notes: n = number of points counted
Qm = % monocrystalline quartz grains
Qp = % polycrystalline quartz grains
Qs = % strained quartz grains
%M = % Mud (muscovite)
Mode = Median grain size in mm
Grade = sand size (vf = very fine; f = fine; m = medium)

Table 9.1. Petrographic analysis of thin sections from cores at archaeological sites around Sheguiandah. Note that no feldspar or lithic fragments were found in any of the samples examined. The mud component may represent degraded feldspar (epimatrix).

Petrographic analysis

In this study petrographic methods are used to examine the textures, degree of straining and recrystallization, and to examine the raw-material selection at a finer scale. Standard petrographic analysis of geological specimens involves preparation of a 30-micron thick slice of rock, mounted in epoxy on a glass slide. This procedure is followed by systematic identification and counting of detrital sand grains (framework components), detrital matrix (mud and clay trapped between the sand at the time of deposition), voids (spaces between grains) and cements (minerals introduced into spaces between sand grains during burial and consolidation). In this study a minimum of 500 framework grains were counted using a fixed interval moving stage.

Results of earlier petrographic analysis of the geological materials are presented in Figure 9.2. In these data sets the abundance of framework quartz, feldspar, and lithic grains (Q, F, L) has been recalculated to equal 100%, while the matrix, cements and voids are given as a percentage of the whole rock. Quartz is the dominant mineral in thin sections, both as detrital grains and cement. As can be seen in Figure 9.2, there is little to distinguish many of the geological sources examined, based on their bulk petrography, as all samples contain abundant detrital quartz, and plot as quartz arenite (>95% of framework grains are quartz). Samples from the Baraboo include quartz arenite, sub-

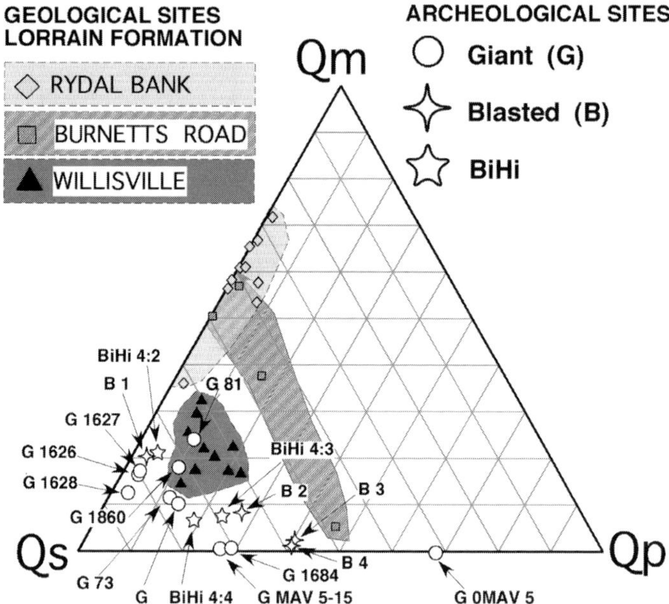

Figure 9.4. Plot of the ratio of monocrystalline (Qm) to polycrystalline (Qp) and strained (Qs) quartz grains in geological from the upper part of the Lorrain Formation in the vicinity of Sheguiandah.

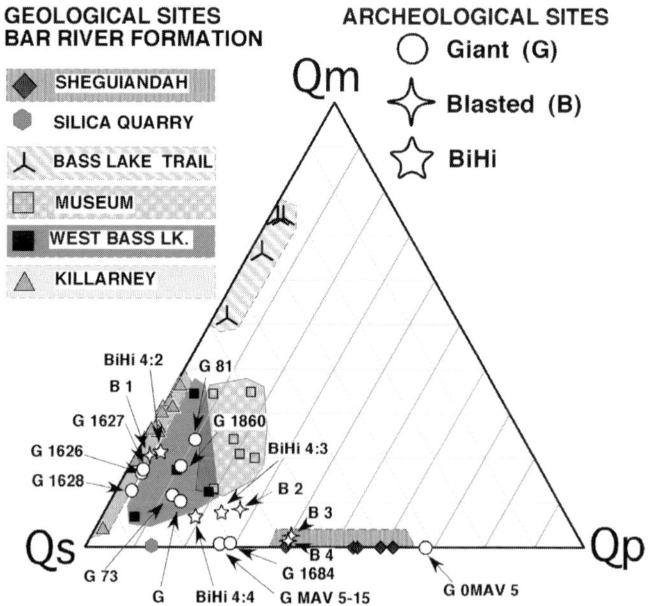

Figure 9.5. Plot of the ratio of monocrystalline (Qm) to polycrystalline (Qp) and strained (Qs) quartz grains in geological from the Bar River Formation in the vicinity of Sheguiandah.

arkose and arkose, while those from the Goodrich are all arkosic arenite (Fig. 9.2). Detrital matrix (clay, replaced by micas) form a significant proportion of some samples from the Mesnard, Lorrain, McCaslin, Bar River, Ajibik and Baraboo. Chert grains are present in most samples of the Ajibik, Mesnard, Baraboo and Hinkley sandstones, but are uncommon to rare in samples of the Lorrain Formation, being found only in samples from the upper part of the formation from Rydal Bank, well to the north of Sheguiandah. Chert was not observed in any of the artifacts or the geological samples from the Bar River and upper Lorrain Formation in the vicinity of Sheguiandah.

Note that all of the artifacts examined plot in the field of quartz arenites (>95% quartz; Table 9.1). Clearly a simple QFL plot is insufficient to delimit the geological source of the artifacts; hence the character of the quartz grains has to be taken into account in determining the provenance of the samples. Quartz grains derived from intrusive rocks are typically unstrained (Qm), while rocks that have been subject to dynamic metamorphism typically produce strained quartz (Qs). Polycrystalline quartz grains (Qp) may have more complex histories, including strain recrystallization into polygonal quartz domains along grain boundaries (Folk 1980). Earlier observations have demonstrated that in plots of quartz types, samples of the Bar River Formation from Sheguiandah can be clearly distinguished from other formations, and even from other areas where the same formation is exposed, by the abundance of polycrystalline grains (Long *et al.* 2002).

New observations

Comparison of the petrographic analysis of the artifacts with data from Julig *et al.* (1998) and Long *et al.* (2002) indicates that all core samples are quartz arenite with modal grain size from very fine to medium sand grade, consistent with observations on parts of the Bar River and Lorrain Formation in other areas. Comparison of the ratio of unstrained (Qm), strained (Qs) and polycrystalline (Qp) quartz grains shows partial overlap with earlier data from the Lorrain and Bar River Formations (Figs 9.4 and 9.5). Note that only two of the archaeological samples (from the Giant site) show overlap with any of the existing geological data from the Lorrain Formation (Fig. 9.4, Samples G81, G1860), and even this is coincident with data from well outside the Sheguiandah area (~25km north – at Willisville).

Seven of the ten samples from the Giant site overlap with data from the Bar River Formation collected at West Bass Lake (Figs 9.5 and 9.6). One sample has sufficient polycrystalline grains to fall near the field for Sheguiandah (Fig. 9.5, Sample GOMAV 5). Samples from the BiHi 4 collection appear to have similar provenance. Two samples from the Blasted Cave site (Fig. 9.5, Samples B1 and B2) appear to have similar Qm/Qs/Qp ratios to the Bar River Formation along the Bass Lake Trail (which is along strike), while two show comparable properties to bedrock and artifacts collected earlier from the Sheguiandah site (Fig. 9.5, Samples B3 and B4). Typical thin sections are shown in Figures 9.6 to 9.9.

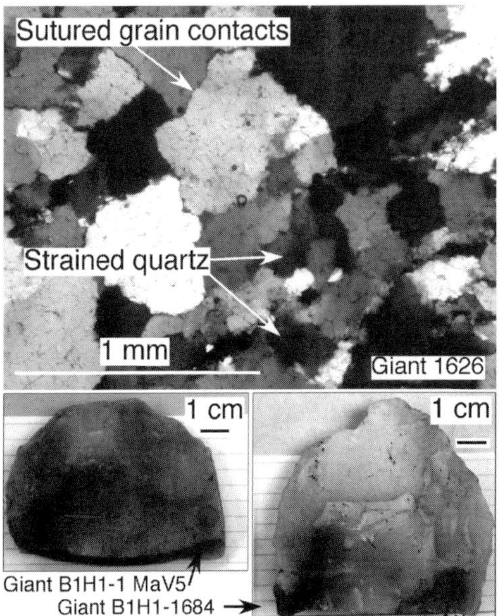

Figure 9.6. Typical thin section and core samples from the Giant site (thin sections were cut from the corner of the samples indicated by a dot). The thin section is typical of much of the upper part of the Lorrain Formation. It is dominated by medium sand sized grains of strained quartz (Qs), that shows distinctive undulose extinction in cross-polarized light. Note the lack of well-developed cement between grains and the resultant abundance of sutured grain contacts.

Figure 9.7. Core and thin section from the Giant site. Note that this is developed in a very fine grained sandstone (quartz arenite) with weakly developed schistosity due to shear related alignment of metamorphic muscovite grains. This fabric may have allowed thin flakes to be produced by fracturing along these planes. Although some polygonal grains have developed along grain boundaries, these are far less abundant than in samples from the Sheguiandah site.

Results

Artifacts from sites away from the main Paleo-Indian Quarry at Sheguiandah do not have the fine grain size, strong preferred fabric (schistocity) and exceptionally high abundance of polycrystalline quartz grains seen in samples and artifacts from the main quarry site in the Bar River Formation. Artifacts appear to be expedient in that they reflect selective sampling of facies with abundant strained and polycrystalline grains and aligned micas. Desirable facies for biface performs exist in both the upper member of the Lorrain Formation and the Bar River Formation, although material may have been difficult to extract in workable sized blocks where joint spacing was large. Samples derived from the Bar River Formation are mostly fine or very-fine sand grade. Lorrain Formation samples may include fine and medium grained sandstones, but typically lack a strong preferred alignment of quartz and mica grains. In all sites ratios of Qm/Qs/Qp appear to cluster, which would allow for recognition in parts of larger collections.

Figure 9.8. Cores and thin section from medium to fine sand grade artifacts from the Lorrain Formation at the Blasted Site. Note extensive development of polygonal quartz at grain boundaries indicating recrystalization of stressed quartz grains during retrograde metamorphism. The absence of a strong schistosity would make production of thin flakes more difficult.

Figure 9.9. Core and thin section from the NW Sheguiandah site (about 500 m NW of the Giant site). This medium to fine grained sandstone material from the Lorrain Formation has minor polygonal quartz developed along grain boundaries, but lacks strong schistocity.

Conclusions

Paleo-Indian quarry sites in the vicinity of Sheguiandah are located on metamorphosed Paleoproterozoic quartz-arenite of the Lorrain and Bar River Formations (Fig. 9.1 right). Our previous work (Julig *et al.* 1998; Long *et al.* 2002) has shown that the most extensive quarries are in a fine grained glassy facies of the Bar River Formation that has been subject to recrystallization of stressed quartz grains during retrograde metamorphism. At the Sheguiandah site these have little to no monocrystalline grains present (Fig. 9.5), and have a strong preferred grain fabric (schistocity), enhanced by strong alignment of muscovite grains. These characteristics, accompanied by regular joints, 10–15cm apart (Fig. 9.3) enhanced extraction of cores for preforms, and permitted manufacture of thin blades. Our previous research determined that only part of the Sheguiandah site contained abundant extensively strain-recrystallized quartz arenite that had been selectively quarried for cores. The current study demonstrates that Paleo-Indian artisans also preferentially selected other quarry sites along strike in the Bar River Formation (Blasted Cave), and Lorrain Formation (Giant Site: Fig. 9.10) in places where extensive strain recrystallization is evident.

Figure 9.10. Glassy blade-core from Giant site (BlHl-1). Note abundant flakes of mica (light spots), which have a strong preferred fabric.

Acknowledgements

We thank the Canadian Museum of Civilization for allowing us to undertake petrographic analysis of cores from selected sites in the vicinity of Sheguiandah. This research was in part funded by the Social Sciences and Humanities Research Council of Canada, and the National Research Council of Canada.

10 The Life and History of Prehistoric Quarry Extraction Tools Excavated from the Skene Motion and Workshop, Hartford Basin, Champlain Valley, New York, USA

Philip C. LaPorta, Scott A. Minchak and Margaret Brewer-LaPorta

Summary

The Skene quarry and associated workshop yield particular insights into the types of tools necessary for the extraction of cherts from low inclination (14–15º) rock beds and for the processing of extracted ore in a setting deficient in abundant raw materials. The Skene quarry typically yields numerous exhausted quarry implements; however, less than expected numbers were recovered. The workshop associated with the quarry revealed a wealth of recycled quarry and processing tools, including wedges and debris resulting from the refashioning of mining implements into forms necessary for ore processing.

Background

"The stone hammer, the greatest of all Stone Age tools, remained imperfectly understood by students of prehistoric culture until within recent years" (Holmes 1919, 283–284). William Henry Holmes' bold statement, while hopeful, is far from true – even for the beginning of the twenty-first century. Holmes (1919, 284–303) attributes hammerstones and anvils as percussion instruments, while he assigns discoidal hammers and picks as performing crumbling functions (Holmes 1919, 332–338). This rough separation was also employed in his description of hammers at quarries (*ibid.* 159–273) and represents the full extent of his classification.

William Ritchie (1929, 5) refers to quarry hammers weighing from 0.7–22.7kg (1.5–50 pounds) as "...abundant." His assertion was based on the examination of greater than 3,000 hammerstones collected by Arthur C. Parker at Flint Mine Hill in Coxsackie, New York and was corroborated by the research of Roy Drier (1961a, 1961b) at Isle Royale, an 80 × 8km (50 × 5 mile) island in Lake Superior, north of Michigan. Drier (1961a, 21) presents evidence suggesting that native inhabitants used fire, stone hammers, copper wedges, chisels and gouges to mine veins that resulted in the removal of rock from shafts as deep as 15m (50 feet) and from trenches as long as 30m (100 feet). So prevalent were stone tools in the area that a historic mining engineer estimated in 1871 that nearly 1,000 tons (200,000 to 300,000 hammerstones) were used in the mining process (Drier 1961a, 24). Drier (1961a, 23–24; 1961b, 30) classified the hammers as mauls, grooved (rare) and not grooved.

The works of Holmes (1890; 1919), Ritchie (1929), and Drier (1961a; 1961b) only scratch the surface in terms of the types of hammers, and absent from their presentations are details of fragments and the smaller tools needed for finer work. However, their work assumes that only the most basic methods and tools were used for quarrying. Historical mining texts (Pryor 1965; Richards and Locke 1940) list primary breaking methods as blasting, use of hand-held hammers, mechanical hammers and breakers, and mechanical rolls. Mechanical methods were used by the Greeks and Romans (see Hoovers' footnotes in Agricola 1950 [1556], 149). This leaves hand-held hammers, but eliminates what is historically and currently used to extract and process ore. Richards and Locke (1940, 1) define ore as 'a natural aggregation of minerals from which a metal or metallic compound can be recovered with profit on a large scale.' Pryor (1965, 815) more broadly defines ore as, 'a naturally occurring complex of minerals from which any fraction of commercial value can be extracted and used'. Flawn (1966, 11–13) further broadens this to include liquids and gases, using the terms resources and reserves – dividing them into known (recoverable, marginal, and sub marginal) and unknown.

Presented in this paper is a more refined view of prehistoric hammers and tools that takes into account the accepted model of ore processing documented since the Renaissance (Agricola 1950 [1556]). However, a further refinement is needed due to different properties of the ore and to account for artifacts and varying forms of quarry tools that differ from historic analogs. In this respect, analysts can hope to achieve a broader data set from which they may infer prehistoric behavior. A prehistoric quarry and associated workshop from Hartford Basin, New York, USA serves as a test example of study.

Hartford Basin, New York, USA: Geology and setting

The prehistoric quarry and related workshop discussed in this paper are located in the Hartford Basin of northeastern New York, USA. Fenneman (1938, 203) placed the Hartford Basin in the Hudson-Champlain section of the Ridge and Valley province of the eastern United States. The valley floor of the Hudson-Champlain section is unique due to glaciation and longitudinal drainage, with streams flowing to the north. Fenneman (1938, 216, 218) specifically noted that the Champlain Valley has sand and clay flats (interpreted by Connally (1973) as pro-glacial lake deposits), and is underlain by rocks co-eval to those in the Hudson Valley. The quarry, and quarry related sites, are located on flat topography far from water sources. The Skene Motion quarry and Skene Workshop site are underlain by the chert bearing Skene Dolostone of the Whitehall Formation (Fisher 1984).

Skene Motion and Skene Workshop sites

The Skene Motion quarry (Fig. 10.1) is located in the Cambrian-Ordovician Whitehall Formation, Skene Dolostone (LaPorta 2000, 23–24). LaPorta and Associates (2000) characterized quarries in the chert bearing Skene Dolostone as being represented by two types: i) on cliff faces, and ii) in horizontal strata. One of the latter was situated in the northwest corner of an 8.1ha (20-acre) modern mine footprint. The site was

Figure 10.1. Skene Motion quarry site, prior to excavation.

investigated from the spring of 2002 to the summer of 2003, having been discovered during reconnaissance work as a series of upturned blocks. The aim of the investigation was: i) to expose the anatomy of the ore, as controlled by ancient sedimentary and tectonic processes in the study area, ii) to explore the extent of the prehistoric quarry, iii) to investigate the methodologies employed during extraction and to identify task subdivision occurring at the quarry; and iv) to attempt to identify the intensity of the quarrying activity. A 4 × 5m grid was placed over the upturned blocks and six of the twenty 1m sq units excavated.

The Skene Workshop site (Fig. 10.2) is located 125m southwest of Skene Motion and is based around a large block of high-grade Skene chert. While completing additional work at the Skene Motion in 2004, surficial evidence of a large chert block, and associated chert workings, was revealed on a newly cleared path from the site. Lithic remains were located in a dolomite trough-ledge, placed between a hump and scarp to the west and a dolomite outcrop to the east. The Skene Workshop was excavated in 2005 with a 4 × 3m grid placed over the upturned blocks and excavated in $1m^2$ units. Three additional $1m^2$ units were placed to the northeast of the block, following the trough-ledge to trace encountered artifacts.

Methods and models: research questions

LaPorta and Associates (2001) asked a series of ambitious research questions about quarries that included task organization, spatial and temporal relationships, raw material extraction technology, evolution of quarry tools, petrofabric constraints and

Figure 10.2. Skene Workshop site, prior to excavation.

habitation. These behavioral questions necessitated a refined version of quarry products and by-products that go beyond the outmoded archaeological two-step process of raw material acquisition to blank (Amick 1982; Bradley 1975). Previously proposed prehistoric quarry terminology (for example, see Brumbach 1985; 1987) of block, chunk, shatter, waste flake, and trim does little to advance behavioral considerations of quarrying and processing beyond the blank. Instead, it shows the need for a revision of terminology. The use of these terminologies is disconcerting, given the amount of literature generated on historic mining, modern mining and economic geology literature, where standardization of terminology is present (Agricola 1950 [1556]; Flawn 1966; Richards and Locke 1940; Simons 1924). This is the prime example of the "Law of the Hammer" (Moore and Keene 1983, 4) by using methods "not because they fit the task at hand, but because they are the methods we know and can easily apply." With revised terminology, the interrelationships of instruments, tasks, and associated mine tailings are brought to light – thus providing researchers with key behavioral data required for interpretation.

The artifact typology developed for the Skene Motion is based on the quarry model developed for the geochronologically correlative Cambrian-Ordovician cherts of the Wallkill River Valley in New York-New Jersey, USA (LaPorta 1994; 1996) and can be used to summarize the chain of operation. The model consists of four task subdivisions: i) zone of extraction (direct quarrying); ii) zone of milling (where the surrounding dolomite is crushed to free the ore); iii) zone of beneficiation (chert is appraised and winnowed using a variety of physical properties) and; iv) zone of refinement (high tenor ore is flaked into bifaces or cores). Each of these tasks is associated with mining tools. Levers and wedges are used to accentuate open joints in order to free the ore in the zone of extraction. Large boulders (impact hammers) are occasionally found in this zone. Milling areas are generally associated with blocky and elongate clay-rich sandstones. Chert processing (beneficiation) areas require circular-oblate hammers fashioned from highly elastic materials. Zones of refinement are associated with anvils and small, elastic hammers. This is a generalized pattern based on research of prehistoric quarries on Cambrian-Ordovician chert quarries of the Wallkill River Valley.

The general quarry tool availability, as well as success in extraction, are dependent upon the presence of abundant glacial till containing quartzites and metaquartzites (LaPorta 1994); but in addition, rest on two assumptions: i) hammers fashioned from rock accompany the use of wood, splints, antler, and the application of fire and; ii) the tools also break and evolve into other instruments. Armed with the above model and quarry tool hypotheses, certain questions can be posed (LaPorta and Associates 2001):

1. Are diagnostic quarry tools present at all types of quarries?
2. Are the materials of quarry tools brought from outside the Smiths Basin study area?
3. Do the quarry toolkits differ from location to location?
4. Can we ultimately link morphological and petrological classes of hammers to a discrete class, or range, of mine tailings and an inferred function?
5. Will there be inter-quarry variations in the resulting chain of operation unveiled at each quarry?

Hammerstones and instruments at the Skene Motion and Skene workshop

Little variation in classification exists for prehistoric quarry tools aside from the terms hammerstones, anvils, and picks. The non-mechanical and non-combustible techniques employed by historical and modern miners include the use of hammers and wedges. Agricola (1950, 149–153 [1556]) separates mining or digging tools into hammers of varying sizes, wedges, crowbars, and picks/shovels and differentiates between hammers (all have handles) as being one-handed or two-handed, the largest of the latter category is used to drive wedges into cracks. For preliminary breaking, Richards and Locke (1940, 6–7) identify three different types of hammer used "for breaking the lumps that are too large for the machine breakers" as; hand sledges, spalling hammers and cobbing hammers. Hand sledges are two-handed hammers (10–20lbs) to break lumps too large for mechanical breakers. Spalling hammers are lighter two-handed tools (4–8lbs) for breaking moderate sized lumps into uniform size with swift light blows. Cobbing hammers are small single-handed tools (1.5–7lbs) with one flat face and a wedge shaped peen parallel to the handle that is used to clean and hand pick ore. Richards and Locke (1940, 7) note that hand breaking, while requiring cognitive effort, is also more expensive than machine breaking. So, while historical analogs can help as a guide in prehistoric hammer use, two important items require a revision of hammerstone terminology; the hardness of chert requires a different method of processing, and there is no analog for prehistoric chert quarrying in northeastern United States.

Quarry tool classifications

Prior to analysis, investigation began with the knowledge of historic examples for hammers and other instruments used to quarry and process rock and ore. In addition to the documentary evidence, the geological/archaeological investigations of greater than 300 prehistoric quarries in the Wallkill River Valley, carried out over a 20-year period, (LaPorta, 2009) allowed for a more in-depth view of extraction tools in the previously mentioned four quarry zones, resulting in recognition of 26 tool types. While the Wallkill cherts are correlative, the authors assumed variations in tool types as being present due to the shallow dip of Skene beds in the Hartford Basin.

In a bulk analysis of the artifacts collected from the Skene Motion and Skene Workshop, analysts separated pieces into the categories ascribed for ores and instruments. Thus, all tools were placed into the "hammer" category. Once separated, these were weighed, inspected for the presence/absence of heat, petrologically identified, described, and sub-divided into one of 17 categories (Table 10.1). Nine types reflect direct-use (anvil, abrader, focal hammer, beaked hammer, hammer, impact object, milling instrument, pick, and refinement hammer), five reflect indirect use (focal chisel, flat wedge, round wedge, chisel, and plug-and-feather chisel), one reflects combined uses (a combination of any of the previously mentioned), and two reflect residual activity (spalls and fragments). In addition, there were unmodified pebbles and gravel clasts that were placed into the hammerstone category as a means of preliminary mass sorting.

Raw material sources

There is no glacial till nearby to provide an abundant source of hammerstone material with the requisite physical properties. Winchell Creek, Potsdam, and Finch-Mosherville sandstones and quartzite, further to the north and the east, provide possible sources for raw material for tools. In 2000, a Finch-Mosherville (also Whitehall Formation) quartzite hammerstone quarry was located to the north of the Skene Motion. A greater physical investment was then required for hammerstone raw material procurement. Aside from the bedrock sources, bedrock till as mapped by Connally (1973) is a minimum of 3.5km (2 miles) from the site area.

Tools at Skene Motion

Eighty three (83) quarry tools (0.34% of 24,138 artifacts excavated in the six 1 × 1m units) were recovered from the Skene Motion quarry, but few are considered diagnostic of specific or multiple tasks of direct working. Chisels, fragments, wedges, and spalls are indirect and residual aspects of quarry tool use. The analysis identified five (6% of the tools) artefacts that reflect direct chert working. Two anvils (SKM.136.6 and SKM.160.1) fashioned from garnet amphibolite gneiss were located in Stratum 2 of Unit 13 and on the bedrock of Unit 19, while two hammers were found that exhibited the same

Classification and Description
IMPACT OBJECT – large, oval, glacial erratic, usually contains many scallop-shaped flake scars along edges; may be internally cracked, pounded, or pulverized along the edges
ANVIL – is a rock on which blows are laid; characterized by pitting in a localized spot(s)
ABRADER – is a hammer or hammer fragment that contains grooves from abrading chert
MILLING INSTRUMENT – elongate, blocky, often rectangular in outline; usually fashioned from clay-rich sedimentary and metasedimentary rocks; upper surfaces may be conical or flaked, while lower surfaces are cuspate and pounded; lower surfaces may also be concave
BEAKED HAMMER – ore splitters fashioned from a single glacially-derived boulder; upper surface bears impact scars and may be pulverized; lower surface consists of coalescing radial flake scars forming a point, or beak that is pitted and rounded
ROUND (BLUNT) WEDGE – glacially-derived cobbles; employed to focus compressive stress on joint surfaces of rock; upper surface is pitted and pulverized; lower surface is flat and slightly concave, containing radial flake scars
FLAT WEDGE – cortex fragment derived from the rupture of an impact object, spalls containing outer cortex are jammed into the open joint spaces; the distal portion of the flat wedge contains numerous elongate striations while the back end is pulverized from impact
HAMMERSTONE – fashioned from glacially-derived cobbles; circular, oval, flat, or biconvex in cross-section; characteristically exhibits pitting and spall negatives
REFINEMENT HAMMER – a small class of hammer, pitted on ends, used for working within a lithon packages
PICK – an instrument fashioned to a point and used to split or remove
FOCAL HAMMER – small wedge with blunt ends
CHISEL – are elongate instruments with tapered wedge shaped ends that are used to focus compressive forces
FOCUS CHISEL – very small class of chisel with irregular facets on all surfaces
PLUG AND FEATHER CHISEL – see chisel; specially used for holes to further accentuate joints
SPALL –a chip removed from an instrument resulting from use or intention; spalls exhibit similar characteristics of flakes such as a platform and bulb of percussion
FRAGMENT – these are failed and broken pieces of hammerstones
COMBINATION – a combination of any of the above categories, except for fragments

Table 10.1. Descriptions of tool classifications from the Skene Motion quarry and Skene Workshop sites.

characteristics: glacial rounding and small negative spalling. Finally, a double beaked hammer (SKM.22.1), found in Stratum 2 of Unit 4, is fashioned from Winchell Creek sandstone. This is plano-convex and has two well-pitted (to the point of rounded) beaks. Analysis also found a refit of SKM.22.1 with SKM.16.1 (Fig. 10.3a), a fragment of a third beak on the hammer.

There are 11 wedges (Table 10.19, 13.3% of the tools) from the excavations that can be further subdivided into flat (n=8) and round (blunt) types (n=3). Seven of the eight

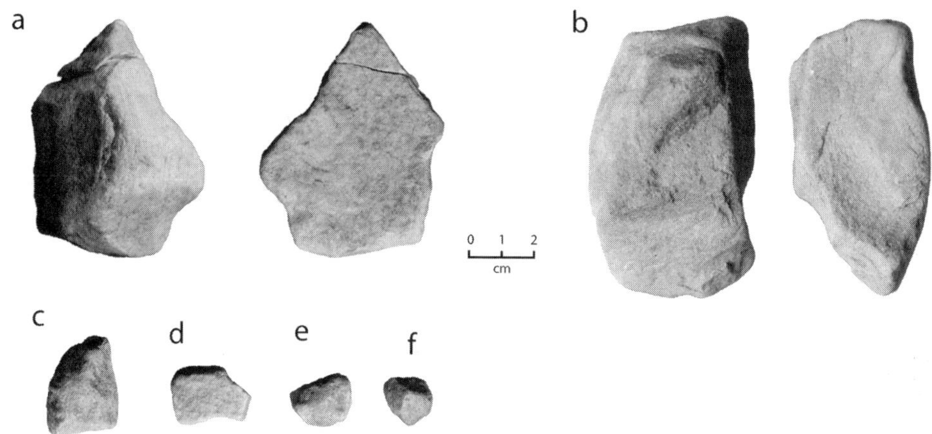

Figure 10.3. Skene Motion quarry instruments: (a) Refit SKM.22.1 and SKM.16.1; (b) round wedge SKM.163.1; (c–d) focal chisels (SKM.87.121, SKM.87.146, SKM.87.190, and SKM.87.214).

flat wedges are fashioned from quartzite, and one is from quartz. The three round wedges are fashioned from unidentified sandstone and quartzite, and Winchell Creek sandstone. The latter example is a rounded cobble with negative spalls detached in order to create the shape, and with step scar battering on the blunt end (Fig.10.3b). Eight chisels (9.6% of the tools) were recovered that are, in general, faceted, but more elongate than the focal chisels and, like them, are fashioned from quartzite, although there are two exceptions (SKM.99.125 and SKM.113.164) from Stratum 1 of Unit 7 and Unit 10 respectively. A majority (n=32, or 38.6%) of the tools are focal chisels (Fig. 10.3 c–f), the petrography of which is quartzite and sandstone.

The second most numerous (n=16, or 19.3% of the artefacts) tool types are fragments of implements, unidentifiable as to a more specific artefact type. An additional small fragment was located during an exploratory excavation of the organic horizon of Unit 2 and is not shown in the table. Petrology of the fragments suggests a wider range of raw material use. Several (10) of the smaller fragments are quartzite, quartz, and sandstone. Others are of chert, garnet amphibolite gneiss, as well as local Winchell Creek and Potsdam sandstones. One Winchell Creek sandstone piece (SKM.16.1) is a beak fragment, found in Stratum 2 of Layer 4, that refits with the multiple beaked hammer SKM.22.1.

Tools at Skene workshop

Investigators recovered 548 quarry tools (11.9% of 4,603 artifacts excavated in the fifteen 1m sq units) at the Skene Workshop site. Eleven (2%) sole-use diagnostic tools included: anvils (n=2), abraders (n=2), beaked hammers (n=2), a milling instrument (n=1), a plug and feather chisel (n=2), a pick (n=1), and a refinement hammer (n=1). A 1.5kg split cobble from Stratum 1 of Unit 9, is from a larger implement and was identified as a

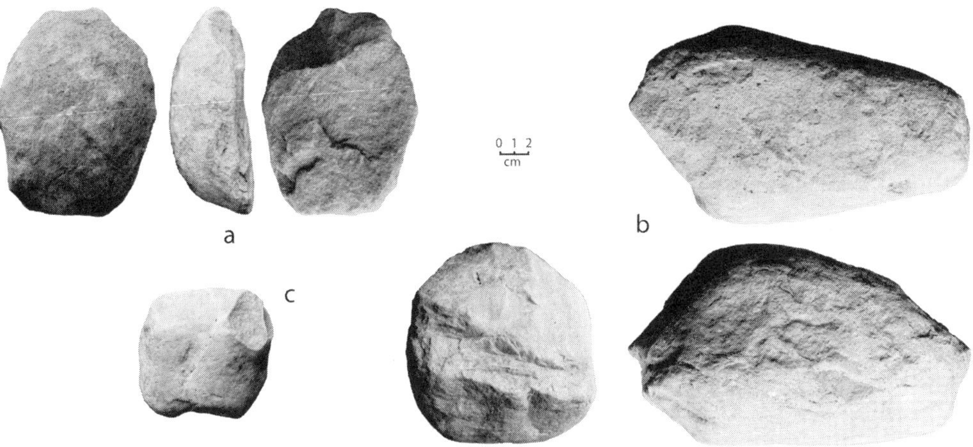

Figure 10.4. Skene Workshop instruments: (a) SKW.65.1 milling instrument; (b) SKW.32.1, impactor/ anvil; and (c) SKW.84.1, hammer/anvil.

milling instrument (Fig. 10.4a SKW.65.1). The higher clay content conforms to that from similar tools from the Wallkill River valley. Use in milling is inferred due to: weight, petrology, and heavy post-breakage pitting and battering on the edges. The single refinement hammer (SKW.139.1) from Stratum 5 of Unit 12, has heavy battering and pitting on one end. Twelve (2.2%) combination-use (anvils, abrader, hammer) tools were identified. Of these, an impact object/anvil (SKW.132.1) is a very large (9 kg) instrument fashioned from an elongated glacial cobble/boulder, heavily battered on one end, as evidenced by deep step scars, negative spalls emanating from the end and pitting (Fig. 10.4b). A hammer/anvil (from SKW.84.1) exhibits two negative spalls from use as a hammer and minor pitting on the flat portion from ephemeral use as an anvil (Fig. 10.4c). A plug-and-feather chisel was recovered from Stratum 5 of Unit 12 (SKW.139.3) and resembles a blade or blade-like flake with two parallel lateral edges (Fig. 10.5a). A prominent bulb of percussion dominates the dorsal face, while the reverse has two prominent ridges and the distal end of the flake is tapered and heavily battered. A tool identified as a pick (SKW.15.2) is fashioned from Potsdam Formation material, elongated, tapered to one end, and faceted in a prismatic fashion except for a face that still has glacial polish (Fig. 10.5b).

Hammers (n=49, 8.9%) are fashioned from glacial cobbles and gravels and exhibit pitting, battering, and spalling. They are fashioned from a variety of raw materials that include; sandstone, quartzite, chert, siltstone, dolomite, and garnet amphibolite gneiss. Their general morphology is similar to that described from the quarry, elongated with a tapered end. Focal hammers (n=8, 1.5%) are fashioned from sandstone and quartzite and their general morphology is also similar to that described from the quarry.

Twenty chisels (3.7%), similar in form to those from the quarry were recovered from the workshop all fashioned from sandstone and quartzite. The 45 wedges (3.7%) were sub-divided into two categories: flat (21 examples) and round (blunt) (14 examples).

Figure 10.5. Skene Workshop instruments: (a) SKW.139.3 plug and feather chisel; (b) SKW.15.2, pick; and (c) SKW.148.1, flat wedge.

They are fashioned from sandstone and quartzite and the round examples on glacial cobbles. One flat wedge SKW.148.1 (Fig. 10.5c) is well curated, with one face retaining glacial polish and knobs, or bits, from successive uses. It was found in Stratum 1 of Unit 8 and is fashioned from quartzite and weighs 516.4 g. The most numerous instruments in the workshop, as in the quarry, are focal chisels (n=217, or 39.6%). These are used to accentuate joints in order to pry open the rock. The petrology of these implements is primarily quartzite and sandstone, with few examples of quartz, chert, and gneiss.

One hundred and twenty one fragments (22.1%) were recovered. Four (SKW.14.2, SKW.36.3, SKW.36.4, and SKW.59.1) from units 4, 7, and 9 were refitted (Fig. 10.6) and formed an elongated hammer with a slightly battered and spalled end that has been heat-treated. A further refit in Unit 9 (SKW.59.13 and SKW.59.14) derives from a pebble, while another three-piece refit with sub-parallel breakage (SKW.73.1, SKW.73.2, and SKW.73.3) from Stratum 5 of Unit 9 formed a faceted focal chisel, plano-convex in cross-section which had failed on the plano face.

Tool trends and conclusions

The spatial association of artifacts for the two sites is currently being analyzed, but it is possible to observe several trends through: i) intrasite and ii) inter-site comparisons. Intrasite spatial and compositional trends show different activities based on the tools excavated. Skene Motion quarry tools and fragment numbers increase to the northeast, while the number of chert artifacts increases to the southwest. The few larger implements are located to the north. Skene Workshop artefacts correlate to the northeast position of the chert ore block. Inter-site spatial and compositional comparisons show a difference in the two sites. A larger number of tools and fragments were excavated at the

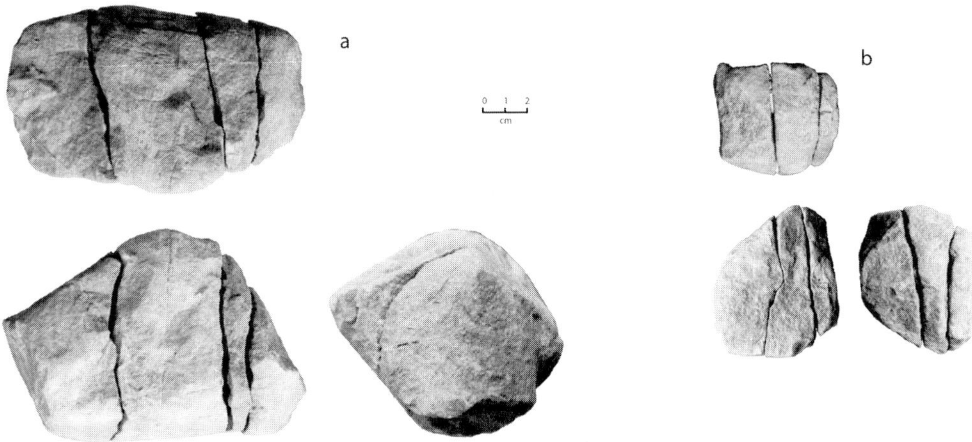

Figure 10.6. Skene Workshop Refits: (a) SKW.14.2, SKW.59.1, SKW.36.3, and SKW.36.4; (b) SKW.73.1, SKW.73.2, and SKW.73.3.

workshop. Skene Motion contained a higher frequency of implement fragments, while Skene Workshop tools are, in general, larger than those found at Skene Motion.

Skene Motion is a quarry where a distinction can be observed between Zone 1 (the zone of extraction) and Zone 2 (the zone of milling), a place where prehistoric quarry workers crunched the stone to extract the ore and free it from the surrounding dolomite. Skene Workshop contains Zone 3 (the zone of beneficiation) where prehistoric technologists winnowed the varying grades of ore for future use. The quarry and workshop, when viewed through the extraction implements distribution and typology, represents a continuum of use. Tools, or their remnants, were used at the quarry and reused or recycled at the workshop. At the quarry, higher frequencies of fragments represent attrition while smaller pieces represent tools that were no longer viable. Artefacts are winnowed along with the chert to further refine the ore, a behavior resulting from the deficiency of abundant raw materials to produce them.

Acknowledgements

The following paper is based on a poster presented at the 71st Annual Society for American Archaeology (SAA) meeting in San Juan, Puerto Rico. The data and research are a result of work at the Smiths Basin mine site by LaPorta and Associates, L.L.C. in preparation for a modern high friction aggregate quarry for Jointa Galusha, L.L.C. Thanks to John Davidson, Jointa Galusha, and their parent company D. A. Collins for affording us the opportunity and funding to accomplish this work.

11 Subsistence Activities at Quarries and Quarry-related Workshops: Testing the Holmes and Bryan Alternatives with Blades from the Gault Site, Central Texas, USA

Scott A. Minchak

Summary

Prehistoric quarries in North America are poorly understood and thus problematical when making inferences about past behavior. William Henry Holmes hypothesized that quarries were exclusive producers of blanks (pre-forms) that were further refined in villages away from the quarry. In contrast, Kirk Bryan postulated that Holmes' "blanks" were usable tools and that quarries also served as factories for working other materials. A microwear analysis of Clovis blades from the 2000 Texas A&M University excavations at Gault serves as a test for the alternative hypotheses, indicating that determining non-extraction activities at quarries and quarry-related workshops is also more problematical than thought.

Introduction

Quarries can be defined as places where rock is removed from the earth or from a large mass of associated rock. As fixed points in the landscape, they will have been an important resource for prehistoric groups and, given the preservation of stone artifacts, allow an assessment of an economy of stone use that can denote exchange and even territoriality. Prehistoric behavior at quarries is rarely treated or discussed in literature, with sites interpreted as sources with "cradle to grave" implications (Bryan 1950, 34; Dockall and Shafer 1993; Lech 1981; Torrence 1986).

In the United States, William Henry Holmes and Kirk Bryan shaped the direction of prehistoric quarry studies. Holmes (1890) viewed quarries as exclusive producers of blanks (pre-forms) that were further reduced and refined away from the quarry, while Bryan (1950) viewed quarries as factories where the quarried stone was also used to work other materials. Task subdivision can be identified at some quarries (LaPorta 1994; 1996 and this volume) which denotes a spatial separation of ore processing and other activities. Based on his work on early farming communities in Poland, Jacek Lech (1983) offered a useful separation between different types of flint workshops: i) mine-related and ii) village-related. While vital for differentiation of technological behavior, sub-divisions do not identify alternative craft activities at quarries or quarry-related workshops. The intention of the paper is to test alternative hypotheses using microwear analysis of Clovis blades from the Gault site, a quarry-workshop in central Texas, USA (Minchak 2007).

Holmes and Bryan, competing and complimentary hypotheses for the presence of alternative functions at quarries

In William Henry Holmes' earliest writing on the Potomac Formation quartzite gravels at Piney Branch (outside of Washington D.C.), he stated that, "having reached a definite conclusion that the blades [Holmes' term for bifaces] were the exclusive product of the property, I was led to investigate their subsequent history" (Holmes 1890a, 17–18). He conceded that some "rude" forms may have been used in emergencies or shaped for a special reason (such as quarrying soapstone or girdling trees), but these quarry forms were made for use. In his short treatment of Flint Ridge (1919, 181), he mentioned "minute flake blades, which probably served as knives" and further noted that "this is the only quarry so far studied in which this particular work was extensively carried on" (Holmes 1919, 181).

Kirk Bryan (1950, 3) posited two hypotheses: i) that many previously termed "blanks" and "rejects" were used as tools and; ii) that many flint quarries were also places where wood and bone were also worked. His work was based on three sites (Bryan 1950, 8–18): i) "Spanish Diggings" in Oklahoma; ii) Alibates quarry (Permian dolomite-replaced chalcedony) near Amarillo, Texas and; iii) Cerro Pedernal quarry (Abiquiu Formation chert) in New Mexico. He (1950, 21) noted the presence of a great quantity of flakes and blades, true blade or blade-like flakes, that were "utilized on wood and bone and then discarded."

The Gault site and Clovis blades

The Gault site (41BL323) is located along the Buttermilk Creek in southern Bell County, Texas, USA (Fig. 11.1a) in the extreme western portion of the Grand Prairie of the Edwards Escarpment (Fenneman 1938, 105–106). The characteristic topography is a nearly level plain with steep slope erosion valleys. The surface takes on a relief of ≤30.5m (100 feet). Gault is located at the head of a low-relief valley and is underlain by the Cretaceous-age, chert-bearing Edwards Formation limestone/dolomite (Fischer and Rodda 1969) and non-chert-bearing Cretaceous age, Comanche Formation limestone (Proctor *et al.* 1974). A spring, with Buttermilk Creek dissecting the site, provide ample water for use during and since the Clovis occupation and, as a result of University of Texas investigations, Ernest Lundelius (1998) confirmed faunal and floral presence at Gault as far back as the Clovis period.

The 2000 Texas A&M excavations produced an extraordinarily large number of Clovis (*c.* 11,500–10,000 B.P.) artifacts in bounded sediment units (Fig. 11.1b), 3a (ponded clay) and 3b (overbank deposit). Clovis artifact assemblages are typified by fluted lanceolate points, large prismatic blades, large flake tools, polyhedral blade cores, and bone artifacts (Collins 1999; Stanford 1991). Blades are associated with a prepared core

a

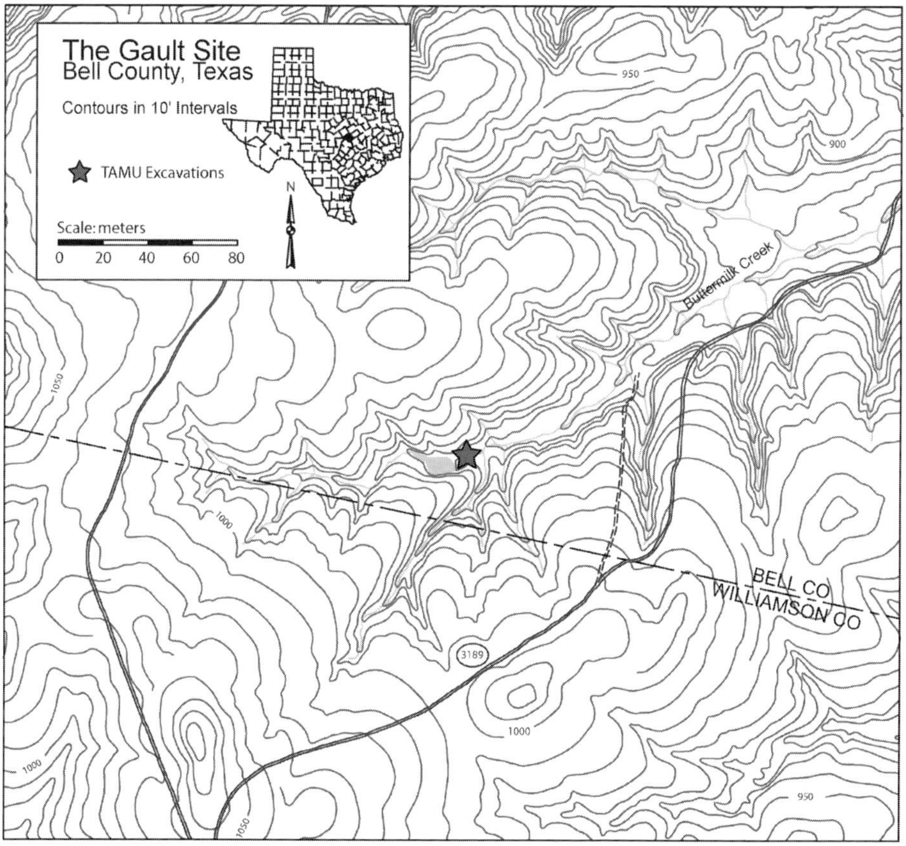

b

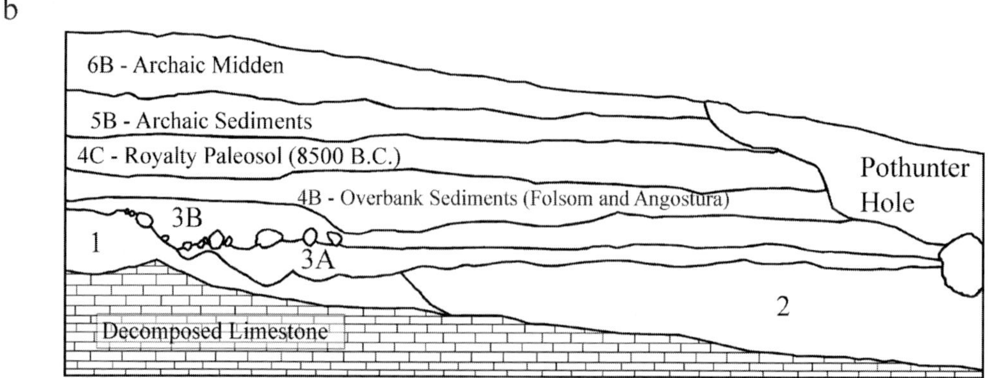

Figure 11.1. a) location of the TAMU Gault Site excavations on the 7.5 minute Youngsport quadrangle; b) generalized profile showing locations of the 3A and 3B units.

and blade technique, showing that a blade is not a random flake. A "true" blade is a specialized elongated flake with parallel or sub-parallel lateral edges; the length being equal to, or more than, twice the width (Bordes and Crabtree 1969, 1; Crabtree 1972, 42). Another distinction is that blades are associated with a prepared core and blade technique, showing that a blade is not a random flake. The excavations uncovered 498 blades and blade fragments from Gault, revealing that blades are fashioned from the Edwards Formation chert which underlies part of the site.

Microwear analysis

Seitzer-Olausson (1980, 48) distinguishes between microwear as being the microscopic study of alteration on human modified materials and use-wear as the alteration of material due to use. Techniques and methods were devised for microwear analysis in order to look at a number of variables (micro flaking, edge rounding, striations, and polishing), comparing them to the microscopic patterns found on archaeological materials, taking into account natural and incidental modification (such as trampling) (Levi-Sala 1988; 1996). As such, a microwear study is heavily dependent on external context (for example: raw material, sedimentary environment in which the artifact was found, and associations). Traceology is now used to describe the work of S. A. Semenov and the Russian school, who studied "traces" of wear on experimental tools and artifacts and which employs the use of striations to provide evidence on how a tool was used and lesser degree on what it was used (Kay 1996, 316; Semenov 1964, 16, 21, 50, 68–83). During the 1970s and 1980s, the high power (HP) versus low power (LP) debate dominated the microwear literature. The interpretation of types of polish is the prime use in high power, or "Keeley Method" (Kay 1996, 316; Keeley 1980, 23), as opposed to rounding and microflaking in low power analyses (Tringham *et al*. 1974). While the "Keeley Method" has seen great use over the past two decades, this study utilizes both methods. Equipment used for microwear analysis included the Leica M12.5 Stereomicroscope (with a magnification range of 12×–160×) and the Leica DM LA Automated Laboratory Microscope (with magnifications settings of 100×, 200×, and 500×) (see Minchak 2007, 14–25, 105–122 for full treatments of microwear methodology).

Experimental program results

Soft contact material experiments (Fig. 11.2) consisted of: i) reaping grass (experimental blades FUTB44 and NNWXP2); ii) circumscribing cane (experimental blade FUTR42); iii) sawing cane (experimental blade FUTR43); iv) cleaning sinew (experimental blade NWXP3); and v) cutting rawhide (experimental blade NWXP4). Hard contact material experiments (Fig. 11.3) consisted of: i) scraping wood (experimental blade GRT4–1); ii) sawing wood (experimental blade NNWXP2); iii) sawing horn (experimental blade NWXP1) and; iv) scraping horn (experimental blade NNWXP2). There are a number of issues raised by these experiments relating to the effects of raw material; mechanical failure; microtopography change and the relationship between these in determining hard versus soft contact materials.

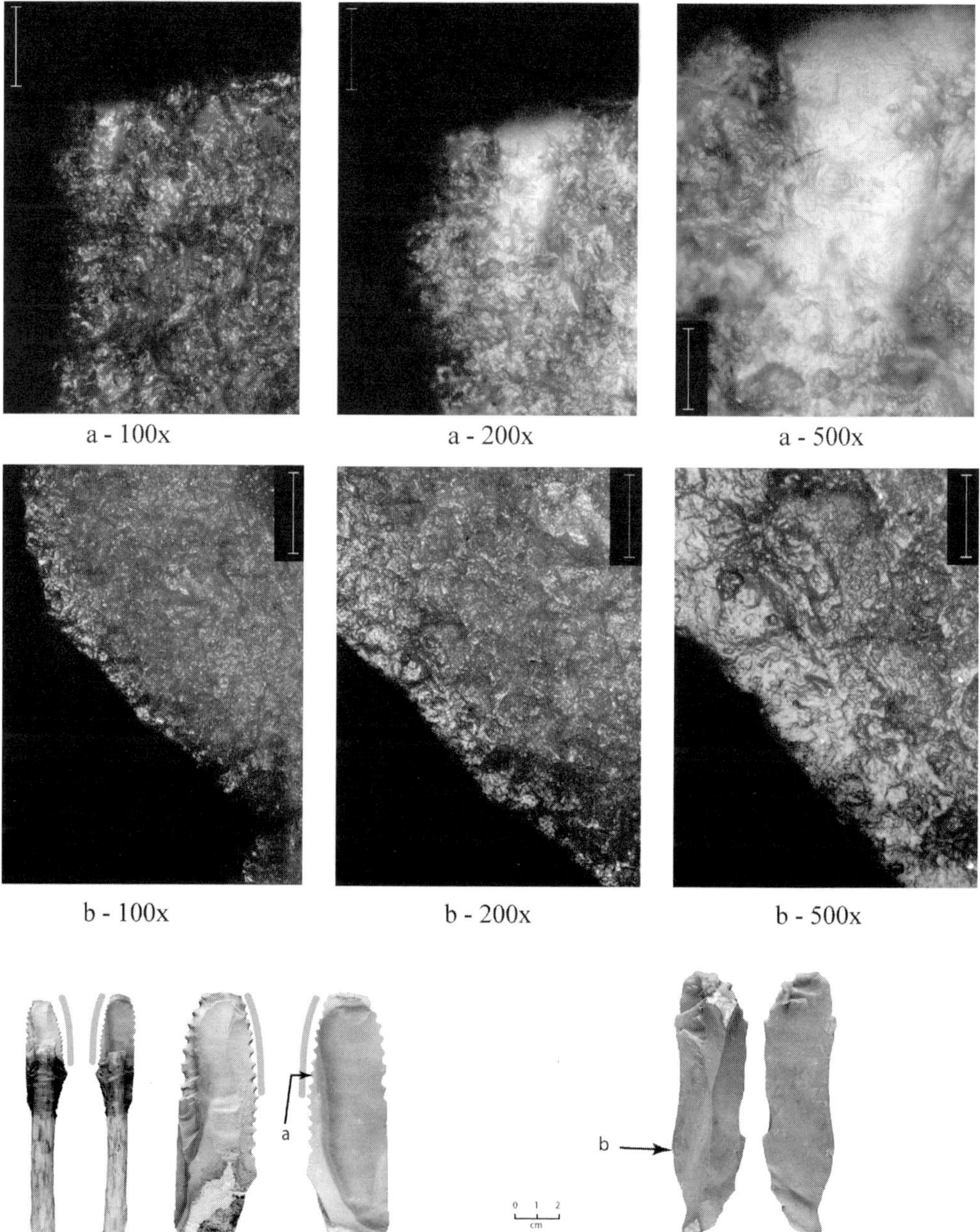

Figure 11.2. Soft Contact Experimental Blades: a) NNWXP1, polish from reaping grass; and b) NWXP3, polish from cleaning sinew.

The raw material undoubtedly plays a role in the recording of use-wear on rock. The right lateral of experimental blade NNWXP2 (Fig. 11.2a) is what might be termed the late diagenetic phase of the chert that is yellow, coarser grained than chert, and white inclusions. The white inclusions are chalcedony, an early phase of quartz development (Folk and Weaver 1952; Hesse 1990a; 1990b; Knauth 1994; Maliva *et al.* 2005; Meyers 1977; Siever 1957) that is softer than chert. This means that it takes on polish and striations faster than the early diagenetic chert. The yellow coarser grained material also takes on polish and rounding quicker that the early diagenetic chert, but less than the chalcedony. Since chalcedony takes on more wear than the surrounding chert, it is susceptible to wear (cultural or natural). More experiments are required to test this hypothesis.

Microflaking was present when using the experimental blades on hard contact materials. Mechanical failure at the edges is most notable in the wood sawing experiment with the serrated blade NNWXP1. While this was the most notable occasion, microflaking was also noticeable while using all hard contact material experiments, as well as the soft contact material experiment of cutting rawhide (NWXP4). Otherwise, soft contact material experiments did not sustain much edge damage. The edge angle (66°) of the distal planing end of NNWXP1 (Fig. 11.3b) resulted in microflaking during use, but the edge did not fail. FUTB44 (5–9° and 24° spine angles) received little to no attrition. What does happen, as seen with both NNWXP2 (after 1,000 and 2,000 strokes, see Fig. 11.2a) and FUTB44 (after 2,000 strokes) is pronounced evolution of edge rounding – one not seen in the hard contact experiments.

Microtopography, polish, and striations are prime indicators not only of use, but also hardness of contact material and direction. In terms of defining use, the hardness of the contact material has a direct relationship with the alteration of the surface microtopography. Soft contact materials, in general, have a greater range of polish on the microtopography, such as that seen in NNWXP2 (Fig. 11.2a), NWXP3 (Fig. 11.2b), and NWXP4. Hard contact materials hit the projections, arêtes, or high points as seen in GRT4–1 (Fig. 11.3a) and NWXP1 (Fig. 11.3b). More surface area polished is achieved by planing of the projections, such as in NNWXP1 and NWXP1.

Characterizing the degree of hardness of the contact materials by use-wear was the main goal of these experiments and the results depict some overlap. Soft contact materials result in less microflaking, a lack of mechanical edge failure, polish of more surface topography, and a rounding of the edges. Hard contact materials result in more microflaking, pronounced to beginning mechanical edge failure, generalized polish confined to the projections, and a lack of edge rounding. These categories overlap in the rawhide cutting experiment and in the evolution of macro- and microscopic characteristics, most specifically polishes.

Gault blade analysis results

The initial separation of blades by geological unit is followed by the technologically based divisions of Gault blades by William Dickens. Blades can be separated into four basic techno-types: i) cortical blades, ii) secondary blades, iii) interior blades and, iv) modified blades. The 498 blades and blade fragments were separated into their vertical provenance within sediment units 3a and 3b. Artifacts from the transitional 3a/3b

Figure 11.3 Hard Contact Experimental Blades: a) GRT4_1, polish from sawing wood; and b) NWXP1, polish from planing horn.

layers were eliminated as were blades from layer 4b, leaving 464 blades for study. Initial analysis was accomplished by eye with the aid of a Bausch and Lomb 16× hand lens. The variables that were noted included: flake scar patterns, rounding, possible residue, amount of cortex and subcortex, burnt pieces. The criteria for further study included presence of: an edge without cortex, non-burnt, flake scars on edge. Vaughan (1984–1986) recommended separating pieces that appear to have edge removal from the collection for use-wear analysis, thus eliminating pieces unlikely to yield use-wear information (*i.e.* patinated, heavily burnt, or coarse raw material pieces), such edge damage being an important variable when determining possible use-wear (Keeley 1980, 19; Tringham *et al.* 1974, 180; Vaughan 1985, 22–23). The general rule is that the more acute the edge angle of an artifact, the more likely it is to be heavily damaged from use or by other means. As a result, certain ranges of edge angles have been described by Vaughan (1985, 59) and Keeley (1980, 42) as being used for certain tasks.

Following the initial sorting, the remaining 233 (3a= 143, 3b= 85, and Modified= 5) blades were subjected to analysis using the steromicroscope. Variables noted included: flake scar patterns, edge and ridge rounding, polish, possible residue, position of, and relationship between all the above. Criteria for further study included: rounding, polish, and residue (especially if a combination was visible). The final stage of analysis was carried out on 24 blades and blade fragments on which the classic variables of polish, striations, residue, and microflaking were most apparent.

The three Clovis Blades from layer 3a exhibit lateral edge modification. Of these, the refit of AM326B2 and AM322 (Fig. 11.4a) displays the best evidence for ephemeral use and lateral edges form an almost complete serrated blade. Patina obscured most of the dorsal viewing, with a few patches of polish and rounding on projections and in scars visible and with a thin band of polish on the ventral edge on the peninsulas of the denticulates (location A – spine angle of 26° and an edge angle of 47°). Polish on the edge of the scars, as well as right up to the steps, suggests an angled position favoring the ventral face, such as that seen for the dorsal face of the sinew cleaning (NWXP3) and rawhide cutting (NWXP4) experiments. The location of the polish, on the distal facing portion of the denticulate, suggests one motion directed toward the distal end, similar to NNWXP2 (reaping grass). Owing to the unusually well preserved denticulation, minor rounding, and shallow invasiveness, use is most likely on soft material, relatively ephemeral and of short duration. Polish on AM424E2 (Fig. 11.4b) is weak, though it grades into heavier patches towards the edge on the ventral face of the mid left lateral edge (location B, 68° spine angle just catching part of another blade removal). The striations are wide and u-shaped, except for those near the area of microflaking (dense and u-shaped). The polish pattern is similar to that seen on experimental blade NWXP3, which was used to clean sinew (38–41° spine angle). If any experimental work matches the striations, it is NWXP4 (cutting rawhide). The degree of polish, similar directions of striations, and lack of heavy microflaking suggest a multiple direction (see 100× images) motion (most likely sawing or a mixture of sawing and cutting) of a harder soft material comparative to rawhide, but at a longer duration.

Of the Clovis Blades from layer 3b, blade AM291H (Fig. 11.5a), a distally and laterally modified whole blade, shows two directions of u-shaped striations arcs going transversal to the lateral edges and distal end. The striations are densely packed and of varying sizes. The arc-shaped striations overlap with the oblique straight shaped striations (location A at 200× and 500×). This location has a spine angle of 42° and an edge angle of 60°. The blade was used for scraping, or possibly planing hard materials (hard wood or most likely bone) due to its similarity to the horn planing of experimental blade NNWXP1 (with a used edge angle of 66°). On blade AM285B (Fig. 11.5b), a distally and laterally modified complete blade, with deep, thin, and densely packed u-

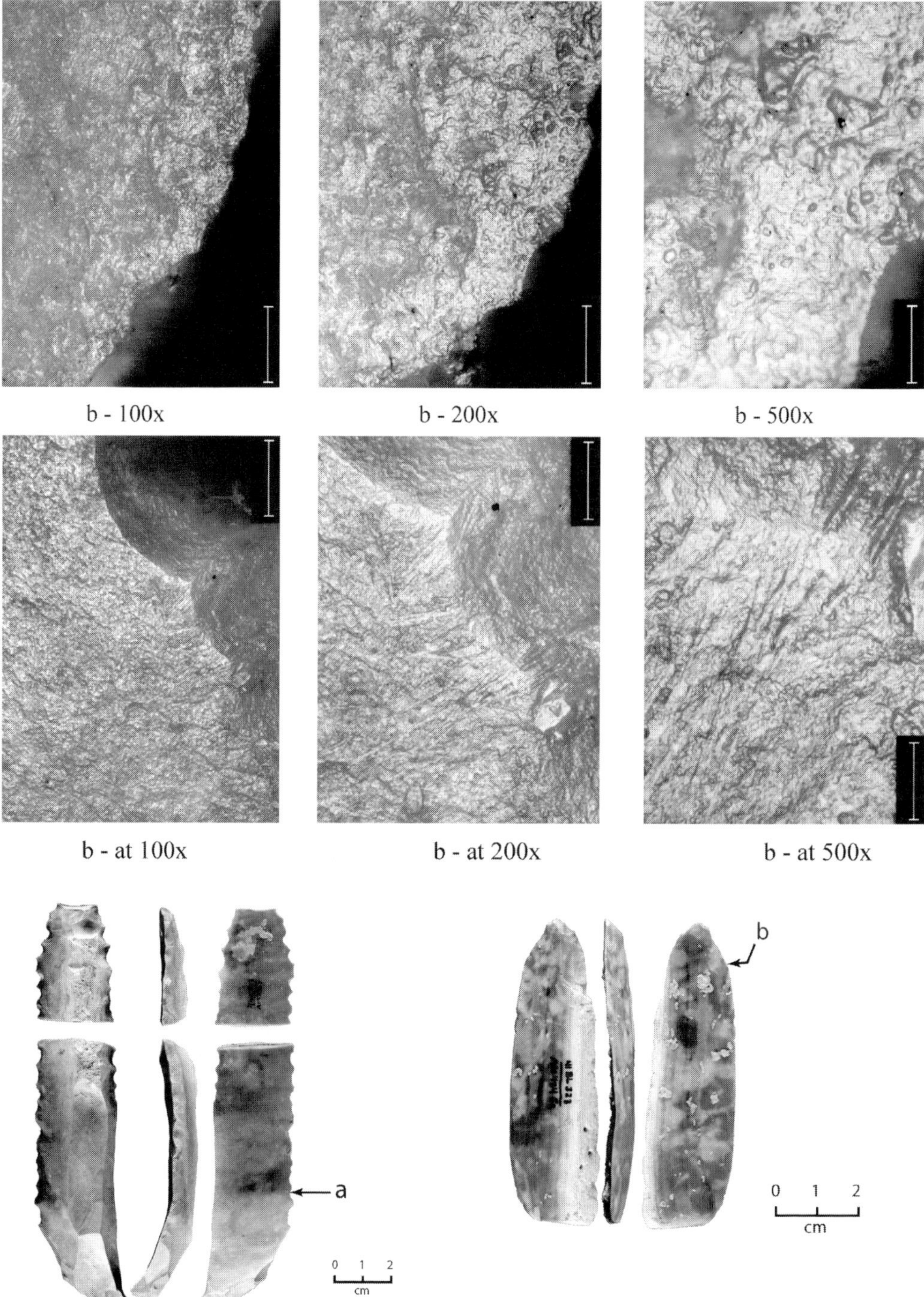

Figure 11.4. Clovis 3a Blades: a) Refit AM322 (Cat #279) and AM326B2 (Cat #278); and b) AM424E2 (Cat #698).

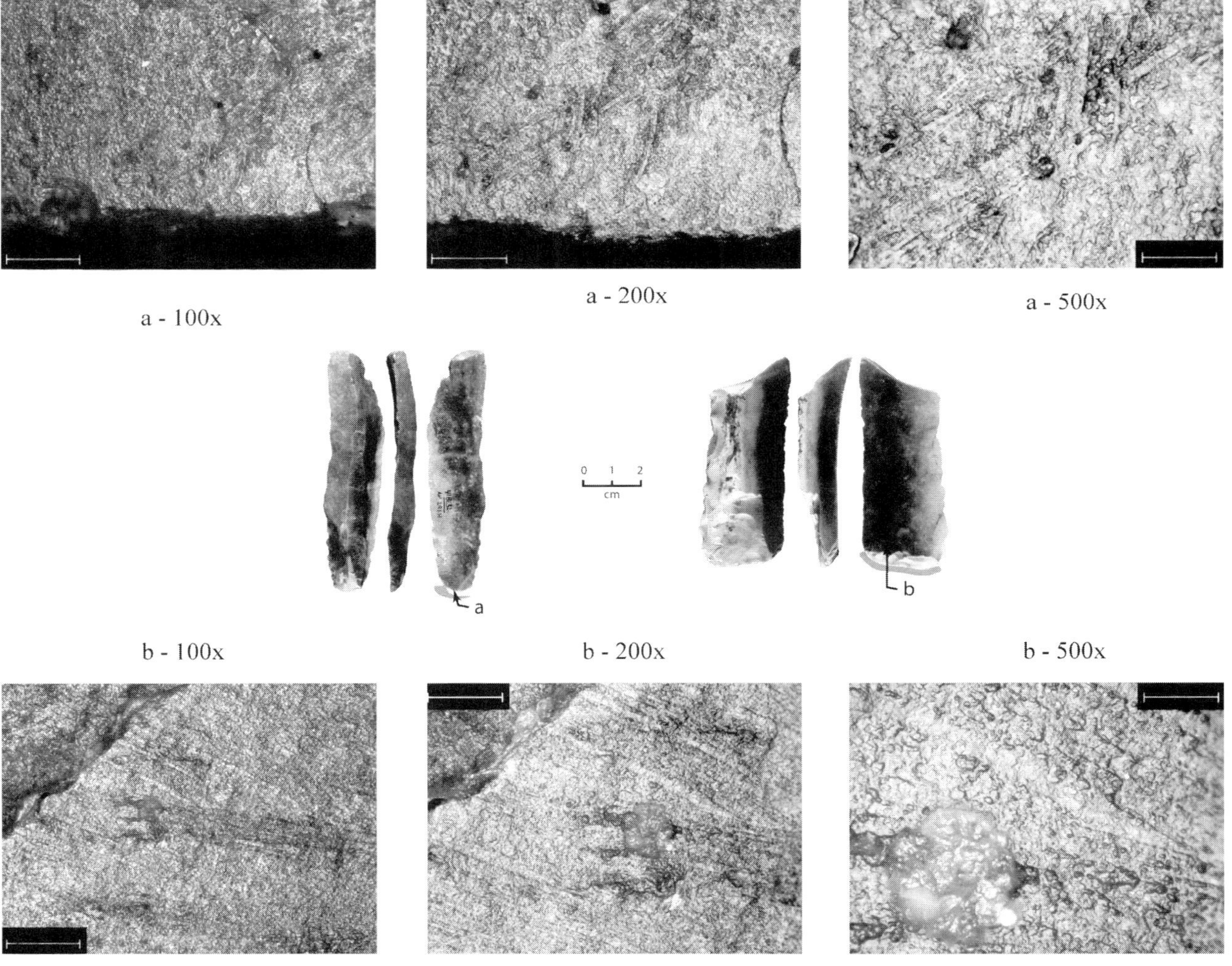

Figure 11.5. Clovis 3b Blades: a) AM291H (Cat #443); and b) AM285B (Cat #265).

shaped striations that are transverse to the distal edge, the microtopography is visible between the thin striations but not in the wider u-shaped striations in-between. A pattern emerged of a package of dense striations (six visible in the 500× image of location A), followed by one wide striation, followed by a further package of dense striations, and so on. A faint trace of this pattern was visible in the flake scars. The piece was evidently used for planing, or possibly scraping hard materials (most likely bone) due to its similarity to the horn planing of experimental blade NNWXP1 (proximal edge of 66°), the motion of AM285B was one direction on a consistent surface. A lack of polish on the rest of the blade gives rise to the inference of only distal edge use.

Non-quarrying/chert processing activities at Gault: conclusions, discussion, and recommendations

A very small number of blades from 3a and 3b, eight Clovis 3a blades, or 3.0% of the total Clovis 3a blade/blade fragment population (n=264), exhibit use-wear. In addition, six Clovis 3b blades, 3.3% of the total Clovis 3b blade/blade fragment population (n=182), exhibit signs of wear. Others with weakly developed wear traces, approximately 3% of used blades identified from the blade populations, lead to an inference of limited use. Certain differences are macroscopically visible between some of the utilized blades of Clovis units 3a and 3b. Distal modifications are limited to unit 3b, while blades/blade fragments with lateral modifications are found almost completely in unit 3a. This observation in morphological difference is not necessarily one that results from function and use. Stereomicroscope observations also point to scarring and rounding on blades/blade fragments from Clovis 3a than Clovis 3b. Polish and striation patterns observed under compound analysis, when compared to experimental blades, show a further difference between blades and blade fragments from 3a and 3b. Polish patterns from 3a correspond to the soft contact experiments, while polish and striation patterns from 3b correspond to the hard contact experiments. In general, the polish and striations on blade and blade fragments in both units are not well developed.

Microwear analysis of TAMU Clovis blades, along with comparisons with other experiments, illustrates that multiple craft or subsistence activities were in operation at Gault, in addition to quarrying and workshop activities. While it is tempting to make greater statements about behavior at the Gault site, there are certain caveats: i) blades and blade fragments are only one aspect of the chert chipped stone industry and are not a proxy for the other lithics or non-lithics; and ii) due to the high amount of chert (within bedrock, eroded, and in streams) in and around the site, assumption of blade use over other forms was made.

It was not the intention of this test to provide a definitive answer to the broad-scale differing views of Holmes and Bryan. Microwear analysis provides a tool, not a model, for testing. More detailed investigations, along with further microwear testing at quarries, may provide enough data to refine the views expounded in the various hypotheses. To address the roles of quarries and quarry-workshops, two items require further investigation. First, a more detailed contextual framework (physiography, geology, hydrology, *etc.* ...) is needed that is based on predictable resources through time. Sites require detailed contextual statements in order to provide the necessary detail to account for variation and provide enough data for even the most basic inter-site connections. Secondly, microwear analysis is needed at other sites to test for alternative quarry functions.

Note – The scales for the microscope images are as follows: 100× = 200 um, 200× = 100 um, and 500× = 50 um.

Acknowledgements

The work reported on here was done under the auspices of Texas A&M University This paper is based on a poster presented at the 71st Annual Society for American Archaeology (SAA) meeting in San Juan, Puerto Rico. The data and research are a result of the author's thesis work at Texas A&M University. Special thanks to Dr, Michael Waters, Dr. Harry J. Shafer, and the late Dr. Robson Bonnichsen for providing the opportunity to work on Gault and for their support. Thanks to my fellow Texas A&M Gault graduate researchers for fostering an open and encouraging working environment. Philip LaPorta deserves thanks for providing guidance and a sounding board for questions. His geological knowledge on the formation of chert and archaeological ideas on prehistoric quarry-workshops proved invaluable to making important determinations of raw material constraints.

12 The Organisation of Lithic Procurement at Silver Mound, Wisconsin: Source of Hixton Silicified Sandstone

Dillon Carr and Robert Boszhardt

Summary

Strategies concerning the acquisition of Hixton Silicified Sandstone from the quarry at Silver Mound, Wisconsin, are evaluated here using an 'organization of technology' framework. Implementing an organizational perspective shifts the focus of research toward assessing the roles that quarries play as one segment of prehistoric lithic procurement strategies, and recognizes the use of quarries is an active, agent driven factor instead of a passive accompaniment to lithic technological systems. Diagnostic hafted bifaces recovered from the quarry at Silver Mound indicate the use of a cyclical procurement strategy by western Great Lakes Late Paleoindians. Building upon data obtained from the quarry, regional distribution and the condition of hafted bifaces manufactured from Hixton Silicified Sandstone are analyzed. It is suggested that different responses to tool-kit needs, such as variable emphasis on reliability and maintainability, will produce differing archaeological signatures even among a population engaged in a cyclical procurement strategy.

Introduction

Our research employs an organizational perspective in evaluating strategies concerning the acquisition of Hixton Silicified Sandstone (HSS) from the Silver Mound quarry in Wisconsin. Such a perspective shifts research focus from one of primarily lithic raw material extraction and re-orients analysis toward assessing the role(s) that quarries played as one component of lithic procurement strategies. This organization of technology framework recognizes that prehistoric quarrying is an active, agent driven, occurrence instead of a passive accompaniment to lithic technological systems. Evaluating the organization of procurement at Silver Mound in this manner provides a broader understanding of how research at quarries can be better integrated within studies that seek to reconstruct the overall organization of lithic technological systems.

Understanding the complex relationship between prehistoric quarries and lithic procurement strategies requires integration of data from individual quarry sites with data pertinent to the transport and use of curated raw materials 'off-site'. Quarry sites play an essential role in understanding supply within procurement strategies by providing data complementary to that obtained from the wider region. The latter acts as a proxy measure for the 'management end' of procurement strategies in operation

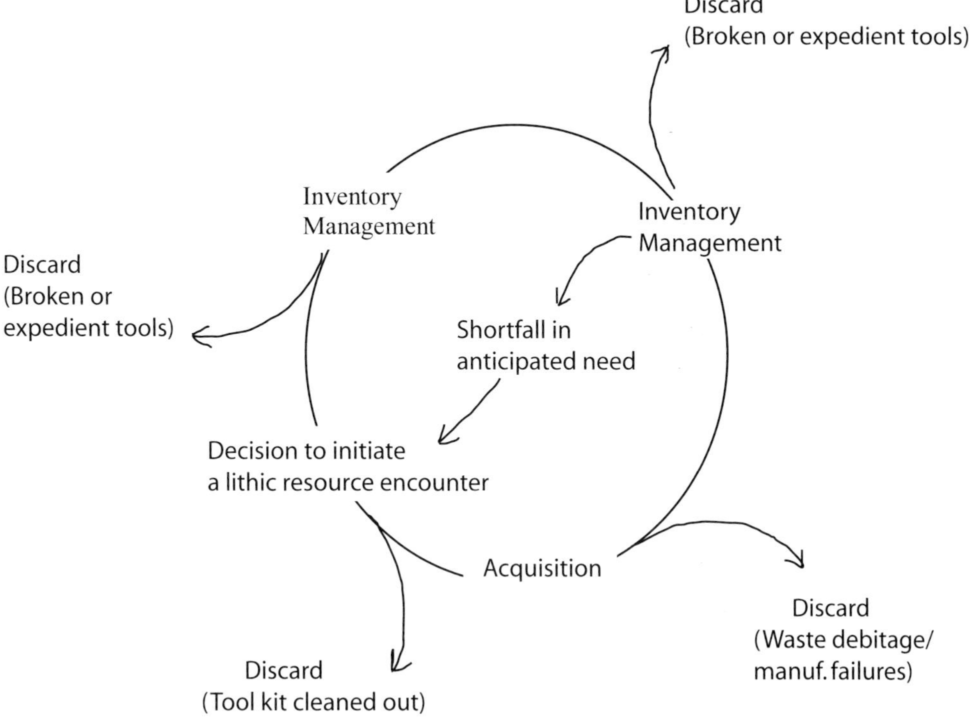

Figure 12.1. Continual processes of lithic procurement.

away from primary quarry areas. In the context of this study, the analysis of diagnostic western Great Lakes Paleoindian hafted bifaces (*c.* 10,500–10,000 uncal BP) recovered from the Silver Mound quarry has indicated the use of a cyclical procurement strategy. Regional scale data regarding the distribution and condition of HSS hafted bifaces are then used to reconstruct how Late Paleoindian populations positioned themselves on the landscape in order to procure HSS.

Organization of Lithic Procurement

The replacement of stone tools within lithic tool-kits is a multi-faceted, recurring concern for prehistoric stone tool using societies. Lithic procurement, though not necessarily acquisition, should therefore be viewed as a continuous, rather than episodic, process (Fig. 12.1). Conceptualizing procurement in a continuous manner emphasizes the fact that strategies are responsive to both the anticipated and situational needs of a population (Bamforth 1986; Binford 1979; Carr 1994; Ellis and Spence 1997; Kuhn 1989; 1994; Nelson 1991). The role of anticipated needs becomes apparent when considering that during procurement decisions are made regarding the necessary amount of material to be acquired. These decisions are based on the estimated volume of tool stone required until the next anticipated opportunity to visit a lithic source. Also, because situational needs may arise, such as accidental loss and breakage, inventories of available materials should be monitored in relation to projected tool stone requirements. Managing tool kits in this manner ensures the decision to procure additional raw materials is made prior to any critical shortfall in available materials.

It can also be suggested that sources of lithic raw material constitute stable, predictable resources in terms of both location and known labor requirements necessary to satisfy need. Given this predictability, the nature of lithic resource encounters (*i.e.* visits to the quarry) contrasts with other activities, such as hunting, where successful resource encounters are often erratic and produce variable return rates. Likewise, it is the stability of tool-stone sources that enables a population to initiate resource encounters in anticipation of need.

The capacity to initiate lithic resource encounters provides for a considerable degree of flexibility to how stone resources are utilized. No doubt among prehistoric populations, who relied extensively on the use of stone tools, maintaining a functioning tool kit would be a paramount concern. However, the procurement of stone resources is also influenced by interests beyond the replacement of stone tools discarded from tool kits. For instance, exchanging stone resources is of value for the maintenance of social networks and indirectly, through risk buffering strategies, the stabilization of subsistence economies (*e.g.* Hayden 1982, 117; Wilmsen 1970, 75–76). Interrelated is Ellis' (1989; see also Carr 2005; Ruggles 2001) suggestion that the selective use of raw material sources operates as a means to maintain intragroup social identity. Moreover, Gould (1980, 228) suggests that the procurement of lithic materials may become influenced by spatial proximity to ceremonial or sacred locations, and highlights the fact that stone resources can have ideological meaning as well. Less explicit is the likelihood that certain lithic sources, frequently associated with prominent landforms, become encoded with meaningful "senses of place" within a community's cultural landscape (*e.g.* Basso 1996; Kornfeld *et al.* 2001). Although difficult to predict archaeologically, these concerns do ultimately influence the range of lithic raw materials being procured by prehistoric populations.

Hixton Silicified Sandstone and Silver Mound

Colloquially referred to as 'sugar quartz', HSS is a distinctive Type 1 orthoquartzite distinguished visually via well rounded sand grains cemented together with silica (Ebright 1987; Porter 1961). Among archaeologists working in mid-continental North America, HSS is recognized as a high quality, visually distinctive, lithic tool stone utilized by pre-contact societies (Ebright 1987; Fowler 1991, 14; Green and Rodell 1994; Hill 1994; Loebel 2005; Tankersley 1990). The significance of HSS during prehistory is exemplified by evidence for extensive quarrying of the material at its only known outcrop; an outlier hill of Cambrian sandstone named Silver Mound located in west-central Wisconsin (Carr and Boszhardt 2005). This quarrying coupled with evidence for the widespread transport of the material for in excess of 800 km is, in part, the basis for the site's recent (February 2006) designation as a National Historic Landmark.

The fact that HSS crops out only at a single location is part of the reason why the material can be distinguished via a number of methods including macroscopic, microscopic and geochemical identification (Boszhardt 1998; Julig *et al.* 1999; Schaffer and Tankersley 1989; Tankersley 1990; Porter 1961). It also means that artifacts manufactured from HSS can be traced back to a single point of origin rather than being attributed more generally to a geological formation, which oftentimes span large geographic areas. This ability to trace the movement of HSS back to a single geographic point is further strengthened by Silver Mound's location in the Driftless Area, an area of south-western Wisconsin that remained unglaciated during the Pleistocene, meaning secondary sources of the material within glacial tills are entirely non-existent. Relating HSS back to a single, known geological location provides considerable resolution when reconstructing lithic procurement strategies; a point that will be elaborated more upon later.

Late Paleoindian use of Hixton Silicified Sandstone

A distinguishing characteristic of Great Lakes and northeastern Paleoindian lithic assemblages is their manufacture from a very restricted range, often a single source, of high quality, visually distinctive, lithic raw material which has frequently been transported upwards of 300km from known sources (Buckmaster and Pauquette 1988; Deller and Ellis 1984; Ellis 1989; Ellis and Deller 2000; Lothrop 1988; Seeman 1994; Shott 1993; Simons *et al.* 1984; Witthoft 1952). This preference contrasts significantly to later periods of occupation in the region (*e.g.* Luedkte 1976). Preferential use of a single lithic source in this manner has been described as a cyclical procurement strategy, referring to the practice of making cyclic returns to a single lithic source on an annual or semi-annual basis (Custer *et al.* 1983; Gramly 1980).

The ensuing analysis is restricted to the earlier of the Late Paleoindian complexes defined in the western Great Lakes region, and can be distinguished through occurrences of diagnostic unfluted, lanceolate shaped, hafted bifaces morphologically similar to those associated with the Agate Basin complex (Carr and Boszhard 2003; Frison and Stanford 1982). The data set employed here is available through the Paleoindian Database of the Americas maintained at the University of Tennessee (Anderson *et al.* 2005), and has been adapted from Carr (2004).

Late Paleoindian use of Hixton Silicified Sandstone: The supply end

Our initial concern is evaluating the degree to which Late Paleoindians were preferentially exploiting HSS, perhaps as part of a cyclical procurement strategy. Preferentially exploiting a single lithic source in a cyclical manner requires periodic visits to the quarry. Because few/no other lithic sources are exploited on a regular basis, the expected result is that a very high percentage (*e.g.* 90%) of curated tools manufactured from HSS discarded and replaced at the quarry. Thus, any artifacts discarded at subsequent visits to Silver Mound would invariably have been manufactured from HSS obtained during previous visits.

The logic outlined above stems, in part, from Michael Gramly's (1980; see also Ingbar 1994) work at quarries in eastern North America where he examined the raw material composition of curated tools. Specifically, at the West Athens Hill, Normanskill chert quarry site in New York, Gramly (1980, 828) observed that the formal tools discarded near the quarry by Paleoindians dominated (>85%) the assemblage. Such a pattern is interpreted to reflect a population utilizing principally the Normanskill source and this contrasts significantly with evidence from the Mount Jasper rhyolite quarry in Vermont, where exhausted tools were seldom (<5%) manufactured from the local rhyolite, instead being comprised of a variety of raw materials procured from elsewhere (Gramly 1980, 826–828).

Important with such reasoning is the role tool curation plays within the organization of lithic procurement strategies; defined here as the transport of stone tools from one location to another in anticipation of future use, even if they are not to be used at that location (Binford 1979, see also Bamforth 1986; Odell 1996; Torrence 1983). While it is difficult to attribute the decision to curate stone tools to a single source of influence, such as mobility (Binford 1979) or time stress (Torrence 1983), as Bamforth (1986, 48) suggests, the availability of lithic raw materials is likely to have considerable influence on the decision to curate. In other words, the limited availability of raw materials forces a population to curate stone tools, and transport them to locations of use *regardless of whether the shortage is caused by the physical distribution of resources across a landscape or by cultural constraints that serve to restrict access* (*e.g.* visually distinctive raw materials, Carr 2005; Ellis 1989).

Curated tools discarded during return trips to Silver Mound are represented by a sample of 50 unshouldered lanceolate hafted bifaces recovered within 40km of the quarry. Table 12.1 summarizes the lithic raw material sources used to manufacture each of the sampled bifaces. It is apparent that HSS represents the most dominant raw material, used to manufacture 38 of the hafted bifaces. Of the additional non-HSS raw material sources identified in the sample, no other single raw material was used in the manufacture of more than two (4.0%) bifaces. Locally available raw material sources utilized include Prairie du Chien chert, Galena Formation chert, and Cataract Silicified Sandstone (CSS), which can be distinguished from HSS on the basis of coloring, texture and structural differences visible under low powered magnification (Boszhardt 1998;

	Observed	%	*Expected*	%
HSS	38	76.0%	22	44.0%
Prairie du Chien chert	2	4.0%	10	20.0%
CSS	2	4.0%	10	20.0%
Unidentified	2	4.0%	2	4.0%
Galena chert	1	2.0%	1	2.0%
Knife River Flint	1	2.0%	1	2.0%
Obsidian	1	2.0%	1	2.0%
Knife Lake Siltstone	1	2.0%	1	2.0%
Jasper Taconite	1	2.0%	1	2.0%
Quartzite	1	2.0%	1	2.0%
			G = 28.66182	p = 0.001

Table 12.1. Identified raw materials among discarded points at Silver Mound and results of G-test indicating preferential use of HSS.

Carr and Boszhardt 2003: Julig *et al* 1999). The remainder of the non-HSS materials present in the sample are either unidentifiable or come from various non-local "exotic" chert sources such as Knife River Flint and obsidian. The extreme distances (700–900km) between Silver Mound and these source areas suggest that these non-local materials were acquired indirectly, or at the very least, were not acquired during the normal course of population movement.

It can be anticipated that the Late Paleoindian population preferentially exploited HSS, at least for the curated part of the tool kit. If the alternative were true, and additional lithic sources were being utilized during the regular course of annual movement, then the discard of reworked and expended tools manufactured from those additional materials would be evident. Based on Gramly's (1980, 826–828) observations at the Mount Jasper quarry, a conservative estimate would be for, at least, moderate percentages (*e.g.* 20–25%) of non-HSS materials to be found discarded among the hafted bifaces recovered near Silver Mound. Assuming the use of the two nearsest sources, Prairie du Chein chert and CSS, a G-test indicates that the observed dominance of HSS at Silver Mound is, in fact, statistically significant (p=0.001). In other words, the very high percentage of HSS (76%) in the sample is consistent with the expectation for a population engaged in a cyclical procurement strategy.

Late Paleoindian Use of Hixton Silicified Sandstone: The Management End

Utilising the 'organization of procurement' framework presented earlier contributes an important element to the discussion: the acknowledgement that there is a purposeful decision made to discard materials from the tool kit. More so, this decision is a component of the overall lithic procurement strategy being employed arising from the interrelated concerns of current tool-kit inventory, anticipated tool-kit requirements, and length of time until the next anticipated opportunity to acquire fresh tool stone. Of significance is that exercising a decision to discard directly results in the formation of the archaeological record.

A sample of 99 unshouldered lanceolate hafted bifaces manufactured from HSS were examined, and variability within the available data interpreted in three dimensions: 1) length of bifaces at discard, 2) condition of bifaces, and 3) the spatial relationship between discarded bifaces and Silver Mound. Combined, all three variables serve as a proxy for intentional decisions to discard stone tools from the tool kit (Table 12.2). For instance, the discard of longer hafted bifaces, these presumably retaining utility, reflects either low anticipated need, or an imminent opportunity to acquire fresh tool stone. Likewise, recycling of broken bases, inferred from a lower average length of broken bases and tips, is a sign of raw material conservation indicating that it may be some time yet before the next anticipated opportunity to visit a lithic source.

Examining the condition of points discarded within a 40km radius of the quarry offers some insight into how Paleoindians were positioning themselves on the landscape in order to acquire fresh HSS from Silver Mound. One pattern that emerges is related to the length of bases discarded near the quarry. On average, they are some of the longest (45.15mm), particularly when compared to bases discarded at distances greater than

Spatial Relationship to Silver Mound	*N*	*Mean Length*	*Std.*	*CV*
< 40-km to Silver Mound				
- Complete points	25	63.01	15.62	24.79
- Broken bases	15	45.15	18.42	40.80
> 40-km Southeast of Silver Mound				
- Complete points	16	73.67	29.21	39.65
- Broken bases	12	29.83	13.07	43.81
> 40-km Northwest of Silver Mound				
- Complete points	17	67.47	17.35	25.71
- Broken bases	14	29.57	11.68	39.50

Table 12.2. Summary of length, condition, and spatial relationship to Silver Mound for sample of HSS hafted bifaces (CV – Coefficient of Variation).

Distance from Silver Mound	N	Mean	Std.
Local (<40 km)	15	45.15	18.42
Non-local (>40 km)	26	29.69	12.09
	t =		3.248
	Sig.(2-tailed)		0.002

Table 12.3. T-test comparing length of discarded bases among sample of hafted bifaces.

40 km from Silver Mound. A t-test comparing the length of bases discarded within 40km of Silver Mound (Table 12.3) with those recovered further away indicate that the observed differences in length are statistically significant (p=0.002).

One explanation for the relatively long bases discarded at Silver Mound is that they were intentionally curated as part of a buffering strategy against shortfalls in available raw material. Selectively curating longer bases would certainly facilitate their ability to be reworked into functional tools and, upon returning to areas near Silver Mound the curated bases would be no longer needed. Although it seems unlikely that a population would not re-tip the bases at the first available opportunity to do so, one advantage to this practice is retaining the flexibility to recycle curated bases into a variety of tool forms. An alternative explanation involves a population residing in the immediate vicinity of Silver Mound for at least part of the year and engaged in some form of logistical mobility. Broken bases brought back in hafts would be discarded near the quarry and because of the spatial proximity to Silver Mound there was little incentive to rework damaged points.

The 'management end' of lithic raw material procurement strategies is closely associated with the continual monitoring of tool-kit requirements. Tool-kit design centers on the competing concerns of time and risk (Kuhn 1994; Bamforth and Bleed 1997). The result is a greater emphasis on the over design of tools to ensure their reliability (Bleed 1986; Bousman 2005, 195–196; Myers 1989). In contrast, the daily but less intensive use of tools places an increased importance on the management of time.

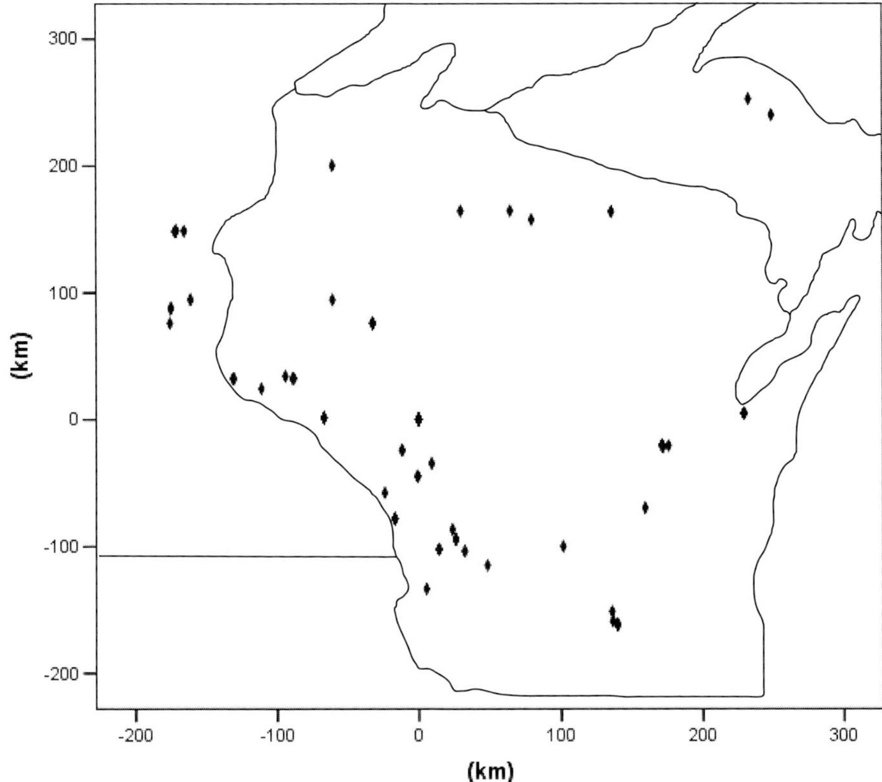

Figure 12.2. Plot of discarded bases to the southeast of Silver Mound.

The likely result is on concern about tool maintainability over their reliability (Bleed 1986; Bousman 2005, 196: Myers 1989; Torrence 1983). In short, emphasis is placed on how the decision making process influences strategies of stone procurement, tool design, use and eventual discard of stone artifacts on archaeological sites.

The presence of discarded bases to the south-east of Silver Mound indicates that the area was occupied for a significant period of time, at least long enough to warrant the re-hafting of points (Fig. 12.2). One explanation for the observed discard of bases to the southeast of Silver Mound is that the bases resulted from indirect acquisition of HSS by a population residing in the area. However, the lengths of complete hafted bifaces to the southeast are on average the longest (73.67mm), and the discard of seemingly functional bifaces would be expected of a population with ready access to an additional supply of HSS. In other words, this decision more closely reflects that made by a population anticipating a return trip to Silver Mound in the foreseeable future.

An alternative explanation is that discard occurred as part of a "gearing up" strategy as described by Kuhn (1989). Groups targeting specific resource patches might anticipate an intensive period of activity. The emphasis in this situation is on reliability over maintainability (see Bamforth and Bleed 1987) and provides incentive to clean out (e.g. gear up) tool kits beforehand. Refurbishing tool kits in this manner would certainly result in the discard of hafted bifaces that seemingly retained their utility. Also, this strategy appears to fit well with the notion that caribou were the focus of Paleoindian subsistence pursuits in eastern North America (Jackson 1997; Loebel 2005, 402–413; Meltzer 1988). Targeting caribou during the temporally restricted annual spring and fall migrations would certainly represent an intensive, and important, period of activity for Paleoindians.

The length and condition of hafted bifaces discarded to the northwest of Silver Mound contrasts with the use of areas south and east of the quarry described above. The overall uniform length of discarded point bases in this region, combined with the lack of overlap between lengths of point bases and complete points, certainly suggests that bases were intentionally discarded only when they were unable to be reworked into functioning weapon tips (Fig. 12.3). One potential cause for the observed pattern is that populations were repeatedly occupying this area while practicing a subsistence and settlement strategy similar to that described by Binford (1980) for foragers. Emphasis among foragers is often placed on the maintainability of the tool kit (Bamforth and Bleed 1987: Bousman 2005: Torrence 1983). In short, consistent maintenance of tools results in the discard of points at the stage when they are unable to be resharpened or, in the case of broken bases, reworked. In addition, the longest bifaces are located closest to Silver Mound with a weak linear relationship (r=0.303) between length and distance from the quarry. A population positioned closer to Silver Mound would have more opportunities to visit the lithic source, or could do so more easily in the event of unexpected shortfalls. Because of the reduced pressure to conserve raw materials the discard of longer complete points in the areas closer to the quarry is expected. However, a population positioned further away from the source, as might be expected, would curate points for longer periods of time.

Discussion

Analysis of diagnostic hafted bifaces from the quarry at Silver Mound indicates that a Late Paleoindian population in the western Great Lakes preferentially exploited HSS to the avoidance of other local tool-stone sources. Expanding upon data from the Silver Mound quarry site, regional scale data regarding the distribution and condition of HSS hafted bifaces were used to reconstruct the 'management end' of lithic procurement strategies. The results suggest that different responses to tool-kit needs, such as variable emphasis on reliability and maintainability, produce differing archaeological signatures. As both signatures are present, even among a population engaged in a single, generalized procurement strategy, it should be recognized that prehistoric lithic procurement strategies are intended to be flexible and responsive to a variety of concerns external to the lithic tool-kit itself.

Evaluating lithic procurement from an organizational perspective provides a framework for more fully understanding the relationship between quarry sites and generalized strategies. Such a framework is essential for developing a holistic picture of how lithic raw materials were being acquired, utilized and eventually discarded by

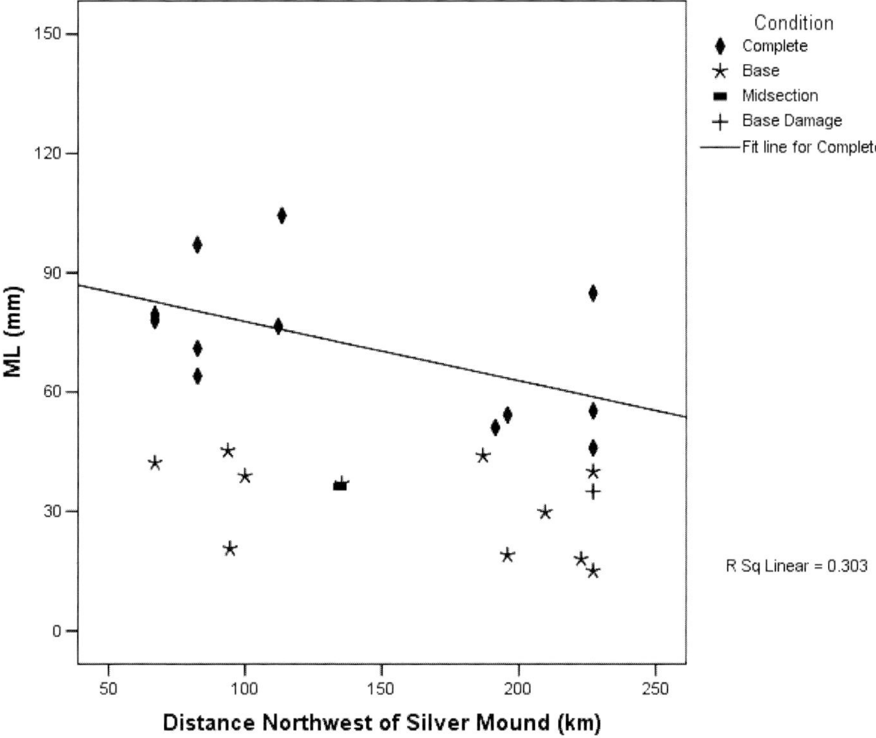

Figure 12.3. Plot of bifaces found to the northwest of Silver Mound.

prehistoric societies. Quarry sites themselves provide valuable data to help reconstruct the supply end of lithic procurement strategies. However, it is also clear that interpreting the 'management end' of lithic procurement requires analysis of quarried materials discarded 'off-site'. Both forms of data were employed here in reconstructing the organization of western Great Lakes Late Paleoindian lithic procurement strategies.

Acknowledgements

We would like to thank Virgil Noble and Erika Seibert of the National Park Service both for securing funding and their tremendous help during the NHL nomination process for Silver Mound. Also, the paper benefited greatly from earlier comments by Brian Deller, Chris Ellis, Roger King, Bill Lovis, John Norder, and Mike Spence. However, we alone are responsible for any errors or omissions; substantive and otherwise.

13 Close to Home? Pipestone Quarry Utilization in the Mid-continental United States

Sarah U. Wisseman, Randall E. Hughes, Thomas E. Emerson and Kenneth B. Farnsworth

Summary

Major pipestone quarries have been identified in several states in the mid-continental (e.g. Ohio, Illinois, Missouri, Kansas, and Minnesota) United States. However, each quarry source has a different history, some being used in both ancient and modern times while others, like the source of flint clay near St. Louis, Missouri, being used for only a short time over a millennium ago. Archaeometric analyses and experimental archaeology support the similar workability of pipestones from multiple quarry sources, whether from Minnesota catlinite to Sterling or Feurt Hill pipestones, so this factor cannot explain why abundant sources were used differentially through time. Other factors, such as the locations of quarries in relationship to changing regional centers, local cultural histories, and new patterns of ritual and exchange must be taken into account to explain variation in pipestone utilization by Eastern Woodlands native peoples.

Background

Pipestone is a generic term for a group of carvable, fine-grained, sedimentary and metamorphic rocks including argillite (catlinite), flint clay, and limestone. Often red, this raw material was employed by several different cultures in the American midcontinent to manufacture high-status, often sacred, items such as animal effigy pipes and "red goddess" figurines.

Traditional procurement and exchange models are often based on universalist economic rationality theories. They portray the movement of stone across the landscape in terms of people seeking "exotic" materials from distant sources because they carry a high prestige value (derived from their rarity and high cost of transport) while local stone sources (because of ease of access) had little or no prestige and were often used for the manufacture of utilitarian objects. In examining several case studies of pipe manufacture and distribution in pre-Columbian eastern North America, we found these theories fall short of explaining actual quarry use and the complexity of the production and consumption revealed in the archaeological record (Emerson *et al.* 2003; 2005).

Pre-Columbian pipestone quarries have been identified in Ohio, Minnesota, Wisconsin, Illinois, Kansas, and Missouri (Fig. 13.1) and, although some problems remain in delineating the extent of natural variation within each source, for the most part we have demonstrated that they are mineralogically distinctive. Chemically, many pipestone

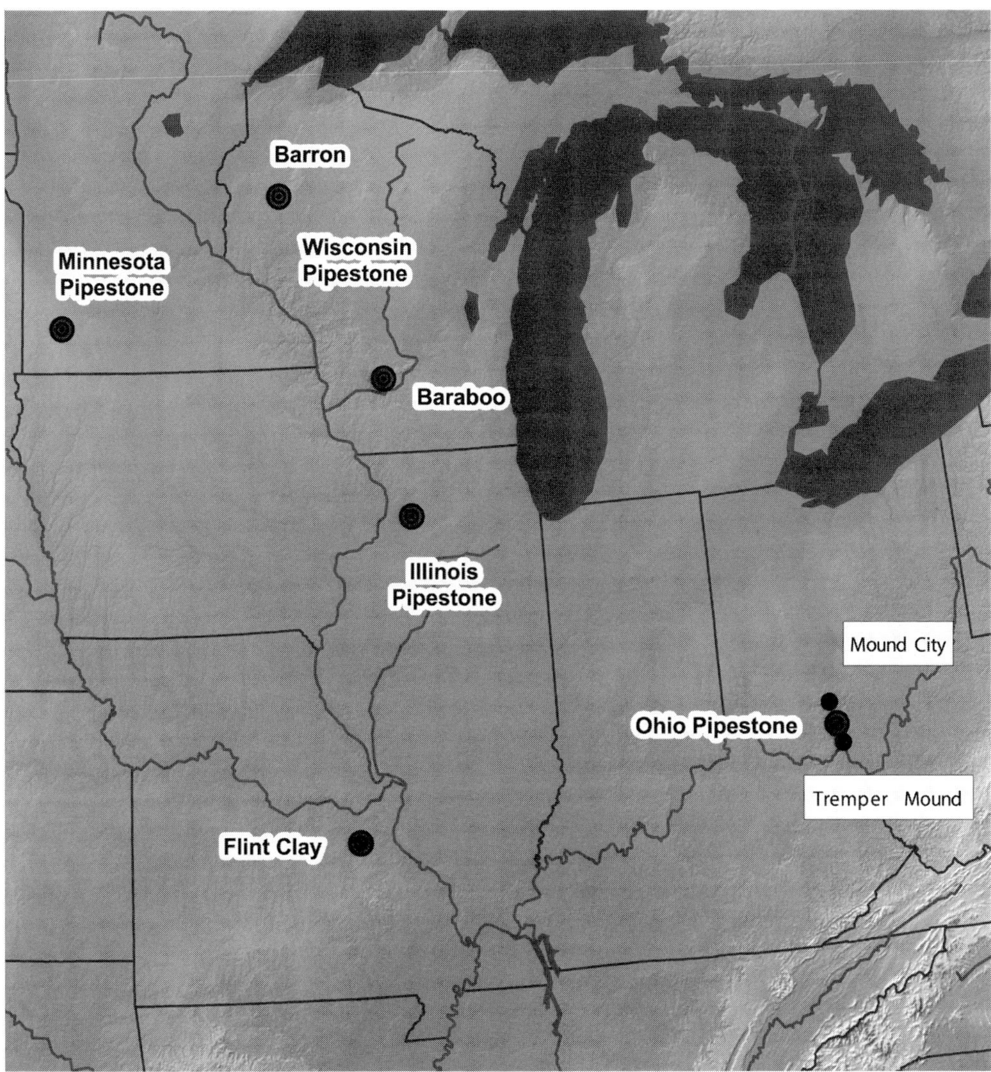

Figure 13.1. Map of pipestone quarries.

sources are similar, but the way elements are combined into minerals and the structural details of those minerals give almost a 100% separation between the various pipestone groups. The identities and percentages of minerals in pipestones reflect their geological origins. For example, those minerals in Minnesota catlinites indicate they were probably formed in normal, drained and oxidizing soils, whereas those in Missouri and Ohio flint clays show likely reduction during burial and exposure to higher temperatures.

More recently we have begun to investigate the relationship of geological composition and pipestone workability by native crafts people. While we are making strides in defining the geological nature of the quarries, we continue to ponder the mismatch between the quality of pipestones and the intensity of their use. We have evidence for the initial regularized native use of pipestones by at least Terminal Late Archaic times (*c.* 3500 years ago) yet most prime sources of pipestone were used only sporadically or for limited time periods. The exception appears to be the Pipestone National Monument in Minnesota, the source for the red pipestone called catlinite that is still in use today. In this short article, we begin the process of evaluating the native use of pipestone in relation to its workability, quarry location, and cultural context.

Geological Methods

Our approach to pipestones and quarry sourcing is first to characterize the mineral composition and its variance using PIMA (Portable Infrared Mineral Analyzer) spectroscopy and occasional X-Ray diffraction (XRD).

X-Ray diffraction, a standard laboratory technique, is performed on hand samples and rock powders at the Illinois State Geological Survey (ISGS). XRD analyses have been at times supplemented by targeted studies of chemical and structural variations within individual minerals using ICP and other techniques described elsewhere (Hughes *et al.* 1998; Emerson and Hughes 2000). Our research strategy takes into account different degrees of polishing, burning, and weathering of samples from archaeological and geological contexts.

The PIMA is a portable instrument first used by geologists in Australia, the U.S., Canada, and South America to locate precious metals, assess ore quality, study the degree of crystallinity of minerals, and to map zones of alteration in rocks changed by hydrothermal processes. At the University of Illinois, we are using the PIMASPTM manufactured by Integrated Spectronics Pty Ltd, Australia, to study archaeological materials for the first time (Hughes *et al.* 1998: Emerson and Hughes 2000; 2001; Emerson *et al.* 2002; 2003; Wisseman *et al.* 2002).

This shoebox-size instrument (Fig. 13.2) can be operated in the field or in a museum setting. It is totally nondestructive; there is no induced radiation damage or sample modification. PIMA spectroscopy provides mineral identification in stone and low-fired ceramic artifacts, as well as in candidate stone and ceramic source materials. It is an excellent precursor to standard laboratory analysis by the complementary technique of X-ray diffraction or more costly elemental techniques such as neutron activation analysis. The PIMA requires no sample preparation if a small, preferably flat, surface of the sample can be brought up to the 1cm diameter window of the instrument.

The PIMA uses the short wavelength infrared (SWIR) part of the electromagnetic spectrum (from 1300–2500 nanometers or 7692 to 4000cm-1) and measures the reflected radiation from the surface of a sample, part of which will have been absorbed by the sample. These absorption features reveal the inter-atomic bond energies characteristic of specific minerals, specifically the overtone and combination tones of longer wavelength (OH) bending and stretching vibrations. Features at about 1400 nm represent the first overtone of the fundamental OH stretching vibration, whereas features around 2200–2500nm are due to a combination of stretching and bending vibrations. PIMA works best on materials containing hydroxyls and water: the absorbed or structural

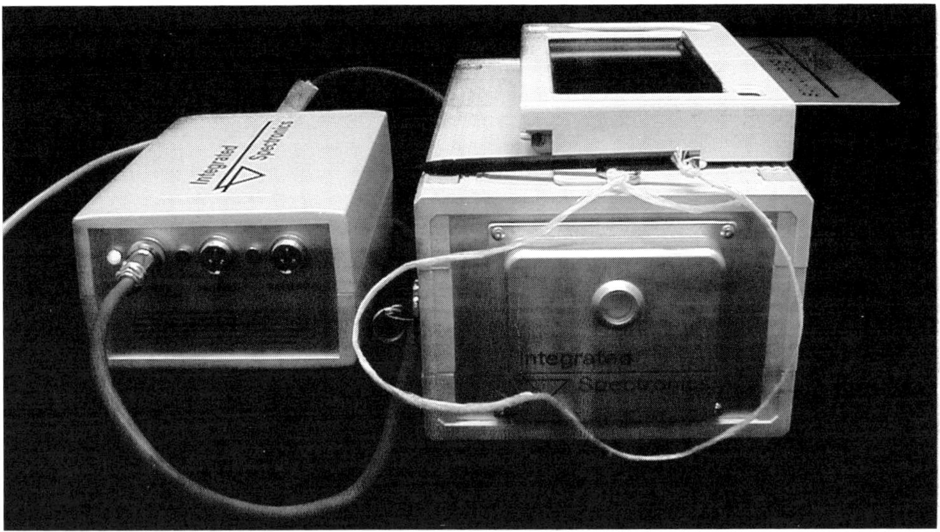

Figure 13.2. Portable Infrared Mineral Analyzer from Integrated Spectronics, Ltd., Australia.

parts of minerals such as phyllosilicates (same as layered silicates), epidotes, zeolites, and amphiboles. Non-silicate oxyanions, such as $CO_{3}2$, NO_3, PO_4^{3-}, and SO_4^{2-}, also have signals in the PIMA range.

The instrument can be held either horizontally or vertically (using a stand) and has settings that compensate for dark samples. One reading takes only thirty seconds, allowing the rapid collection of a large number of analyses. Measurements can be made on whole or partial artifacts, sherds, rock chips, thin sections, powders, and soil and sediment samples and cores. PIMA spectroscopy is also a quick way to get a preliminary, non-destructive assessment of compositional differences between original and restored areas without removing an artifact from its museum setting (*e.g.* Wisseman *et al.* 2004).

Archaeological Case Studies in the Midcontinental United States

Our work to date has included identifying the materials and quarries used to manufacture Middle Woodland pipes and Mississippian figurines, as well as defining the true nature of catlinite, its variation, and its use over time. In each case, our goal has been to characterize the rock types used to make artifacts, locate their sources, determine their range of variation, and then use that information to reevaluate existing archaeological models of trade and exchange of both raw materials and finished products. Since our analyses of pipestones from some prominent quarries used to craft native pipes and figurines and our interpretation of their cultural implications have been extensively published elsewhere (Hughes *et al.* 1998; Emerson and Hughes 2000; 2001; Emerson *et al.* 2002; 2003; 2005; Wisseman *et al.* 2002; 2004), the focus here will be on what we have come to think of as the "catlinite problem." However, we will

Figure 13.3. Hopewell platform pipe, Illinois River valley, c. *50 BC–250 AD.*

briefly summarize our work with several other pipestone quarries (*i.e.* Feurt Hill and Missouri CBP) in order to illustrate the potential of our approach. In each instance our analysis served to "turn-upside-down" existing archaeological interpretive models of manufacture and distribution.

The Feurt Hill and Missouri CBP Quarries

Middle Woodland (*c.* 50 BC–AD 250) platform and effigy pipes (Fig. 13.3) made by the Hopewell people were for many years assumed to be of Ohio manufacture, with the primary source of raw material being from the Feurt Hill pipestone quarries in Scioto County, Ohio. Our combined analyses (Figs 13.4 and 13.5) by PIMA, XRD, and other techniques have demonstrated that in addition to this source, Hopewellian craftsmen used a surprising amount of pipestone from sources in northwestern Illinois, near the towns of Sterling and Rock Falls (Emerson *et al.* 2002. Hughes *et al.* 1998. Wisseman *et al.* 2003). Previously it had been thought that Ohio pipestone pipes were traded to Illinois; instead, we demonstrated that most Hopewell pipes appeared to have been manufactured in Illinois and then shipped to Ohio. Our second discovery arose from detailed examination of pipes from the Tremper Mound site caches in southern Ohio: many so-called "red Ohio pipestone " pipes are in fact made from Minnesota catlinite (Emerson *et al.* 2005). The implications of this discovery will be discussed further below.

The large red stone figurines (Fig. 13.6) crafted by 12th century Mississippian peoples at the site of Cahokia, near St. Louis, Missouri, are some of the most spectacular prehistoric works of arts in North America. Examples of these figurines and effigy pipes have been found in archaeological sites within an area stretching from Wisconsin to Mississippi and from Oklahoma to Alabama. Representing both mythological and actual individuals, they are a rich source for understanding Mississippian symbolism,

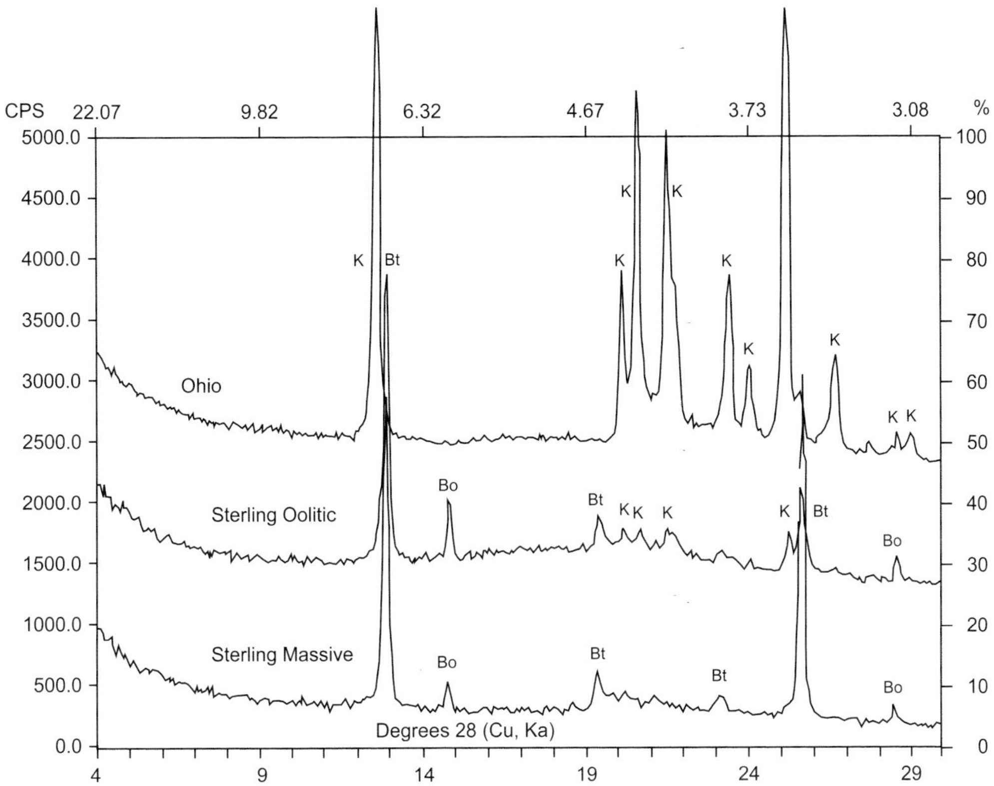

Figure 13.4 XRD traces of OH and NW IL pipestones.

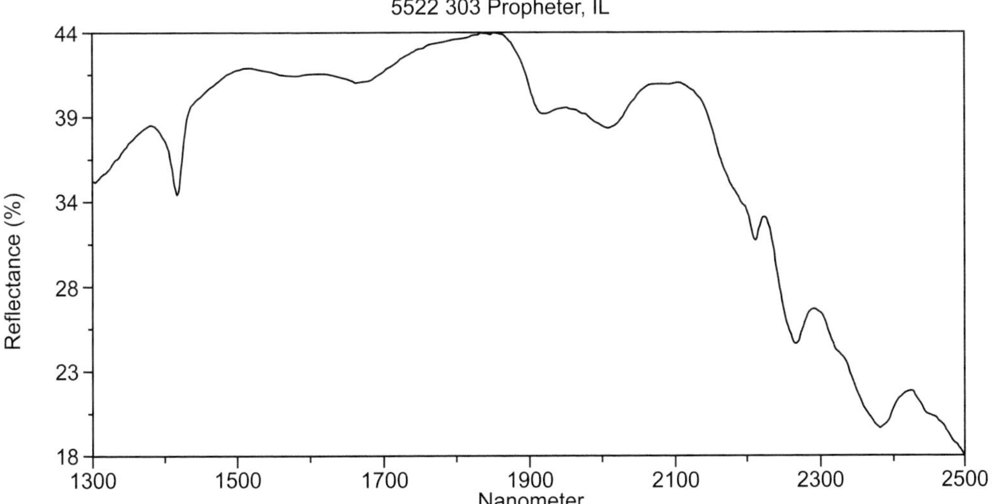

Figure 13.5. PIMA spectrum of berthierine-rich pipestone from NW IL.

Figure 13.6. Keller figurine, Cahokia site, 12th century AD

iconography, and lifestyles. For nearly seventy-five years these figurines were interpreted as having been carved from Arkansas bauxite by Oklahoma Caddoan groups and then traded north hundreds of miles into the St. Louis area. After extensive testing of quarry specimens and museum artifacts, we demonstrated that all of the "red goddess" figurines were created from a single source of flint clay near St. Louis, Missouri. (Fig. 13.7) (Emerson and Hughes 2000; Emerson *et al.* 2003). This flint clay is characterized by a distinctive combination of chlorite with a 7Å/14Å mixed-layering, abundant boehmite and heavy-metal phosphate mineral (CBP) suite that is a unique flint clay (Fig. 13.8). In fact, red goddess figurines were made in Cahokia near St. Louis and only then moved hundreds of miles to the south into the Oklahoma Caddoan area (Fig. 13.9).

In addition to the Ohio, Minnesota, and Missouri quarries (Fig. 13.10), we have characterized at least two pipestone sources in Baraboo and Barron counties, Wisconsin, and one in Rice County, Kansas. Baraboo pipestone, catlinite, and Kansas pipestone (Fig. 13.11) lack or have minor amounts of quartz, so they are relatively soft, even though

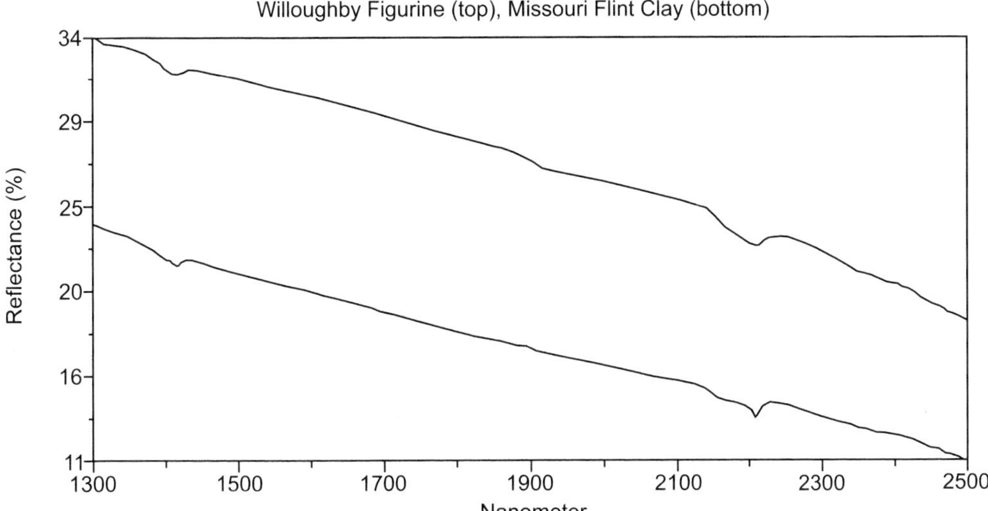

Figure 13.7. Comparison of PIMA spectra for a Cahokia figurine and flint clay from a quarry near St. Louis, MO.

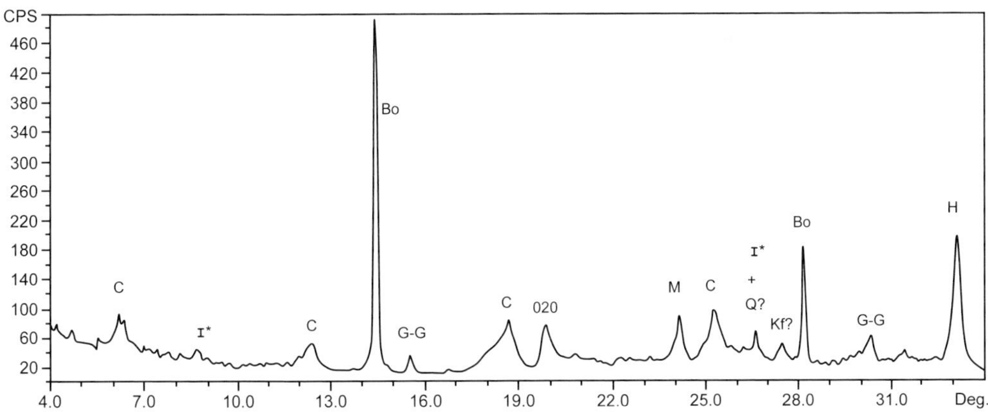

Figure 13.8. XRD trace of typical, "unburned" Missouri pipestone, with cookeite-like chlorite (C), illite and mixed-layered illite/smectite (I), boehmite (Bo), gorceicite-goyazite (G-G; a heavy-metal phosphate mineral), the 020 peak that is common to clay minerals, hematite (H), questionable quartz (Q?), and questionable K-feldspar (Kf?).*

they were metamorphosed to temperatures that produced pyrophyllite and fine-grained muscovite (mica). These red pipestones, the flint clays, and a small number of very pure limestones and dolomites are unique in the central US in lacking quartz.

Our growing database of PIMA spectra and XRD traces allows us to make some comparisons of pipestones from different sources that were not possible before. For example, Missouri and northwestern Illinois flint clays are chemically very similar, but

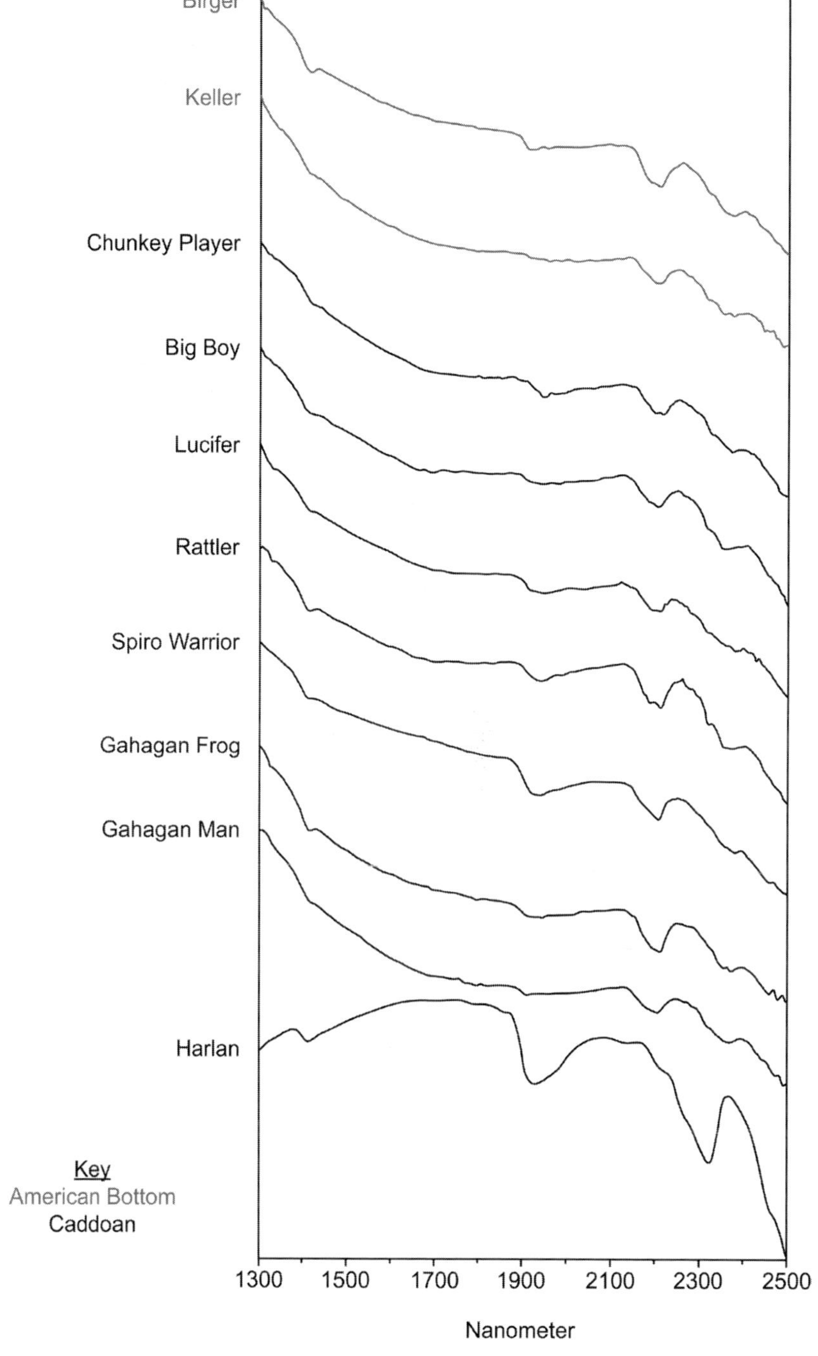

Figure 13.9. PIMA spectra of multiple Cahokia figurines.

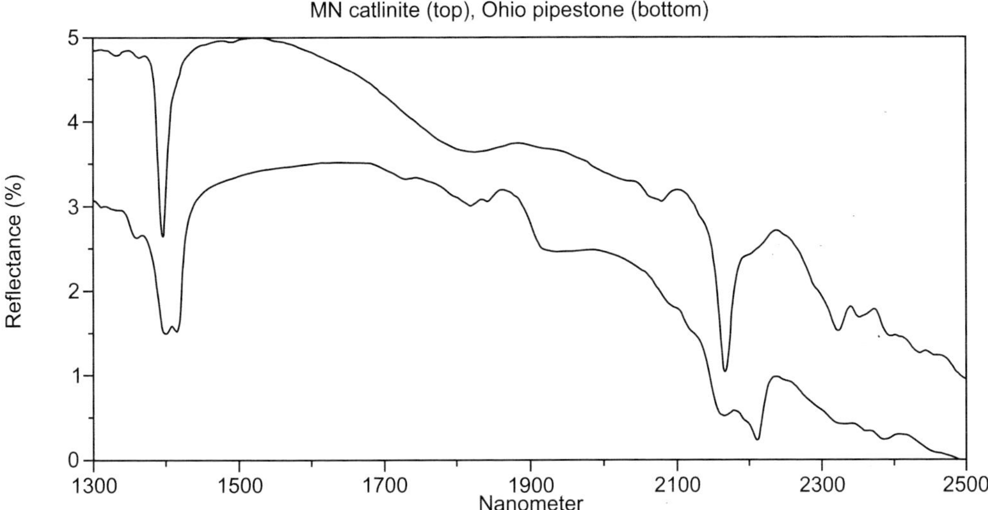

Figure 13.10. Comparison of Ohio and Minnesota pipestones.

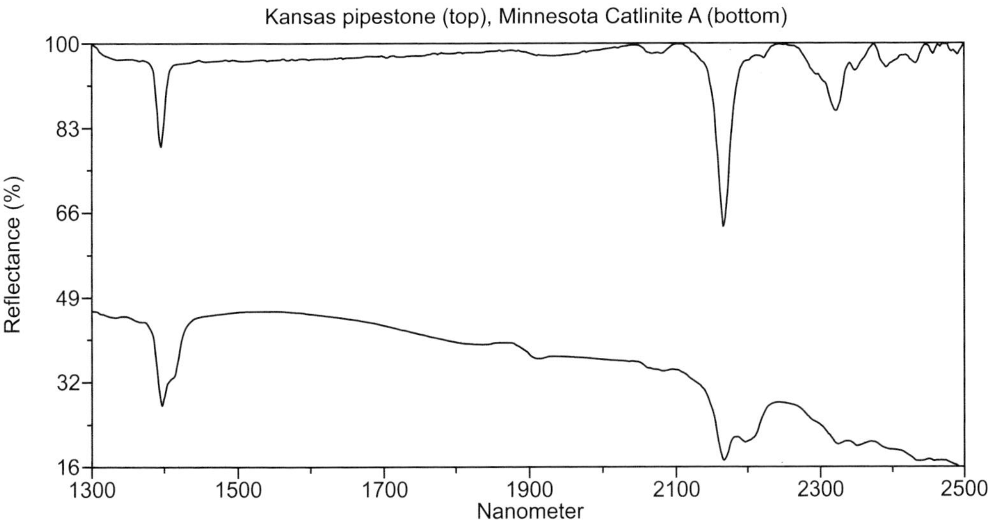

Figure 13.11. PIMA spectra Minnesota and Kansas pipestones.

greater temperature probably altered the berthierine in the Missouri clays to a cookeite-like mineral, which contains the same amount of lithium. Both have boehmite, but the kaolinite is less in the Missouri source.

We have also performed minor experiments in workability of the different pipestones, both in the field while collecting samples and back in the lab. Using Moh's hardness scale, most of our pipestones fall in the 2 to 4 hardness range (from easily scratched with a fingernail to easily scratched by a steel knife). Hardness is a derivative of the structure of the mineral, so it varies in different directions within all non-isometric minerals. The clay minerals and micas in pipestones are typical examples of minerals that are very soft along the weak bonds of their platy surface directions (along the sheets of building blocks), and they are much harder directions across the plates. It appears that pipestones must be cut by flint (chert= near 7), and polished/drilled by quartz (=7) silt and grinding stones.

To illustrate the range, Missouri CBP flint clay is easily carved but many of the blocks we collected fell apart with exposure to air. The explanation for this is case hardening, which is a widespread phenomenon of relatively soft rocks that are hardened and partly weathered beneath a long-exposed soil surface. In contrast, northwestern Wisconsin pipestones from Baraboo and Barron counties have enough silica cement to make them difficult to carve.

The "Catlinite Problem"

Separating catlinite from other visually similar red pipestones, is the common thread in all our subprojects and has proven to be one of our easiest tasks using PIMA spectroscopy (Emerson and Hughes 2001; Emerson *et al.* 2004; 2005). Any red stone used by native societies to make smoking pipes (*calumets*) and other artifacts is often referred to as "catlinite," but true catlinite is a mineralogically distinct fine-grained argillite whose occurrence is restricted to the area in and around Pipestone National Monument (PNM) near the town of Pipestone in southwestern Minnesota. This source was a dominant political and religious site in the 18th and 19th centuries.

We are fortunate in having detailed historical accounts and archaeological, geological and mineralogical studies of the major pipestone and catlinite quarries in the Midcontinent. Many of these historical and archaeological documents have been compiled in a volume by Alan Woolworth (1983), and the primary geological and mineralogical studies have either been referenced or conducted by James Gundersen (1987; 1988; 1991; Gundersen and Tiffany 1986; Penman and Gundersen 1999).

Gundersen's extensive work (1991) with these various Midwestern argillites established that they are primarily comprised of five distinct minerals: diaspore, kaolinite, muscovite, pyrophyllite, and quartz. His analysis using X-ray diffraction (XRD) of known pipestone sources and artifacts demonstrates that the identification of the three dominant minerals in a specimen is often sufficient to determine geologic provenance. The argillites from the PNM catlinite quarries are uniquely distinguished by the dominance of diaspore, pyrophyllite, and muscovite. Kaolinite, as a minor ingredient, may or may not be present. All of the other known pipestones tested by Gundersen contain quartz as a component. It is only at the PNM geologic source that confirmed outcrops of the quartz-free catlinite are exposed for human exploitation.

The general belief that all aboriginal red pipes were made of catlinite (appropriately initiated by Catlin 1973, 202 [1844]) and the inability of many investigators to megascopically distinguish between red siltstones, pipestones and catlinite has led to most archaeological specimens being identified as catlinite. Since few mineralogical

Figure 13.12. Catlinite layers at Pipestone National Monument, MN (photo, NPS website).

studies of archaeological red pipes have been conducted, the actual chronological and spatial distribution of catlinite pipes and other artifacts throughout native societies of North America is impossible to reconstruct in detail.

Historical accounts and archaeological studies have shed some light on the aboriginal use of the PNM quarries. Limited archaeological investigations in 1949 by Beaubien (1983, 37–80) and Sigstad in 1965–66 (Sigstad 1970) yielded a low density of occupational debris revealing that the locality was intermittently inhabited. However, the quarries may not have been actually systematically utilized until the fourteenth century. Diagnostic lithic artifacts cover the whole spectrum of prehistory while ceramics typically fall into the categories associated with Late Woodland and Plains Village groups such as Cambria, Great Oasis, Oneota, and Mill Creek. Recent reanalysis of these archeological remains has confirmed the earlier chronological and cultural assessments (Dale Henning, personal communication 2000). Henning's (1998a; personal communication 2000) long research in northwestern Iowa, near the PNM, indicates the first local small-scale use of catlinite occurs in the 1300s, substantively increases in the early 1400s, and takes on all the trappings of large-scale utilization at sites like Blood Run after AD 1500. We know from the earliest historical accounts of the region in the late

1600s and early 1700s (summarized in Beaubien 1983), such as those by Groseilliers and Radisson, Father Marquette, Le Sueur, and Raudot, that natives esteemed the red pipes and spoke of a quarry on the *riviere rouge,* shown on Guillaume de L'Isle's 1702 map in the Minnesota vicinity. Most early observers, such as Holmes (1919), believed that the use of catlinite was primarily a historic period phenomenon, although acknowledging that it may have had its origins in late prehistory.

Penman and Gundersen (1999) have conducted significant research on the chronology of catlinite trade and use in the Upper Mississippi River Valley (UMRV). These researchers, using XRD analysis, identified catlinite at a series of late prehistoric Oneota sites, primarily in the Red Wing, Minnesota and LaCrosse, Wisconsin areas. They showed that catlinite use in the late prehistory of the UMRV did not predate AD 1280 (J. T. Penman, personal communication 2000). In Central Illinois, catlinite does not appear in the late prehistoric Spoon or LaMoine River Mississippian cultures (Conrad and Nolan 1991) nor in the large Oneota Bold Counselor sites (Conrad and Nolan 1991: Esarey and Conrad 1998). Catlinite pipes and other objects are commonly recovered in the Lima Lake locality of the Mississippi River Valley (Nolan and Conrad 1998), and sporadically in the Lower Illinois River Valley (Farnsworth and O'Gorman 1998) postdate AD 1300.

There is, however, a very significant exception to the UMRV pattern of catlinite use that has recently been revealed by important research carried out by Boszhardt and Gundersen (2001) and expanded by our recent work (Emerson *et al.* 2005). Performing X-ray diffraction analysis (XRD) analysis on several red tube pipes and several platform pipes from Wisconsin, they demonstrated the artifacts were manufactured from catlinite. Consequently, despite the lack of evidence for either Early or Middle Woodland use of the PNM quarries, it is evident that at least small amounts of catlinite were appearing in some localities within the Hopewell Interaction Sphere as far away as Ohio.

A number of American Bottom artifacts around the great site of Cahokia were identified in the late nineteenth and early twentieth centuries as catlinite. These included red stone Mississippian pipes (McAdams 1882: also Bushnell 1904, 18–19: Moorehead *et al.* 1929, 99). Mound 72 at Cahokia yielded a small ear spool identified by Fowler *et al.* (1999, 137, fig. 10.5) as being made of "red pipestone." One of the best-documented cases of red stone identified macroscopically as catlinite is from excavations at the Cahokia Mounds State Historic Site Interpretive Center (ICT II). Four partially worked fragments and one segment of a pipe stem, all macroscopically identified as catlinite, were retrieved from Stirling phase contexts (AD 1100–1200; Gums 1993). Catlinite is also reported from the Mitchell site, a large multi-mound Mississippian center north of Cahokia. During salvage excavations, Porter (1974, 896–97) discovered a flat unworked slab of "red catlinite" on a prehistoric surface near a circular sweat lodge.

Our initial PIMA work has shown that, in fact, *none* of the above "documented" cases of macroscopically identified early catlinite use are valid (Emerson and Hughes 2001; Emerson *et al.* 2005). In every instance where we were able to analyze the specimens from a Mississippian context, they were either examples of CBP Missouri flint clay or look-alike red stone – but not catlinite.

It is not until Oneota times (post-fourteenth century) that we were able to positively identify true catlinite in the American Bottom region. These specimens are represented by finds at several local sites that range in time from Oneota through historic Illinois Indian (Emerson and Hughes 2001). Red stone pipe fragments were recovered from the surface of two adjacent sites located on an alluvial fan of Prairie du Pont Creek in St. Clair County near Centreville (Booth and Koldehoff 1999, 89–124). These sites both yielded Oneota diagnostic lithic and ceramic artifacts from the late thirteenth Century Bold Counselor phase (cf. Jackson 1998). On a broader perspective such disk pipes are usually associated with the Oneota Classic horizon (mid-fourteenth to mid-seventeenth centuries; *e.g.*, Henning 1998b; Brown 1989).

A tubular pipe stem, thought to be a portion of a catlinite elbow pipe, was recovered from the plow zone near the multicomponent Florence Street site (11S458). Based on style and design, the pipe was most likely discarded by one of the historic native groups who inhabited the area (Temple 1966; Walthall and Benchley 1987).

Excavations at the early 18th century French *River L'Abbe* mission at Cahokia revealed six catlinite triangular-to-trapezoidal drilled pendants. These small ornaments were popular in the first half of the eighteenth century among the Illini groups (Walthall and Benchley 1987, 74–75).

XRD was Gundersen's (1991) methodology of choice to distinguish the geologic sources of red pipestone materials from archaeological sites. He also demonstrated that it is a critical step in separating the relatively rare Minnesota catlinite artifacts from samples of similar and more widespread red pipestones and siltstones from other quarries or from glacial drift deposits (*e.g.*, Gundersen 1984; 1993; Gundersen and Tiffany 1986; Penman and Gundersen 1999). We (Hughes and Emerson 1999; Emerson and Hughes 2000) have shown that the technique is useful in distinguishing the red flint clay of Missouri that is often found in Mississippian contexts in the American Bottom. This is important because red flint clay can be mistaken macroscopically for one of the red pipestones or catlinite.

Combining XRD and PIMA analyses of numerous quarry samples of catlinite (from the Gundersen and Sigstad collections now in Lincoln, Nebraska, as well as some other samples we obtained) and archaeological collections from Mound City, Ohio and Tremper Mound, Ohio, have enabled us to distinguish two types of catlinite from essentially the same geological source, the Pipestone National Monument. Catlinite A has equal or nearly equal amounts of muscovite and pyrophyllite (muscovite: pyrophyllite peak ratio greater than 0.5), whereas Catlinite B has significant but far lower amounts of muscovite. The key features are between 2100 and 2200 nanometers (Fig. 13.13).

Our characterization of the pipestones used to manufacture pipes found at the site of Tremper Mound, Ohio, shows that contrary to the popular belief that Ohio was the center for a pipe exchange system that covered much of the groups east of the Mississippi River, Hopewellian craftsmen of the Middle Woodland period (50 BC and AD 250) did not produce all of their pipes from the nearby Feurt Hill pipestone quarries in Scioto County. In fact, only about fifteen percent of the production at Tremper was from local stone; eighty-five percent of the pipes were made from pipestone from northwestern Illinois and Minnesota catlinite types A and B. On the other hand, ninety-seven percent of the pipes found at Mound City National Monument only tens of miles away were revealed by analysis to be made from local stones (Emerson *et al.* 2002; 2004). These

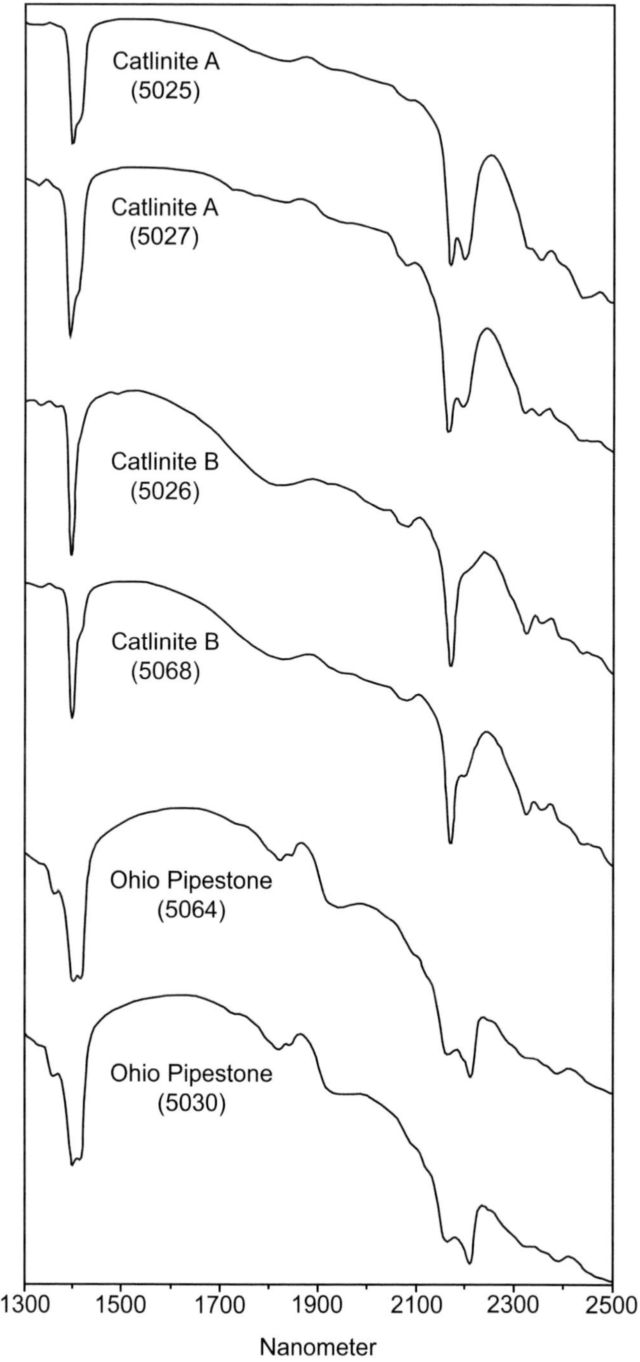

Figure 13.13. PIMA spectra of catlinites and pipestones found at Tremper Mound, Ohio.

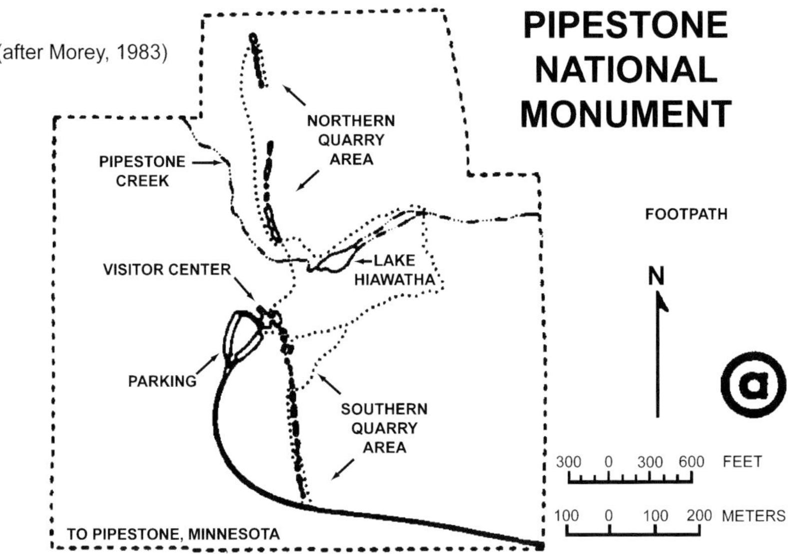

Figure 13.14. Map of Pipestone National Monument (after Gundersen 1991, National Park Service MWR-17).

results have turned our attention back to the only source of catlinite that we know of, the Pipestone National Monument (PNM), and the range of variation within it.

PNM is divided into northern and southern sections (Fig. 13.14), with over eighty-three separate quarry locations that were sampled by James Gundersen. The catlinite layers occur within the Sioux Quartzite. Catlinite is formed at higher temperatures than Missouri flint clay, NW IL, or Ohio pipestone and is a high quality, fine-grained material, easy to carve and polish. At the PNM exposures, the catlinite layers occur mostly underneath the much harder quartzite and are revealed in a roughly north-south line that is two-thirds of a mile long. Gundersen divides the layers into lower, middle, and upper catlinite units, noting that they are limited laterally and are not necessarily contiguous even though they appear at the same stratigraphic level.

A re-examination of Gundersen's 1991 article is instructive because he hints at some internal variation in the PNM quarries even as he concludes that "catlinites are rather homogeneous-appearing argillites" and there is no typical "modal catlinite" or "average catlinite." He also says "red catlinites are characterized by a distinct, limited range of mineral variations within the D-P-M [diaspore, pyrophyllite, and muscovite] ternary field that is not duplicated by any other Plains types" (Gunderson 1991, 57).

Our PIMA analyses of Gundersen's quarry samples now stored in the Lincoln NE National Park Service facility show more variation than expected from Gundersen's conclusions. In the course of this examination we recorded 903 PIMA spectra. In quarry 15, which is in the upper unit of the southern quarry, PIMA sample 5178a shows a catlinite B spectrum on the "light side" and a catlinite A spectrum on the "diagonal

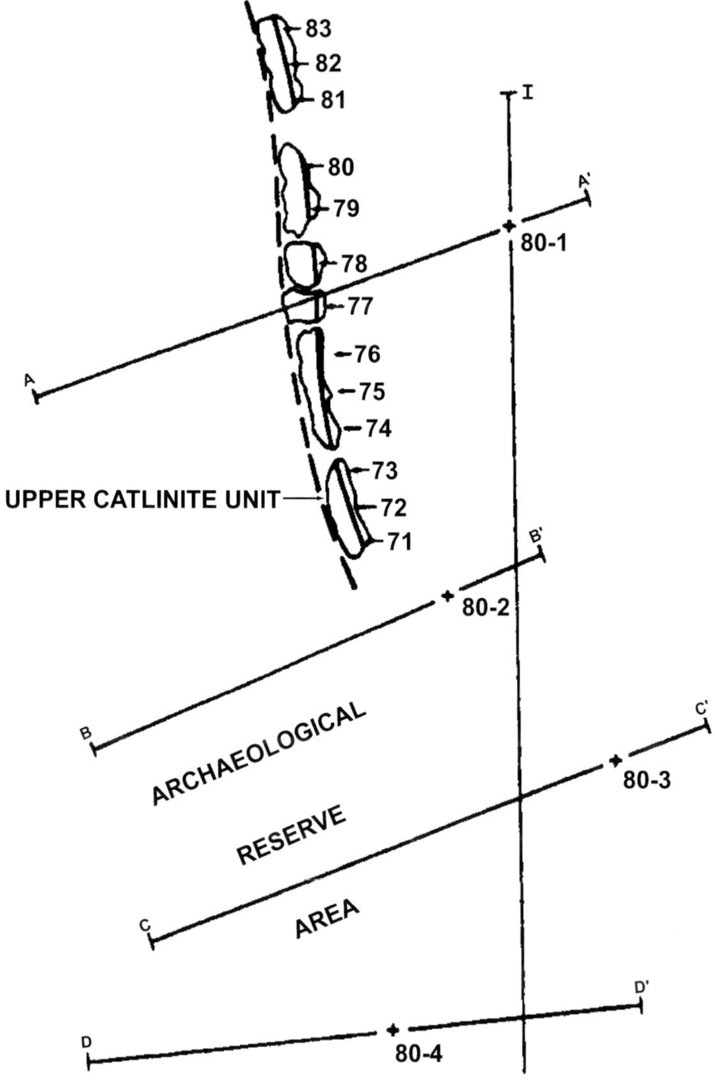

Figure 13.15. Map of north part of northern quarry area (after Gundersen 1991, National Park Service MWR-17).

fracture" of the same piece. Mineralogically, the difference is that the fracture zone contains more muscovite than the "light side."

A brief review of the collections showed several other examples in quarry 15 (Fig. 13.15), plus one each in quarries 78, 82, and 83 of the upper unit of the north quarry, where the "red" or "polished red" side of a sample produced a catlinite B spectrum while the "bleached," "porcelain white" or "greenish" side of the same piece produced a

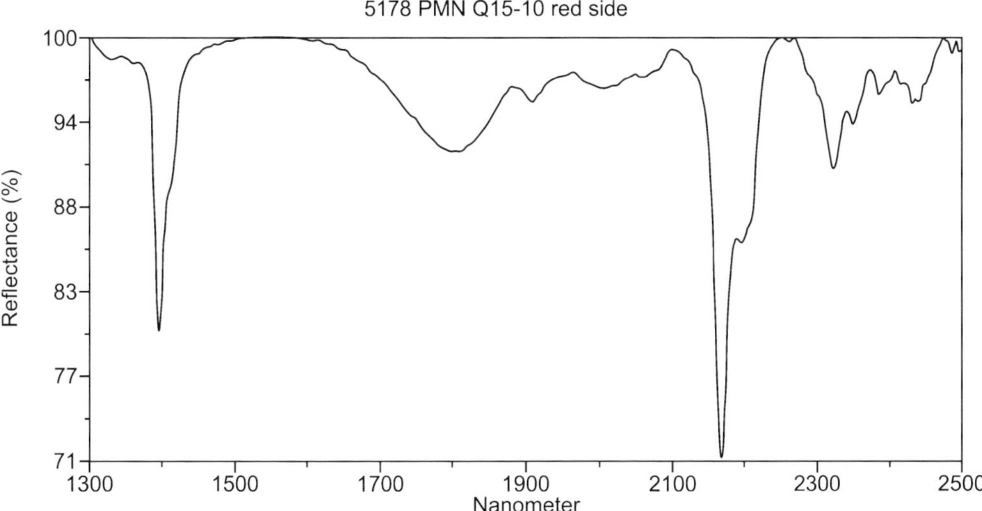

Figure 13.16. Red side of hand sample from quarry 15.

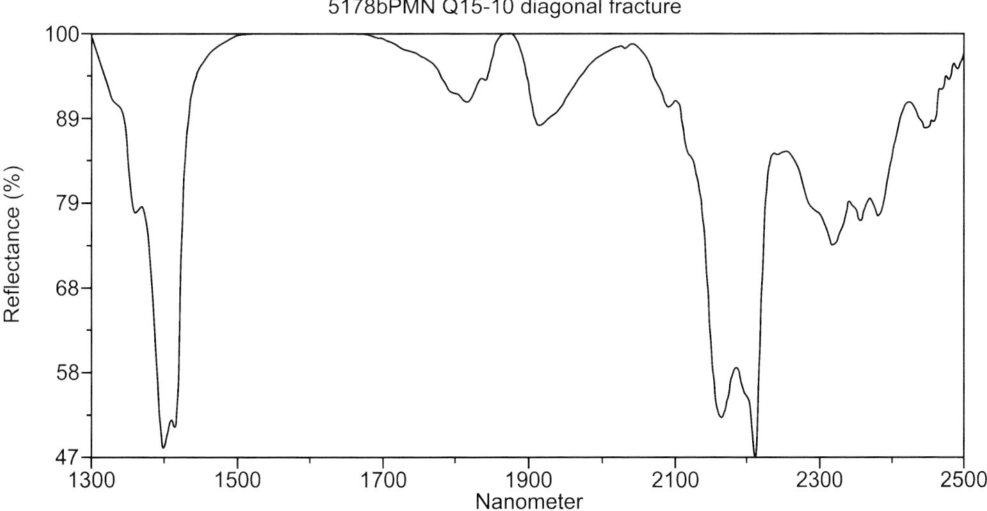

Figure 13.17. Diagonal fracture of same sample from quarry 15.

catlinite A spectrum (Figs 13.16 and 13.17). However, there are instances where different colors or observed weathering on two sides of the same rock sample did *not* produce different PIMA spectra; for example, the "red" and "cream" faces of sample 5936 in quarry 34 (lower catlinite unit, south quarry) both produced good catlinite B spectra.

The A and B variations of catlinite are a result of either 1) the original potassium content in the paleosol, and/or 2) the penetration by potassium-rich hot fluids during metamorphosis. Some of the catlinite layers at PNM are quite thin, presumably with quartzite deposits in between. We have also noticed that archaeological samples, catlinite pipes, are often thin in one dimension. Further analyses of these pipes may show how differences between the top and bottom of specific beds are reflected in the artifacts.

Conclusions

Our long-term pipestone research project has revealed new pipestone sources, has mineralogically characterized these quarries, and, through the extensive analysis of artifact collections in museums, has shown that there is considerable variation in how these sources were utilized over time. In the case of the Ohio pipestone quarries, our results have forced a reevaluation of not only the direction of "trade" and "exchange" of pipestones (from west to east rather than from east to west) but also the mixed utilization of raw materials from Ohio, northwestern Illinois, and Minnesota. Furthermore, it is now clear that major sources were not utilized continuously: the source closest to Tremper Mound, only a mile or two away, saw minimal use during the Middle Woodland period, but was used sporadically a thousand years later during Fort Ancient times. These quarries have also become the source of pipestone for fake Hopewell pipes in modern times.

In sharp contrast, our analyses of Cahokia figurine production in the Mississippian period between AD 1000–1400 shows that "red goddess" figurines were produced without exception from flint clay quarried from nearby Missouri, a source that was used only for a single 100 year period in the twelfth century. However, ultimately these highly charged objects were distributed over the Southeast and may have played a key role in spreading Cahokian ideology throughout the area. This analysis overturned earlier models that assumed the figurines were manufactured in the southeast and then traded north.

We now know that our only catlinite source, the Pipestone National Monument in Minnesota, was utilized only briefly during the Middle Woodland period, was virtually abandoned during Mississippian times, and then skyrocketed in use after *c*. AD 1300. Most of the historic period "red peace pipes" that commonly appear in early travelers accounts and in modern museum are made from catlinite. This quarry is still in use today.

The remote Wisconsin quarries (in Baraboo and Barron counties) show sporadic use during the Early Woodland period, then a peak during the Middle Woodland period. Baraboo pipestone was used again for Aztalan earspools in Mississippian times (Richards *et al.* 2005). Wisconsin pipestone, perhaps due to its hardness and limited deposits, was never a major source of pipes but seems to have been a significant source of pipestone for very localized groups.

Much more work remains to be completed on defining the range of normal variation within each major quarry. However, it is clear that the physical properties of pipestone and proximity to pipestone quarries are not sufficient to explain the idiosyncratic use of this material over time. Individual cultural preferences, including intangible factors such as value placed on exotica, must be taken into account as we reformulate models of quarry utilization and cultural interaction.

Acknowledgements

This material is based upon work supported by the National Science Foundation under Grant nos. 9971179 and 0203010. Any opinions, findings, and conclusions or recommendations expressed in this material are those of the authors and do not necessarily reflect the views of the National Science Foundation. We gratefully acknowledge the assistance and cooperation of Mark Lynott, Tom Theissen, and Douglas Scott, Midwest Archaeological Center, National Park Service in facilitating the study of the Pipestone National Monument samples.

14 Pen Pits, New Grange and Progress in the Archaeology of Extraction

David Field

Summary

The study of prehistoric quarries has an excellent pedigree that mirrors the development of the archaeological discipline. However, the very nature of quarrying means that it has its own very special problems. Recent successes point to methods of overcoming these.

Early interventions

The nature of the exhibits set within the historic fort at San Juan on the Caribbean island of Puerto Rico and visited during the SAA Conference served perfectly to emphasise the continuing, if sometimes intermittent, antagonism between the European colonial powers during the 17th to 19th centuries. In particular, it helps to stress how warfare has so often been a catalyst for change and innovation. This distrust between nations has influenced archaeology as well. In Britain, the fear of Napoleonic invasion inspired the creation of a system of detailed mapping of the countryside, the Ordnance Survey, in order to assist in the military planning of defensive strategies. Important in the survey were the earthworks of previous generations that might be returned to and utilised with military advantage. In central southern England, the work recorded the location of a series of ancient monuments, Iron Age hillforts, Bronze Age burial mounds, Romano-British settlements and medieval earthen castles and, often overlooked but of significance in the present context, a group of ancient quarries. Philip Crocker the surveyor responsible, collaborating with the antiquarian Richard C. Hoare, produced large scale plans of many of these sites a number of which were subsequently published in Hoare's landmark *Ancient Wiltshire* during the year of Napoleon's retreat from Moscow.

One of the earliest sites thus mapped was a series of quarry pits at Zeals Row, Gaspar and Bourton, all referred to as the Pen Pits, situated on either side of the River Stour along the Wiltshire-Somerset border (Fig. 14.1) and close to Hoare's estate at Stourhead. Even then parts of Pen Pits were in the process of being levelled by cultivation (Hoare 1812, 34–6) but the site was said to cover almost 300 hectares and was later considered to have incorporated up to 20,000 pits, all of which lay on a geological deposit incorporating hard cemented layers of sand known as the Upper Greensand. Hoare kept an open mind on whether the pits represented occupation hollows or quarries for obtaining stone, but noted the presence of Romano-British pottery and other artefacts found in association with them. Somewhat later, intrigued by the pits, General Pitt

Figure 14.1. Plan showing the location of quarry pits near Stourhead, Wiltshire surveyed by Philip Crocker and incorporated in the first folio of R. C. Hoare's Ancient Wiltshire in 1810.

Rivers investigated the site in greater detail. His appetite for ancient extraction remains had been sharpened when some decades earlier (as Colonel Lane Fox) he had excavated flint mine shafts at Cissbury, in Sussex, UK, where contemporary opinion held that the quarry hollows may have served a function as cattle enclosures or pig pounds (Irving 1857, 294). The excavations led him to conclude that they were of earlier date than the Iron Age hillfort that overlay them and that the pits were, in fact, for the extraction of flint (Lane Fox 1869; 1876). Concurrently, exploration of the Neolithic flint mines at Spiennes in Belgium was taking place (Briart *et al.* 1868) and, perhaps spurred on by the results here and by the discoveries of his contemporary, William Greenwell at the Neolithic site of Grimes Graves (1870), Pitt Rivers was keen to support excavation at the Pen Pits site.

The Pen Pits Exploration Committee set up by the Somerset Archaeological and Natural History Society to investigate the nature of the site carried out some initial investigations and demonstrated that with little doubt they were quarries for quern or mill stones (Anon 1879; 84; Pitt Rivers 1884; Crawford 1953, 100–2) and further excavations served to confirm this impression (Fig. 14.2). Unfortunately, while fragments of Iron Age and Romano-British pottery were recovered, providing some indication of antiquity and the archaeological relationship of an overlying medieval earthwork castle recalled the association at Cissbury, the thorny question of the date was again left open (Winwood 1884).

Recent work at Pen Pits has added little to satisfactorily resolve these matters. Few extant hollows or heaps now remain extant, though a pipeline that was recently cut through the area (Rawlings 1995) allowed part of the site to be planned and investigated by the Royal Commission on the Historical Monuments of England (Fig. 14.3). Many of the pits had been slighted by a series of medieval field lynchets and trackways demonstrating their antiquity, although others had been used in more recent times. Herein lies a problem associated with many quarry sites. The very process of extraction often destroys earlier workings. Stone or mineral has often been utilised throughout history as well as during prehistory for very similar purposes. According to Gramly (1984) and Boisvert (1992) the rhyolite at Mount Jasper, New Hampshire, USA, for example, was extracted over a period of 10,000 years, while the stone at Graig Lwyd, in Wales, UK, first used for stone axes during the Neolithic period (Warren 1919) was utilised in post medieval and modern times for buildings and wall construction. In such circumstances, this later extraction must have destroyed many of the original prehistoric quarry workings.

I have perhaps dwelt too long on this site, but historical perspective is useful in demonstrating trends in archaeology. Those investigations of the 19th century, even when sites were encountered rather serendipitously, helped establish most of the archaeological quarry-site frame works that we are used to today. Even much of our now-familiar nomenclature was adopted as a result of, for example, William Greenwell employing local gunflint miners from Brandon to excavate at the nearby Neolithic site of Grimes Graves (Greenwell 1870). Similar work took place in North America where, towards the end of the 19th century, William Holmes investigated quartzite and soapstone quarries in the District of Columbia in 1890, Novaculite in Arkansas in 1891, and Pipestone in Minnesota in 1892 (Holmes 1890a; 1890b; 1891; Meltzer and

PLAN OF THE PORTION OF PEN-PITS EXCAVATED BY LIEUT.-GEN. PITT-RIVERS, OCTOBER-NOVEMBER, 1883.

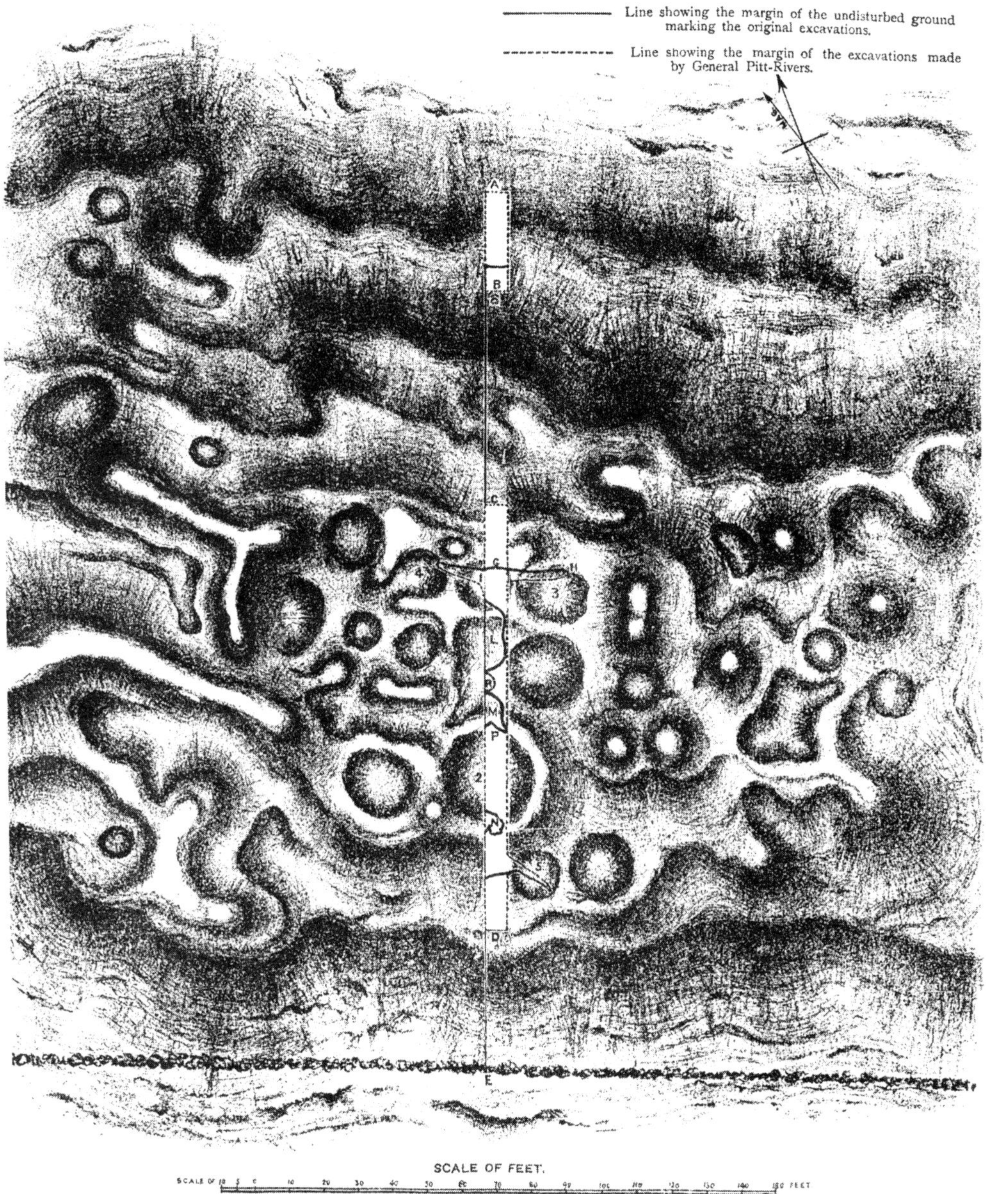

Figure 14.2. Plan of quarry pits near Stourhead, Wiltshire showing position of excavation trench as depicted by Lt Gen Pitt Rivers (from Pitt Rivers 1884).

Figure 14.3. Plan of quarry pits and field lynchets at Zeals Row, part of the Pen Pits group. While some of the pits have been partially obscured by the cultivation others appear to cut through it demonstrating a degree of longevity of extraction.© Crown copyright. NMR

Dunnell 1992), while his contemporary Lindesey Brine had been recording the presence of earthworks associated with early quarrying near Lake Superior (Brine 1966). All of these field studies and more provide a rich store for further work.

Recent work

While Lane-Fox (1869; 1876), investigated how artefacts such as *bos scapulae* might be used as mining tools at Cissbury, Holmes examined the role of hammers and other artefacts (*e.g.* 1890, 324) and his work has recently been followed up by Michael Conrow, Scott Minchak, Philip La Porta and colleagues, notably on the material excavated from the Skene Motion and Workshop in the Champlain Valley, New York (Chapter 10). Such tools are remarkably comparable across both time and space. Examination of hammers from a Bronze Age extraction site at Copa Hill, UK, for example, revealed similarities with tools from sites in northern Chile (Craddock 1994). Given that these tools are often merely battered and bruised pebbles, it may be of no surprise that their resemblances are perhaps as remarkable as their differences thus making them particularly difficult to study.

It is now almost 200 years since the production of Crocker's plan and what must be seen as the first archaeological investigation of a quarry site. It is perhaps worthy of a fresh, considered and comprehensive modern investigation, by revisiting the site using methods now available, such as ground penetrating radar and LIDAR. A multi-disciplinary approach that includes petrological analysis to investigate the distribution of artefacts and their contexts, as well as of the site itself, its variations and processes.

Quern stones have often received less attention than flint tools in archaeological study. Only now, after some 75 years of similar work on ground axes (Grimes 1970), is characterisation and sourcing of Neolithic grinding stones being investigated in Britain by the Implement Petrology Committee and not surprisingly there is much fertile ground. Important investigations by Elizabeth Bloxam, Tom Heldal and Per Storemyr at Aswan in Egypt that were described during the Puerto Rico Symposium point to a late Palaeolithic origin for an extensive grindstone extraction. The origin of the Pen Pits site remains uncertain but may have been partly destroyed or obscured by later extraction and spoil heaps.

Discussing quarry access, Ericson (1984, 3) concluded that a 'methodical framework' is needed in order to analyse stages of on-site quarry activity (see also Bradley and Edmonds 1993). Work by Margaret Brewer, Philip LaPorta and Scott Minchak in the north central Appalachians, indicates that study of petrofabrics, the effects of plate tectonics imparted in rocks and, in particular the jointing and cleavage effects, are likely to have an important effect not only on the quarrying processes taking place within the site itself, but also how methods were applied at individual sites. Adrian Burke's work in Eastern Quebec also demonstrates how the geological characteristics of the material inform the manner in which rock is transformed. In this context, methods of accessing the often difficult to retrieve rock, have been investigated by Tom Heldal, Elizabeth Bloxam and Per Storemyr, who discussed fire setting at the Symposium and concluded that in Egypt there is evidence for a sophisticated use of fire-cracking, tunnelling, creating channels to break into the quarry face (see also Willies 1994 on early historical firesetting or Pétrequin and Pétrequin 2000 on such use in Papua New Guinea). Extraction procedures can then be broken down and sub-divided. Access to soapstone at Fleur de Lys, Newfoundland, for example, according to John Erwin, occurred in four stages, quarry face preparation, pre-form isolation, pre-form extraction, and finishing. The nature of the workshop debris led to a view that children on site may be imitating the work of their parents. This is something considered at the Great Orme, UK, where some of the galleries were considered too restricted for men to pass through, reminding us that caution is required in assuming that extractive work was purely the preserve of men. Indeed, two of the three human skeletons found at flint mines in the UK are of females (Barber *et al.* 1999), while in certain anthropological accounts only females were authorised to enter mines (Flood 1983).

But there is also geographical and social context to consider. There is little evidence of extraction sites being located centrally to settlement catchments. More often they appear in 'marginal' positions and evidently in certain cases at some distance from the areas of greatest artefact use. Perhaps the first stage of the procurement process lies in the journey to the site. Such journeys might be tied in with established nomadic routes that follow game migration as Pierre Desrosiers, Noura Rahmani and Daniel Gendron working at Kangiqsualuk: a Palaeoeskimo quarry in the Eastern Arctic of Canada indicated in their contribution to the symposium, or transhumance patterns or, bearing in mind the difficulty of access of many sites, perhaps a product of rites of passage. Equally, changing social regimes are likely to have had an impact on whether certain quarries continue in use and new methods of obtaining material are adopted, as indicated may be the case in studies by Sarah Wisseman, Thomas Emerson, Randall Hughes and Kenneth Farnsworth on the pipestone material on the Midwest United States.

In the case of Catlin's efforts to get to the pipestone quarries, the journey was exploratory, but his difficulties in reaching the site were not only occasioned by navigation of the physical terrain but also negotiation of the social landscape (Matthiessen 1989). They remind us that negotiation was also needed through supernatural and metaphysical locations and that the journey may have been something of a pilgrimage, perhaps with its own rituals and customs as much as a resource gathering exercise. Indeed the process may have been a crucial component of the experience leading to knowledge in the rituals of extraction. Peter Topping's discussion of ritualised journeys and movement (Chapter 3) introduces interesting new lines of enquiry, not only into the procedures of getting there, but also into the mechanics of exchange and distribution. Considering the movement of material to the Karanovo/Tell Azmak area in northern Thrace from northeast Bulgaria, Ivan Gatsov considers the extent to which material might have been 'exchanged' and transmitted onwards from group to group or, alternatively, from a 'long distance expedition'. Such factors may, for example, point to reasons whereby clusters of ground axes of rock Group I material from southwest Britain are located in the eastern half of the country at the furthest distance from its source (McK Clough and Cummins 1988, 266 Map 2). In this case a considerable part of the route may have been by sea; a potentially dangerous procedure, which in itself is likely to have been informed and serviced by a myriad of spirits and supernatural beliefs. Certainly alpine jadeite, which reached the shores of Britain by at least 3806BC

(Hillam *et al.* 1990) and probably earlier, occasioned a sea journey and, as Gabriel Cooney pointed out in his contribution to the Symposium (unfortunately not included here), the movement of Neolithic ground axes from Teivebulliagh and elsewhere in Northern Ireland to England required likewise. Set on islands with obvious symbolic properties, the sea journey from the mainland of Ireland, to extraction points on Lambay Island and Rathlin Island also reflects the importance of the difficult expedition; particularly as in the latter case porcellanite was more easily obtained on the mainland.

However, as Cooney indicated, the local population may have perceived things slightly differently and while of symbolic significance in its own right, it may be that familiarity and abundance of the material resulted in a reduced economic importance. It was an integral part of the neighbourhood resource system for the local community, but it is this dichotomy between long distance movement of materials and the local people and their beliefs that Cooney finds interesting. The quartz scatter placed against the extraction face transformed the site and in a sense mirrors the role of quartz in certain ceremonial sites across Europe, such as in the stone rows at St Just, France, or New Grange, Ireland. Investigation of the role of quartz with its aesthetic properties of colour, sparkle and reflection, all of which might have been perceived as agents to assist with supernatural or spiritual communication, has intriguing possibilities. The reflective effects, particularly at night (*e.g.* Burl 1976; 1993), and the alignment of some stone rows, passages and entrances constructed of this material have led to suggestions of ceremonies connected with lunar symbolism. The source of the quartz at Lambay is not clear, but the enormous amount needed for the retaining wall at New Grange (Fig. 14.4) is thought to have been obtained from the Wicklow Mountains which are within striking distance of Lambay. Prehistoric quartz quarries are all but unknown. Only those at Lundfors and Nolinge, in Sweden (Lindgren 1995) and Cnoc Dubh, in the Outer Hebrides in Scotland (Ballin 2004) have been investigated in any detail and there is likely to be fruitful field investigation here.

The C^{14} date from quarries at Lambay Island along with carinated bowl sherds places it early in the Neolithic chronology of Britain and Ireland and the site takes its place alongside a number of flint mines (Barber *et al.* 1999) and quarry sites such as Graig Lwyd and Great Langdale, in the UK that, with the limited dating material available appears to occur equally early in the sequence. In each case, later activity emphasises persistent use of such locations.

In her contribution to the Symposium, Ann Teather pursued the symbolic and metaphysical theme of such extraction sites and compared flint mine shafts in the UK with natural shafts, such as that excavated at Down Farm, Dorset, UK (Green 2000). Other natural shafts – swallets or swallow holes – with prehistoric cultural deposits left at amazing depths have been recorded in the Mendip Hills (Lewis 2005) and similar shafts of no apparently obvious practical purpose may have been dug in some sort of mimicry. The carefully placed spoil platform alongside the Monkton-up-Wimborne shaft (Green 2000), for example, is difficult to explain and it raises questions regarding the beliefs and rituals involved in extraction.

Barrett (1991) emphasised how Iron Age people occupied a landscape created during the Bronze Age and the implication is that similar principles applied during earlier times, but this also helps to identify origins – some of the places that at a relatively early

Figure 14.4. New Grange in Ireland with a revetment of quartz throught to have originated in the Wicklow Mountains.

date may have assumed a role that subsequently became of ancestral importance and key among them will be those places from where rock was traditionally obtained.

However, these are by no means the earliest of extraction sites and the search for origins can be pushed back considerably further than the Neolithic. Lower Palaeolithic extraction has been reported from Pakistan (Biagi *et al.* 1997), Egypt (Vermeersch *et al.* 1995), and Israel (Barkai *et al.* 2006) and Late Palaeolithic from Poland (Bando *et al.* 1992), Hungary (Simán 1995) and elsewhere (essays in Korlin and Weisegerber 2006). Indeed we might ask just how widespread was Palaeolithic quarrying and evidently it was not simply to obtain material for cutting tools, for Elizabeth Bloxam, Tom Heldal and Per Storemyr point to a late Palaeolithic origin for grindstone extraction in Egypt at a place where cultural links might have been attached over thousands of years. Such sites are a potential source of ancestral 'dreamtime'-like stories mentioned in an earlier chapter by Peter Topping.

We should be aware that rock and soils from all parts of the landscape might have been used and exploited, not least erratic blocks, as the large number of intimate sites investigated by Philip LaPorta and Scott Minchak demonstrated. Even small or apparently insignificant deposits of material such as Chalosse flint in southern France studied by Pierre Chalard will have been important to hunter gatherer groups and study of them might assist in defining territorial areas. Tracing such sites is a difficult business, although in the UK, the Implement Petrology Committee have achieved a significant degree of success having analysed thousands of Neolithic axes and assigned them to one of over 25 identified rock sources, termed 'axe factories'. Elsewhere, type-sets of flint material are held by a number of institutions, but a significant development are the extensive descriptions established by Rengert Elburg and Paul van der Kroft now to be found online at www.flintsource.net.

Application of Neutron Activation Analysis is increasingly becoming a key role in tracing the parent source of cultural material, for example, in tracing the source of Ramah Chert and Misstasini Quartzite where, having expressed suitable caution, and after appropriate statistical analysis David Le Blanc and colleagues met with a significant degree of success. The method was also used to distinguish between sub-sources of obsidian in the Mount Arci area of Sardinia by Robert Tykot, Carlo Luglie, Teddie Setzer, Guiseppa Tanda and Ronald Webb. It is probably too early to judge the success of the renewal of efforts in the Trace Element Analysis of flint being carried out but the British Museum (Craddock and Cowell 2004: also see Craddock et al. 1983) but results appear encouraging. Work on rock Group I by Mik Markham in the UK also holds out promise, while the use of reflectance spectroradiometry for characterising jadeite axes has had spectacular and far reaching success with the discovery of sources in the Piedmont by Pierre Petrequin and colleagues (*e.g.* Petrequin *et al.* 2006). In the US, artefacts in the upper Mississippi valley manufactured from Hixton silicified sandstone can to be attributed to a single geological source, the Silver Mound quarry complex where work by Robert Boszhardt and Dillon Carr provides a framework for understanding the relationship between discarded tools and the quarry workshops.

The question of contemporary selection of material is difficult. For long it was held that the raison d'être of the Grimes Graves flint mines was the 'floorstone' situated at the base of the shafts, but it is now clear that other seams were widely utilized as well, especially those easy of access, perhaps where they outcrop at the surface on a valley slope. It has also been pointed out that the better seams of flint in the Sussex area were actually ignored and mines developed elsewhere leading to a view that the location itself might be of greater significance than precisely what was obtained from it. However, there were practical considerations also. Patrick Julig and Darrel Long recount how size is ultimately of importance in ensuring adequate core sizes for biface pre-form and blade blank production and that the glassier Sheguiandah Paleo-Indian material, although difficult to quarry, was nevertheless targeted in order to achieve this end.

New directions

The papers in this volume and the conference that spawned it cover a wide geographical area – sites in North America, Europe and the Middle East are all covered. Unfortunately it cannot claim to be global either in space or in depth of material. There are, for example, no contributions from the continents of Asia, Australia, Africa or South America. However, it serves to bring together a significant amount of fresh data, frames some new lines of enquiry and provides a signpost toward some new directions.

A common vocabulary of extraction seems to be something to strive for. Even in Europe there are different expressions for parts of the flint mining chaîne operatoìre. The pillar mines of Poland (*e.g.* Borkowski 1995), for example, would be referred to as galleries in southern England (references in Barber *et al.* 1999). A valiant attempt has been made at provision of a glossary for the earthworks of medieval extraction sites

(Cranstone 1994) though for the moment it is not clear how far it has international approval. All this is made more difficult as the end products, the artefacts, are often known by different terms as well.

While in preparation of this book, the proceedings of the Bochum International Flint Symposium were published (Korlin and Weisgerber eds 2006). An enormous volume that successfully builds upon the catalogues of prehistoric extraction sites in Europe published in 1980 (Weisgerber ed.; republished 1999) and 1995 (Lech ed.). One important task will be to extend the area covered and prepare inventories for other continents.

While the state of fieldwork and research into prehistoric quarries is healthy, some concern might be expressed regarding the conservation of extraction sites. At Widan-el-Faras in Egypt, for example, modern quarries were destroying an important ancient quarry, but investigation and effort by Per Storemyr, Tom Heldal and Elizabeth Bloxam resulted in securing World Heritage Site status for the site. Nevertheless, it is just one of three prehistoric quarry sites now carrying that status. Many sites have, or have had, new threats to contend with, cultivation of course at, for example Church Hill, Findon, UK (Barber *et al.* 1999), transport routes, for example, Jablines, France (Bostyn and Lanchon 1992), not to mention the threat from private collection and looting at such sites as Great Langdale, UK, where artefacts lie loose on the surface. Only three of twenty obsidian quarries visited by Stocker and Cobean (1984) in Mexico and Guatemala were reported as undamaged by looters. In the US another problem has surfaced, that of the rise in interest of traditional crafts, where modern flint knappers seeking good quality material sometimes utilize that from ancient quarry sites. The obsidian from near Adamsville in the Mineral Mountains of Utah is one such, where great stretches of ancient and modern debitage are intermixed.

Per Storemyr, Tom Heldal and Elizabeth Bloxam and their important and successful Quarryscapes programme emphasises how quarry 'landscapes' as distinct from small easily defined sites are in general poorly documented and unregistered (www.quarryscapes.no). Like monument protection systems in many countries, the local system in Egypt is unable to deal with 'landscapes' as distinct from 'sites' and there is little vision of conservation of ancient quarries. Programmes of education that enhance ancient quarry recognition are undoubtedly important, particularly when remains simply appear as a series of earthworks or apparently amorphous undulations on the surface.

There are other successes. Museums or visitor centres have been established at Mount Arci, Sardinia where, as reported by Robert Tykot and colleagues, the obsidian workshops cover many hectares and Flint Ridge, in the US, Spiennes, in Belgium and Grimes Graves and Great Orme in the UK also have centres. Other visitor facilities are present at Rijckholt-St. Geertruid, Netherlands (viewing tunnel), Krzemionki, Poland (accessible shaft) while others such as Mauer-Antonshohe, Vienna, Austria have information boards, all of immense importance in the study of the History of Technology. Offsite the Deutschen Bergbau-Museum at Bochum, Germany is one of the few mining museums that pay serious attention to prehistoric material.

References

Agricola, G. 1950 [1556] *De Re Metallica*. translated by Herbert C. Hoover and Lou H. Hoover. New York: Dover Publications.

Allard, M., Chalard, P. and Martin, H. 2005 'Témoins de mobilité humaine aux Peyrugues (Orniac, Lot) durant le Paléolithique supérieur : signification spatio-temporelle'. In: J. Jaubert and M. Barbaza (dirs.) *Territoires, déplacements, mobilité, échanges pendant la Préhistoire*, 219–232. Actes du colloque du CTHS Terres et Hommes du Sud, Toulouse 9–14 avril 2001, Paris: Ed. du CTHS.

Allen, R. O., Allen, K. K., Holland, C. G., and Fitzhugh, W. W. 1978 'Utilisation of Soapstone in Labrador by Indians, Eskimos and Norse'. *Nature* 271, (5642), 237–239.

Allen, R., Hamroush, H., Nagle, C. L. and Fitzhugh, W. W. 1984 'Use of Rare Earth Element Analysis to Study the Utilization and Procurement of Soapstone Along the Labrador Coast'. *ACS Advances in Chemistry Series* 205. Archaeological Chemistry III, American Chemical Society.

Amick, D. S. 1982 *Topsy: Late Archaic Biface Manufacture on the Buffalo River, Southwestern Highland Rim, Tennessee*. Department of Anthropology, University of Tennessee. Submitted to Tennessee Department of Transportation, Contract No. BRZ 9100(2)-91-031-0303-94. Copies available from the Department of Anthropology, University of Tennessee, Knoxville.

Anders, E. and Grevesse, N. 1989 'Abundances of the elements: Meteoritic and solar', *Geochimica Cosmochimica Acta* 53, 197–214.

Anderson, D. G., Miller, D. S., Yerka, S. J. and Faught, M. K. 2005 'Paleoindian Database of the Americas: 2005 Status Report' *Current Research in the Pleistocene*, 22, 91–92.

Anon. 1879 'Report of the Pen Pits Exploration Committee' *Proceedings Somerset Archaeological and Natural History Society* 25, 7–17.

Anon. 1884 'The result of further excavations at Pen Pits' *Proceedings of the Somersetshire Archaeological and Natural History Society* 30, 149–152.

Arnold, D. 1991 *Building in Egypt. Pharaonic Stone Masonry*. New York and Oxford: Oxford University Press.

Aston, B. 1994 *Ancient Egyptian Stone Vessels*. Heidelberg: Heidelberger Orientverlag.

Aston, B., Harrell, J. A., Shaw, I. M. E. 2000 'Stones' (Chap. 2), in P. T. Nicholson and I. Shaw (eds) *Ancient Egyptian Materials and Technology*, 5–77. Cambridge: Cambridge University Press.

Astruc, J-G., Coustou, J-C., Cubaynes, R., Galharague, J., Lorblanchet, M., Marcouly, R., Pélissié, Th. and Rey, J. 1994 *Notice de la carte géologique de la France, feuille de Gramat* 833, 69.

BRGM 2003 Carte géologique de la France à l'échelle du millionième, 6e édition révisée, 2 cartes couleur.

Ballin, T. B. 2004 'The worked quartz vein at Cnoc Dubh, Uig parish, Isle of Lewis, Western Isles: Presentation and discussion of a small prehistoric quarry' *Scottish Archaeological Internet Report* 11, 2004. www.sair.org.uk

Bamforth, D. B. 1986 'Technological Efficiency and Tool Curation' *American Antiquity* 51, 1, 38–50.

Bamforth, D. B. and Bleed, P. 1997 'Technology, flaked stone technology, and risk' in C. M. Barton and G. A. Clark (eds) *Rediscovering Darwin: Evolutionary Theory and Archaeological Explanation*, 109–139 Archaeological Papers of the American Anthropological Association no. 7, American Anthropological Association, Washington D.C.

Bando, C., Dagnan-Ginter, A., Holen, S., Kozlowski, J., Montet-White, A., Pawlikowski, M. and Sobczyk, K. 1992 'Wolowice: Flint extraction and processing site'. *Recherches Archeologiques de 1990*, 1–25. Krakow: Institute of Archaeology.

Barber, M., Field, D. and Topping, P. 1999 *The Neolithic Flint Mines of England*. Swindon: Royal Commission on the Historical Monuments of England / English Heritage.

Barkai, R., Gopher, A. and LaPorta, P. 2006 'Middle Pleistocene landscape of extraction: quarry and workshop complexes in northern Israel'. In N. Goren-Inbar and G. Sharon (eds) *Axe Age Acheulian Tool-making from Quarry to Discard.* London and Oakville: Equinox Publishing.

Barrett, J. 1999 'The mythical landscapes of the British Iron Age', in W. Ashmore and A. B. Knapp (eds) *Archaeologies of Landscape: contemporary perspectives,* 253–68. Oxford: Blackwell.

Basso, K. H. 1996 *Wisdom Sits in Place: Landscape and Language among the Western Apache* Albuquerque: University of New Mexico Press.

Baxter, M. J. 2003 *Statistics in archaeology*. New York: Arnold.

Beadnell, H. 1905 *The Topography and Geology of the Faiyum Province, Egypt*. Cairo.

Beaubien, P. L. 1983 'Notes on the Archaeology of Pipestone National Monument. In The Red Pipestone Quarry of Minnesota: Archaeological and Historical Reports, compiled by A. Woolworth,' *Minnesota Archaeologist* 42 (whole volume), 37–80.

Biagi, P., Negrino, F., Starnini, E. 1997 'New data on the Harrapan flint quarries of the Rohri Hills (Sind-Pakistan)'. In R. Schild and Z. Sulgostowska (eds) *Man and Flint*, 29–39. Warsaw: Institute of Archaeology and Ethnography, Polish Academy of Sciences.

Binford, L. R. 1979 'Organization and Formation Processes: Looking at Curated Technologies' *Journal of Anthropological Research* 35, 255–273.

Binford, L. R. 1980 'Willow Smoke and Dogs' Tails: Hunter-Gatherer Settlement Systems and Archaeological Site Formation' *American Antiquity* 45, 1, 4–20.

Bleed, P. 1986 'The Optimal Design of Hunting Weapons: Maintainability or Reliability', *American Antiquity* 51, 4, 737–747.

Bloxam, E. 2000 'Transportation of Quarried Hard Stone from Lower Nubia to Giza during the Egyptain Old Kingdom'. In A. McDonald and C. Riggs (eds) *Current Research in Egyptology 2000*, 19–27. BAR International Series 909. Oxford: Archaeopress.

Bloxam, E. 2003 *The Organisation, Transportation and Logistics of Hard Stone Quarrying in the Egyptian Old Kingdom: A Comparative Study,* PhD Thesis, Institute of Archaeology, University College London.

Bloxam, E. 2006 'From complex data to simple transmission: modelling the significance of ancient quarry landscapes', *Proceedings of the first QuarryScapes symposium,* Antalya, Turkey, 27–29. Available at: http://www.quarryscapes.no/workshops.php

Bloxam, E. and Heldal, T. 2007. 'The industrial landscape of the Northern Faiyum Desert as a World Heritage Site: modelling 'outstanding universal value' of 3rd millennium BC stone quarrying in Egypt', *World Archaeology* 39, 3, 305–323.

Bloxam, E. and Kelany, A. 2007 'Chapter 10: The material culture of the West Bank quarry landscape: constructing the social context'. In E. Bloxam, T. Heldal and P. Storemyr (eds) *Characterisation of complex quarry landscapes: an example from the West Bank quarries, Aswan.* QuarryScapes Report. Trondheim: Geological Survey of Norway.

Bloxam, E. and Storemyr, P. 2002 'Old Kingdom Basalt Quarrying Activities at Widan El-Faras, Northern Faiyum Desert', *Journal of Egyptian Archaeology* 88, 23–36.

Bloxam, E. and Storemyr, P. 2005 'Recent Investigations in the ancient quarries of Gebel Gulab and Gebel Tingar, Aswan', *Egyptian Archaeology* 26, 37–40.

Bloxam, E., Heldal, T. and Storemyr, P. (eds) 2007 *Characterisation of complex quarry landscapes: an example from the West Bank quarries, Aswan,* QuarryScapes Report. Trondheim: Geological Survey of Norway.

Bloxam, E., Storemyr, P. and Heldal, T. 2009 'Hard stone quarrying in the Egyptian Old Kingdom (3rd millennium BC): Rethinking the social organisation', in Y. Maniatis (ed.) ASMOSIA 7, Proceedings of the 7th International Conference of the Association for the Study of Marble and other Stones in Antiquity, Thassos, Greece, 15–20 September 2003. *Bulletin de correspondance Hellenique supplement* 51, 187–201.

Boisvert, R. A. 1992 'The Mount Jasper lithic source, Berlin, New Hampshire: National register of historic places nomination and commentary'. *Archaeology of Eastern North America* 20, 151–166.

Boivin, N. 2004 'From veneration to exploitation: human engagement with the mineral world'. In N. Boivin and M. A. Owoc (eds), *Soils, Stones and Symbols: Cultural Perceptions of the Mineral World,* 1–29. London: UCL Press.

Bon, F. 2002 'L'Aurignacien entre Mer et Océan. Réflexions sur l'unité des phases anciennes de l'Aurignacien dans le sud de la France', *Mémoire de la Société Préhistorique Française,* XXIX, 253.

Bon, F., Chauvaud, D., Dartiguepeyrou, S., Gardère, P. and Mensan, R. 1996 'La caractérisation du silex de Chalosse'. In *Hommage à Dominique Buisson. Antiquités Nationales* 28, 33–38.

Bon, F., Gambier, D., Ferrier, C. and Gardère, P. 1998 'Gisement de Brassempouy (Landes): les recherches de 1995 à 1997, bilan et perspectives'. *Bulletin de la Société de Borda* 449, (2ème trimestre 1998), 203–222.

Booth, D. L. and Koldehoff, B. 1999 'Emergency Watershed Protection Archaeological Survey Project' *Illinois Transportation Archaeological Research Program, Research Report No. 62*. University of Illinois at Urbana-Champaign.

Bordes J-G., Bon F. and Le Brun-Ricalens F. 2005 'Le transport des matières premières lithiques à l'Aurignacien entre le Nord et le Sud de l'Aquitaine: faits attendus, faits nouveaux'. In J. Jaubert and M. Barbaza (dirs.) *Territoires, déplacements, mobilité, échanges pendant la Préhistoire,* 185–198. Actes du colloque du CTHS *Terres et Hommes du Sud*, Toulouse 9–14 avril 2001. Paris: Ed. du CTHS.

Bordes, F. and Crabtree, D. 1969 'The Corbiac Blade Technique and Other Experiments'. *Tebiwa* 12(2), 1–21.

Borkowski, W. 1995 *Krzemionki Mining Complex: Deposit Management System* Warsaw: Panstwowe Muzeum Archeologiczne.

Bostyn, F. and Lanchon, Y. 1992 *Jablines: Le Haut Chateau. Une minière de silex au Néolithique* Paris: Editions de la Maison des Sciences de l'homme.

Boszhardt, R. F. 1998 'Additional Western Lithics for Hopewell Bifaces in the Upper Mississippi River Valley', *Plains Anthropologist* 43, 165, 275–286.

Boszhardt, R. F. 1998 *An Archaeological Survey of an Orthoquartzite District in West-Central Wisconsin*, Reports of Investigations no. 306, Mississippi Valley Archaeology Center, University of Wisconsin – La Crosse.

Boszhardt, R. F. and Gundersen, J. N. 2001 'X-Ray Powder Diffraction Analysis of Early and Middle Woodland Red Pipes from Wisconsin' *Midcontinental Journal of Archaeology* 26.

Bousman, C. B. 2005 'Coping with risk: Later Stone Age technological strategies at Blydefontein Rock Shelter, South Africa' *Journal of Anthropological Archaeology* 24, 3, 193–226.

Bowan, H. R., Asaro, F. and Perlman, I. 1973 'Compositional variation in obsidian sources and the archaeological implications', *Archaeometry* 15, 123–127.

Bown, T. M. and Harrell, J. A. 1995 'The oldest paved road, Faiyum Depression, Egypt', *The Ostracon* 6, no. 3, 1–4.

Bradley, B. A. 1975 'Lithic Reduction Sequences: A Glossary and Discussion' In E. Swanson (ed.) *Lithic Technology: Making and Using Stone Tools*, 5–13. The Hague: Mouton Publishers.

Bradley, R. 2000 *An Archaeology of Natural Places*. London: Routledge.

Bradley, R. and Edmonds, M. 1993 *Interpreting the axe trade: Production and exchange in Neolithic Britain*. Cambridge: Cambridge University Press.

Bressy, C., Burke, A., Chalard, P. and Martin, H. (eds) 2006 *Notions de territoire et de mobilité : exemples de l'Europe et des premières nations en Amérique du Nord avant le contact européen*, 169.

Actes deux sessions présentées au Colloque de l'EAA, Lyon, 8–12 septembre 2004, ERAUL, 116, Liège.

Briart, A., Cornet, F. and de Lehaie, A. H. 1868 'Rapport sur les découvertes géologiques et archéologiques faites à Spiennes en 1867'. *Mémoires ... de la Société des Sciences, des Arts ... du Hainaut, année 1866–7*. Mons.

Brine, L. 1966 *The Ancient earthworks and temples of the American Indians* (first published 1894) Royston: Oracle Publishing.

Briois, F., Chalard, P., Grégoire, S., Lacombe, S., Servelle, Ch., Simonnet, R., Jarry, M. and Sevegnes, L. 1999 'Lithothèque des matières premières siliceuses. Région Midi-Pyrénées', *Bilan Scientifique de la Région Midi-Pyrénées*, S.R.A. de Midi-Pyrénées, 1998, 242–243.

Brown, I. W. 1989 'The Calumet Ceremony in the Southeast and its Archaeological Manifestations' *American Antiquity* 54, 311–331.

Brumbach, H. J. and Weinstein, J. 1999 'Material Selection, Rejection, and Failure at Flint Mine Hill: An Eastern New York State Chert Quarry', *Northeast Anthropology* 58, 1–25.

Brumm, A. 2004 An axe to grind: Symbolic considerations of stone axe use in Ancient Australia. In N. Boivin and M. A. Owoc (eds) *Soils, Stones and Symbols: Cultural Perceptions of the Mineral World*, 143–163. London: UCL Press.

Bryan, K. 1950 *Flint Quarries – The Sources of Tools and, at the Same Time, the Factories of the American Indian*. Papers of the Peabody Museum of American Archaeology and Ethnology. 17, No. 3. Cambridge: Harvard University.

Buckmaster, M. M. 1989 'A Report on the Early Component at the Paquette Site, Marquette County, Michigan', *The Wisconsin Archaeologist* 70(4), 430–462.

Buckmaster, M. M. and Pauquette, J. R. 1988 'The Gorto Site: Preliminary Report on a Late Paleo-Indian Site in Marquette County, Michigan' *Wisconsin Archeologist* 69, 2, 101–124.

Buisson, D. 1996 'Brassempouy : présentation du site et problèmes posés par les fouilles récentes'. In *Pyrénées Préhistoriques Arts et Sociétés*, 423–437. Actes du 118e Congrès National des Sociétés Historiques et Scientifiques. Pau, 25–29 octobre 1993. Ed. C.T.H.S.

Burke, A. L. 2002 'Les carrières du Paléoindien récent à La Martre et la géologie du chert du mélange de Cap-Chat', *Recherches amérindiennes au Québec* 32, 91–99.

Burke, A. L. and Chalifoux. E. 1998 'Stratégie d'acquisition du chert Touladi et production lithique durant la période du Sylvicole au Témiscouata', in R. Tremblay (ed.) *L'éveilleur et l'ambassadeur: Essais archéologiques et ethnohistoriques en hommage à Charles A. Martij*, 33–51. Montreal: Recherches amérindiennes au Québec.

Burl, A. 1976 *The stone circles of the British Isles*. New Haven and London: Yale University Press.

Burl, A. 1993 *From Carnac to Callanish*. New Haven and London: Yale University Press.

Bushnell, D. I. 1904 *The Cahokia and Surrounding Mound Groups*. Cambridge, Massachusetts: Peabody Museum of American Archaeology and Ethnology, Harvard University, Vol. III, No. 1.

Callahan, E. 2000 *The Basics of Biface Knapping in the Eastern Fluted Point Tradition: A Manual for Flintknappers and Lithic Analysts*. Fourth edition. Lynchburg VA: Piltdown Productions.

Capdeville, J-P., Gineste, M-C., Turq, A. and Vergain, P. 1997 *Notice explicative, carte géologique de la France* (1/50 000), feuille Hagetmau (978). Orléans: BRGM, 70.

Card, K. D. 1978 'Geology of the Sudbury-Manitoulin area, Districts of Sudbury and Manitoulin'. *Ontario Geological Survey Report* 166, 238. Accompanied by Map 2360, scale 1 inch to 2 miles (1:126 720), and 4 charts.

Carr, D. H. 2004 *The Paleoindian Use of Hixton Silicified Sandstone: Examining the Organization of Western Great Lakes Paleoindian Lithic Raw Material Procurement Strategies*. MA Thesis, London: University of Western Ontario.

Carr, D. H. 2005 'The Organization of Late Paleoindian Lithic Procurement Strategies in Western Wisconsin', *Midcontinental Journal of Archaeology* 30, 1, 3–36.

Carr, D. H. and Boszhardt, R. F. 2003 'The Kriesel Cache: A Late Paleoindian Biface Cache from Western Wisconsin', *Plains Anthropologist* 48, 3, 225–236.

Carr, D. H. and Boszhardt, R. F. 2005 *National Historic Landmark Nomination for the Silver Mound Archaeological District*, Unpublished manuscript on file at the Mississippi Valley Archaeology Center, University of Wisconsin-La Crosse.

Carr, P. J. (ed.) 1994 *The Organization of North American Prehistoric Chipped Stone Tool Technologies*, International Monographs in Prehistory, Archaeological Series no. 7, Ann Arbor.

Catlin, G. 1973 [1844] *Letters and Notes on the Manners, Customs, and Conditions of the North American Indians.* 2 vols. New York: Dover Publications, Inc.

Caton-Thompson, G. and Gardner, E. W. 1934 *The Desert Fayum*, vols 1–2. London: Royal Anthropological Institute.

Cérane, Inc. 1984 *Deux millénaires d'archives archéologiques: Occupations préhistoriques, historique et contemporaines de la région de Washidimi, Réservoir LG-2, Baie James*, Unpublished repport, Ministère des Affaires culturelles, Direction régionale du Nouveau-Québec, Québec.

Chalard, P. à paraître 'L'industrie du Magdalénien ancien: caractérisation des silex'. In E. Ladier (dir.) *Le gisement magdalénien ancien de l'abri Gandil à Bruniquel (Tarn-et-Garonne).*

Chalard, P. and Briois, F. 2002 'Caractérisation des matières premières du gisement mésolithique d'Al Poux', In C. Amiel and L-A. Lelouvier (coords) *Gisements post-glaciaires en Bas-Quercy. Variabilité des espaces et des statuts de deux occupations mésolithiques sauveterriennes de plein air*, 49–55. Archives d'Ecologie Préhistorique, Centre d'Anthropologie et INRAP Ed., Toulouse.

Chalard, P. and Servelle, C. 2003 'La circulation des matières premières lithiques au cours de la Préhistoire', In V. Rousset and M. Vaginay (coords) *Histoire des sites, Histoires des hommes. Découvertes archéologiques réalisées lors de la construction de l'autoroute A20 en Quercy*, ASF, DRAC, INRAP, Archéologies, Editions du Rouergue.

Chalard, P., Briois, F., Lacombe, S. and Servelle, Ch. 1995 'Lithothèque régionale. Midi-Pyrénées', *Bilan Scientifique de la Région Midi-Pyrénées*, S.R.A. de Midi-Pyrénées, 1994, 228–229.

Chalard, P., Guillermin, P. and Jarry, M. 2006 'Acquisition et exploitation des silex allochtones au Gravettien: l'exemple de la couche E du gisement des Fieux (Lot, France)', In C. Bressy, A. Burke, P. Chalard, S. Lacombe, and H. Martin (eds) *Notions de territoire et de mobilité en Préhistoir : exemples de l'Europe et des premières nations en Amérique du nord avant le contact européen*, 29–40. Actes deux sessions présentées au Colloque de l'EAA, Lyon, 8–12 septembre 2004, ERAUL, 116, Liège.

Chalard, P., Jarry, M., Lelouvier, L.-A., Marlière, P., Mourre, V. and Valdeyron, N. 2002 'L'industrie lithique du gisement mésolithique du Camp de Jouanet', In C. Amiel and L-A. Lelouvier (coords) *Gisements post-glaciaires en Bas-Quercy. Variabilité des espaces et des statuts de deux occupations mésolithiques sauveterriennes de plein air*, 122–177. Archives d'Ecologie Préhistorique, Centre d'Anthropologie et INRAP Ed., Toulouse.

Chalard, P., Morala, A. and Turq, A. in preparation a, 'Caractérisation des silex de l'industrie solutréenne', In J. Clottes, J-P. Giraud, and P. Chalard (dirs) *Diversités et identités des groupes solutréens et badegouliens en Quercy. L'exemple de l'Abri du Cuzoul à Vers (Lot)*, Publication prévue dans les DAF.

Chalard, P., Morala, A. and Turq, A. in preparation b, 'Caractérisation des silex des industries badegouliennes', In J. Clottes, J-P. Giraud and P. Chalard, (dirs) *Diversités et identités des groupes solutréens et badegouliens en Quercy. L'exemple de l'Abri du Cuzoul à Vers (Lot)*, Publication prévue dans les DAF.

Chalifoux, É. 1999a 'Late Paleoindian Occupation in a Coastal Environment: A Perspective from La Martre, Gaspé Peninsula, Quebec', *Northeast Anthropology* 57, 69–79.

Chalifoux, É. 1999b 'Les occupations paléoindiennes récentes en Gaspésie: résultats de la recherche à La Martre', *Recherches amérindiennes au Québec* 29, 77–93.

Chalifoux, É. and Tremblay, R. 1998 *Entre les Monts Chic-Chocs et la Mer de Goldthwait: L'adaptation des premiers occupants de la vallée de La Martre (synthèse archéologique 1995–1997).* Report submitted to the Conseil régional de concertation et de développement, la Corporation du centre d'interpretation d'archéologie préhistorique de la Gaspésie à La Martre, and the Ministère de la Culture du Québec.

Chapdelaine, C. (ed.) 1994 'Il y a 8000 ans à Rimouski: Paléoécologie et archéologie d'un site de la culture Plano', *Recherches amérindiennes au Québec* 22. Montreal.

Clark, C. P. 1989 'Plano Tradition Lithics from the Upper Peninsula of Michigan', *The Michigan Archaeologist* 35, 88–112.

Clarke, W. G. (ed.) 1915 Report on the excavations at Grime's Graves, Weeting, Norfolk, March-May 1914. London: Prehistoric Society of East Anglia.

Coles, J. 1979 *Experimental Archaeology*. New York: Academic Press.

Collins, M. B. 1999 *Clovis Blade Technology: A Comparative Study of the Keven Davis Cache, Texas*. Texas Archaeology and Ethnohistory Series. Austin: The University of Texas Press.

Connally, G. G. 1973 *Surficial Geology of the Glens Falls Region, New York*. New York State Museum Map and Chart Series 23.

Conrad, L. A. and Nolan, D. J. 1991 *Some Preliminary Observations on the Occurrence of Catlinite in West Central Illinois*, paper presented at the 36th Annual Midwest Archaeological Conference, La Crosse, Wisconsin.

Costamagno, S. 2006 'Territoires de chasse paléolithiques: des méthodes d'études à l'application archéologique'. In C. Bressy, A. Burke, P. Chalard and H. Martin (eds) *Notions de territoire et de mobilité: exemples de l'Europe et des premières nations en Amérique du Nord avant le contact européen*, 63–70. Actes deux sessions présentées au Colloque de l'EAA, Lyon, 8–12 septembre 2004, ERAUL, 116, Liège.

Crabtree, D. E. 1972 *Introduction to Flintworking*. Occasional Papers of the Idaho State University Museum, No. 28. Pocatello.

Craddock, B. R. 1994 'Notes on stone hammers', in T. D. Ford and L. Willies (eds) *Mining Before Powder* Matlock Bath: Peak District Mines Historical Society.

Craddock, P. and Cowell, M. 2004 'Cutting edge', *British Archaeology* 79, 18–21.

Craddock, P. T., Cowell, M. L., Leese, M. N. and Hughes, M. J. 1983 'The trace element composition of polished flint axes as an indicator of source', *Archaeometry* 25, 135–63

Cranstone, D. 1994 'Early surface features of mining: towards a typology'. In T. Ford and L. Willies (eds) *Mining before Powder.* Matlock Bath: Peak District Mines Historical Society.

Crawford, O. G. S. 1953 *Archaeology in the field.* London: Dent.

Cubaynes, R., Faure, Ph., Hantzpergue, P., Pélissié, Th. and Rey, J. 1989 'Le Jurassique du Quercy. Unités lithostratigraphiques, stratigraphie et organisation séquentielle, évolution sédimentaire', *Géologie de la France*, 3, 33–62. Paris.

Cubaynes, R., Ruget, C. and Rey, J. 1989 'Essai de caractérisation des prismes de dépôt d'origine eustatique par les associations de foraminifères benthiques: exemple de la bordure est du Bassin aquitain', *C. R. Acad. Sci., Paris* 308, 1517–152.

Curwen, E. and Curwen, E. C. 1926 'Harrow Hill Flint-Mine Excavation, 1924–5', *Sussex Archaeological Collections* LXVII, 101–138.

Custer, J. F., Cavallo, J. A. and Stewart, R. M. 1983 'Lithic Procurement and Paleo-Indian Settlement Patterns on the Middle Atlantic Costal Plain' *North American Archaeologist* 4, 4, 263–275.

Dartiguepeyrou, S. 1995 'L'industrie lithique gravettienne du Chantier I à Brassempouy. Approche technologique', *Mémoire de maîtrise de l'Université de Paris I Panthéon-Sorbonne*, 99.

De Putter, T. and Karlshausen, C. 1992 Les pierres utilisées dans la sculpture et l'architecture de l'Égypte pharaonique. Guide pratique illlustré. Connaissance de l'Égypte ancienne, Bruxelles.

Delfaud, J. 1970 'Essai sur la géologie dynamique du domaine aquitano-pyrénéen durant le Jurassique et le Crétacé inférieur', *Thèse Doc. Sc. Nat., Bordeaux*.

Deller, D. B. and Ellis, C. J. 1984 'Crowfield: A Preliminary Report on a Probable Paleo-Indian Cremation in Southwestern Ontario' *Archaeology of Eastern North America* 12, 41–57.

Demars, P-Y. 1982 *L'utilisation du silex au Paléolithique supérieur: choix, approvisionnement, circulation, 253.* Cahiers du Quaternaire, no. 5, CNRS, Bordeaux.

Demars, P-Y. 1994 *L'économie du silex au Paléolithique supérieur dans le nord de l'Aquitaine,* 819. Thèse de doctorat d'état, Université de Bordeaux I.

Denton, D. 1998 'From the source, to the margins and back. Notes on Mistassini quartzite and archaeology in the area of the colline Blanche'. In R. Tremblay (dir.) *L'éveilleur et l'ambassadeur. Essais archéologiques et ethnohistoriques en hommage à Charles A. Martijn,* 17–32. *Paléo-Québec,* no. 27, Recherches amérindiennes au Québec, Montréal.

Dockall, J. D. and Shafer, H. J. 1993 'Testing the Producer-Consumer Model for Santa Rita Corozal, Belize', *Latin American Antiquity* 4, 158–179.

Drier, R. W. 1961a 'Michigan's Most Ancient History is America's Prehistoric Copper Mine'. In R. W. Drier and O. J. Du Temple (eds) *Prehistoric Copper Mining in the Lake Superior Region,* 19–25. Published privately by the authors.

Drier, R. W. 1961b 'Pre-Historic Mining in the Copper Country'. In, R. W. Drier and O. J. Du Temple (eds) *Prehistoric Copper Mining in the Lake Superior Region,* 27–31. Published privately by the authors.

Ducasse, S. 2003 L'industrie lithique badegoulienne de la couche 6 du Cuzoul de vers (Lot). L'exploitation des matériaux siliceux au Badegoulien récent, 300. Mémoire de maîtrise de l'Université de Toulouse-le-Mirail.

Ducasse, S. and Lelouvier, L-A. à paraître 'Technologie et typologie des séries en silex au Badegoulien'. In J. Clottes, J-P. Giraud and P. Chalard, (dirs) *Diversités et identités des groupes solutréens et badegouliens en Quercy. L'exemple de l'abri du Cuzoul de Vers (Lot).*

Dumais, P., Larouche, C. and Poirier, J. 1996 'Les Sites Paléoindiens Récents de La Martre et de Mitis: Réflexions sur le Peuplement Plano de l'Est du Québec', *Archéologiques* 10, 54–76.

Ebright, C. A. 1987 'Quartzite Petrography and Its Implications for Prehistoric Use and Archaeological Analysis', *Archaeology of Eastern North America* 15, 29–45.

Edmonds, M. 2001 'Lithic Exploitation and Use'. In D. R. Brothwell and A. M. Pollard (eds), *Handbook of Archaeological Sciences,* 461–470. Wiley, New York.

Egypt State of the Environment Report 2004. Available at: ww.eeaa.gov.eg/English/info/report_soe2005.asp

El-Din, G. E. 2006 'Parliament to scrutinise Toshka', *Al-Ahram Weekly,* 5–12 April 2006, no. 789.

Ellis, C. J. 1989 'The Explanation of Northeastern Paleoindian Lithic Procurement Patterns' in C. J. Ellis and J. C. Lothrop (eds), *Eastern Paleoindian Lithic Resource Use,* 139–164. Westview: Boulder.

Ellis, C. J. and Deller, D. B. 2000 *An Early Paleo-Indian Site Near Parkhill, Ontario,* Mercury Series, Archaeological Survey of Canada Paper no. 159. Ottawa: Canadian Museum of Civilization.

Ellis, C. J. and Spence, M. W. 1997 'Raw Material Variation and the Organization of Small Point Archaic Lithic Technologies in Southwestern Ontario', in P. J. Woodley and P. G. Ramsden (eds) *Preceramic Southern Ontario,* 119–140. Occasional Papers in Northeastern Archaeology no. 9, Ontario: Copetown Press, Hamilton.

Emerson, T. E. and Girard, Jeffrey S. 2004 'Dating Gahagan and Its Implications for Understanding Cahokia-Caddo Interactions', *Southeastern Archaeology*. 23, 1, 57–64.

Emerson, T. E. and Hughes, R. E. 2000 'Figurines, Flint Clay Sourcing, the Ozark Highlands, and Cahokian Acquisition', *American Antiquity* 65, 79–101.

Emerson, T. E. and Hughes, R. E. 2001 'DeMything the Cahokia Catlinite Trade', *Plains Anthropologist* 46, 175, 149–161.

Emerson, T. E., Hughes, R. E., Farnsworth, K. B., Wisseman, S. U. and Hynes, M. 2005 'Tremper Mound, Hopewell Catlinite, and PIMA Technology', *Midcontinental Journal of Archaeology* 30, 2, 189–216.

Emerson, T. E., Hughes, R. E., Hynes, M. R. and Wisseman, S. U. n.d. 'Implications of Sourcing Cahokia-style Flint Clay Figures in the American Bottom and the Upper Mississippi River Valley', *Midcontinental Journal of Archaeology* 27, 2, 309–338.

Emerson, T. E., Hughes, Randall E., Hynes, M. R. and Wisseman, S. U. 2003 'The Interpretation and Sourcing of Cahokian Figurines in the Trans-Mississippi South and Southeast', *American Antiquity* 68, 2, 287–313.

Engelbach, R. 1922 *The Aswan Obelisk*. Impr. De l'Institut Français d'Archeologie Orientale: Cairo.

Engelbach, R. 1938 'The Quarries of the Western Nubian Desert and the Ancient Road to Tushka', *Annales du Service des Antiquitiés de l'Egypt* 38, 369–390.

Ericson, J. E. 1984 'Towards the analysis of lithic production systems' in J. E. Ericson and B. A. Purdy (eds) *Prehistoric quarries and lithic production*, 1–10. Cambridge, London and New York: Cambridge University Press.

Erwin, J. C. 1998 *Preliminary Field Report for the 1997 Fleur de Lys Archaeology Project*. Unpublished report prepared for the Government of Newfoundland and Labrador, Department of Tourism, Culture and Recreation, Culture and Heritage Division.

Erwin, J. C. 1999 *Fleur de Lys Archaeological Project: A Report of the 1998 Field Activities*. Unpublished report prepared for the Government of Newfoundland and Labrador, Department of Tourism, Culture and Recreation, Culture and Heritage Division.

Erwin, J. C. 2001 *A Prehistoric Soapstone Quarry in Fleur de Lys, Newfoundland*. Unpublished PhD Dissertation, University of Calgary, Alberta.

Erwin, J. C. 2003 'Dorset Palaeoeskimo Settlement Patterns in White Bay, Newfoundland', *Northeast Anthropology* 66 (Fall), 5–14.

Erwin, J. C. 2005a 'Revisiting the Dorset Soapstone Quarry in Fleur de Lys, Newfoundland'. In P. Sutherland (ed.) *Contributions to the Study of Dorset Palaeo-Eskimo*, 121–131. Quebec Canadian Museum of Civilization, Archaeology Paper 167. Hull: Mercury Series.

Erwin, J. C. 2005b *Interim Report for the 2003 Field School: The Cow Cove Excavations*. Unpublished report prepared for the Provincial Archaeology Office, Government of Newfoundland and Labrador, St. John's, Newfoundland.

Erwin, J. C. n.d. *Prehistoric Soapstone Vessel Use in Newfoundland and Labrador*. Post-Doctoral Manuscript in Preparation, Memorial University of Newfoundland, St. John's, Newfoundland.

Esarey, D, and Conrad, L. A. 1998 'The Bold Counselor Phase of the Central Illinois River Valley: Oneota's Middle Mississippian Margin', *The Wisconsin Archeologist* 79, 2, 38–61.

Faivre, J.-P. 2004 'L'industrie lithique moustérienne du niveau G7 des Fieux (Miers, Lot): des matériaux, des schémas opératoires, un même objectif', *Paléo* 16, 71–90.

Faivre, J.-P. 2006 'L'industrie moustérienne du niveau Ks (Locus 1) des Fieux (Miers, Lot): mobilité humaine et diversité des compétences techniques', *BSPF*, 1, 3, 17–32.

Farnsworth, K. B. and O'Gorman, J. A. 1998 'Oneota in the Lower Illinois River Valley', *The Wisconsin Archeologist* 79, 2, 62–92.

Fenneman, N. M. 1938 *Physiography of Eastern United States*. New York: Mc-Graw Hill.

Fischer, W. L. and Rodda, P. U. 1969 'Edwards Formation (Lower Cretaceous), Texas: Dolomitization in a Carbonate Platform System', *The American Association of Petroleum Geologists Bulletin* 53, 55–72.

Fisher, D. W. 1984 Bedrock geology of the Glens Falls-Whitehall region, New York. *New York state museum map and chart series* 35.

Fitzhugh, W. W. 1972 'Environmental archaeology and cultural systems in Hamilton Inlet, Labrador', *Smithsonian Contribution to Anthropology*, 16, 239–244.

Fitzpatrick, A. 2003 'The Amesbury Archer', *Current Archaeology* 184, 146–152.

Fitzpatrick, A. 2004 'The Boscombe Bowmen: builders of Stonehenge?', *Current Archaeology* 193, 10–14.

Flawn, P. T. 1966 *Mineral resources*. New York: John Wiley and Sons.

Flem, B. and Bédard, L. P. 2002 'Determination of trace element in BCS CRM 313/1 (BAS) and NIST SRM 1830 by ICP-MS and INAA', *Geostandards Newsletter* 26, 3, 287–300.

Flood, J. 1983 *The archaeology of the Dreamtime*. London: Collins.

Flood, J. 1995 *The archaeology of the Dreamtime* (revised edition). London: Harper Collins.

Flood, J. 1997 *Rock Art of the Dreamtime*. London: Harper Collins.

Folk, R. L. 1980 *Petrology of sedimentary rocks*, 185. Austin, Texas: Hemphill Publishing Company.

Folk, R. L. and Weaver, C. E. 1952 'A Study of the Texture and Composition of Chert', *American Journal of Science* 250, 498–510.

Foucher, P. and San-Juan, C. 2000 'Le niveau D solutréen de l'abri des Harpons (Lespugue, Haute-Garonne). Collection Saint-Perrier du Musée des Antiquités Nationales', *Antiquités Nationales* 32, 17–55.

Foucher, P. and San-Juan, C. 2005 'La circulation des matières premières siliceuses dans le gravettien pyrénéen'. In J. Jaubert et M. Barbaza (dirs) *Territoires, déplacements, mobilité, échanges pendant la Préhistoire*, 199–217. Actes du colloque du CTHS *Terres et Hommes du Sud*, Toulouse 9–14 avril 2001. Ed. du CTHS: Paris.

Fowler, M. 1991 'Mound 72 and Early Mississippian at Cahokia', in J. B. Stoltman (ed.) *New Perspectives on Cahokia: Views from the Periphery*, 1–28 Monographs in World Archaeology no. 2, Madison: Prehistory Press.

Fowler, M. L., Rose, J., Vander Leest, B. and S. R. Ahler. 1999 'The Mound 72 Area: Dedicated and Sacred Space in Early Cahokia', *Reports of Investigations, No. 54.* Springfield, Illinois: Illinois State Museum.

Frison, G. C. and Stanford, D. J. (eds) 1982 *The Agate Basin Site: A Record of the Paleoindian Occupation of the Northwestern High Plains.* New York: Academic Press.

Fritz, C., and Tosello, G. 2005 'Entre Périgord et Cantabres: les magdaléniens de Marsoulas In J. Jaubert et M. Barbaza (dirs) *Territoires, déplacements, mobilité, échanges pendant la Préhistoire*, 311–327. Actes du colloque du CTHS *Terres et Hommes du Sud*, Toulouse 9–14 avril 2001. Ed. du CTHS: Paris.

Funk, R. E. 2004 *An Ice Age Quarry-Workshop: The West Athens Hill Site Revisited. New York State Museum Bulletin 504*. Albany, New York: University of New York and the New York State Education Department.

Gagnon, L. 1988 *La géologie de la colline Blanche, rivière Témiscamie, Québec*, MSc Thesis, Université de Montréal, Montréal.

Gardiner, J. P. 1990 'Flint procurement and Neolithic axe production on the South Downs: a re-assessment', *Oxford Journal of Archaeology* 9, 119–140.

Gatsov, I. and Kurčatov, V. 1997 'Neolithische Feursteinartefakte'. In S. Hiller and V. Nikolov (eds) *Karanovo, Die Ausgrabungen im Sudsektor 1984–1992*, 213–227. Salzburg: Band I.1. Band I.2 Tafeln, Taf. 92–94.

Gatsov, I., Nedelcheva, P. and Kalčev, P. (unpublished) *Azmak-Neolithic and Chalcolithic chipped stone industries. Part I.*

Gellibert, T. B., Merlet, J. C., Ferrier, C. and Legigan, Ph. 2001 'Le gisement badegoulien de Cabannes (commune de Brocas-les-Forges, Landes)', *Archéologie des Pyrénées Occidentales et des Landes* 20, 81–104.

Goodyear, A. C. 1989 'A Hypothesis for the Use of Cryptocrystalline Raw Materials Among Paleoindian Groups of North America' (reprinted). In C. J. Ellis and J. C. Lothrop (eds) *Eastern Paleoindian Lithic Resource Use*, 1–9. Boulder: Westview Press.

Gould, R. A. 1977 'Ethno-archaeology; Or, Where do Models Come From?'. In R. V. S. Wright (ed.) *Stone Tools as Cultural Markers,* 162–177. Canberra: Australian Institute of Aboriginal Studies.

Gould, R. A. 1980 *Living Archaeology.* Cambridge: Cambridge University Press.

Govindaraju, K. 1994 '1994 compilation of working values and sample description for 383 geostandards', *Geostandards Newsletter* 18 (special issue), 158.

Goyon, J.-C., Golvin, J.-C., Simon-Boidot, C. and Martinet, G. 2004 *La construction pharaonique du Moyen Empire à l'époque gréco-romaine.* Paris: Éditions Picard.

Gramley, R. M. 1984 'Mount Jasper: a direct access lithic source area in the Whjite Mountains of New Hampshire' in J. E. Ericson and B. A. Purdy (eds) *Prehistoric quarries and lithic production,* 11–22. Cambridge, London and New York: Cambridge University Press.

Gramly, R. M. 1978 'Lithic source areas in Northern Labrador', *Arctic Anthropology* 15, 2, 36–47.

Gramly, R. M. 1980 'Raw Material Source Areas and "Curated" Tool Assemblages', *American Antiquity* 45, 4, 823–833.

Green, M. 2000 *A Landscape Revealed.* Stroud: Tempus.

Green, W. and Rodell, R. L. 1994 'The Mississippian Presence and Cahokia Interaction at Trempealeau, Wisconsin', *American Antiquity.* 59, 2, 334–359.

Greenwell, W. 1870 'On the Opening of Grime's Graves in Norfolk', *J. Ethnol. Soc. London* (new series 2), 419–439.

Grimes, W. F. 1979 'The history of implement petrology in Britain'. In T. H. McKClough and W. A. Cummins (eds) *Stone Axe Studies,* 1–4. CBA Research Report 23. London: Council for British Archaeology.

Guillermin, P. 2004 'Réflexions sur l'interprétation des industries gravettiennes à partir de l'étude techno-typologique d'une occupation spécialisée: la couche E du gisement des Fieux (Miers, Lot)', *Mémoire de DEA d'Anthropologie* 99.

Guillermin, P. 2006 'Les Fieux: une occupation gravettienne du Causse quercinois', *Paléo* 18, 69–94.

Guillot, P. L., Astruc, J.-G., Feix, I., Humbert, L., Lefavrais-Henry, M., Lefavrais-Raymond, A., Michard, A., Monier, G. and Roubichou, P. 1992 Notice explicative, 76. Carte géol. France (1/50000), feuille de Saint-Céré (810), Orléans, BRGM.

Gums, B. L. 1993 'Groundstone Tools, Modified Rock, and Exotic Materials', in *The Archaeology of the Cahokia Mounds ICT-II: Testing and Lithics, Part III,* Cultural Resources Study 9, Springfield, Illinois: Illinois Historic Preservation Agency.

Gundersen, J. N. 1984 'Provenance Analysis of Plains Pipestone Argillites' Geological Society of America, *Abstracts with Programs* 16, 6, 526.

Gundersen, J. N. 1987 'Wisconsin Pipestone: A Preliminary Mineralogical Examination', *The Wisconsin Archeologist* 68, 1–21.

Gundersen, J. N. 1988 'Pipestones of the St. Helena Phase' in D. Blakeslee (ed) *St. Helena Archaeology: New Data, Fresh Interpretations,* 79–97, Lincoln, Nebraska: J and L Reprint Company.

Gundersen, J. N. 1991 'The Mineralogical Characterization of Catlinite from its Sole Provenance, Pipestone National Monument, Minnesota', *Research/Resource Management Report MWR 17,* Lincoln, Nebraska: National Park Service, Midwest Region, (reprinted in *Central Plains Archaeology* vol. 9, no. 1, 2002).

Gundersen, J. N. 1993 '"Catlinite" and the Spread of the Calumet Ceremony', *American Antiquity* 58, 56–62.

Gundersen, J. N. and Tiffany, J. A. 1986 'Nature and Provenance of Red Pipestone from the Wittrock Site (13OB4), Northwest Iowa', *North American Archaeologist* 7, 45–67.

Hansen, S., Dragoman, A., Reingruber, A., Gatsov, I., Görsdorf, J., Nedelcheva, P., Oanță-Marghitu, S. and Song, B. 2005 'Der kupferzeitliche Siedlungshügel Pietrele an der Unteren Donau. Bericht über die Ausgrabungen im Sommer 2004', *Eurasia Antiqua* 11, 341–393.

Harrell, J. A. and Brown, V. M. 1994 'Chephren's Quarry in the Nubian Desert of Egypt', *Nubica* 3, 1, 43–57.
Harrell, J. A. and Madbouly, M. I. 2006 'An ancient quarry for siliceous sandstone at Wadi Abu Aggag, Egypt', *Sahara* 17, 51–58.
Harrell, J. A. and Bown, T. 1995 'An Old Kingdom Basalt Quarry at Widan el-Faras and the Quarry Road to Lake Moeris', *JARCE* 32, 71–91.
Hayden, B. M. 1982 'Interaction Parameters and the Demise of Paleo-Indian Craftsmanship', *Plains Anthropologist* 27, 95, 109–123.
Heldal, T. and Storemyr, P. 2007 'The quarries at the Aswan West Bank'. In E. Bloxam, T. Heldal and P. Storemyr (eds) *Characterisation of complex quarry landscapes: an example from the West Bank quarries, Aswan*. QuarryScapes Report. Trondheim: Geological Survey of Norway.
Heldal, T., Bloxam, E., Degryse, P., Storemyr, P. and Kelany, A. 2006 'Old Kingdom gypsum quarries at Umm es-Sawan, Northern Faiyum Quarry Landscape, Egypt', *Proceedings of the first QuarryScapes symposium,* Antalya, 11–14. Available at: http://www.quarryscapes.no/workshops.php
Heldal, T., Bloxam, E., Storemyr, P. and Kelany, A. 2005 'The Geology and Archaeology of the Ancient Silicified Sandstone Quarries at Gebel Gulab and Gebel Tingar, Aswan, Egypt', *Marmora* 1, 11–35.
Heldal, T., Bloxam, E., Storemyr, P. and Kelany, A. 2007 'The quarry road network in the Gebel Tingar-Gebel Gulab area'. In E. Bloxam, T. Heldal and P. Storemyr (eds) *Characterisation of complex quarry landscapes: an example from the West Bank quarries, Aswan*. QuarryScapes Report. Trondheim: Geological Survey of Norway.
Heldal, T., Bloxam, E., Storemyr, P. in press a, 'Unravelling ancient stone quarry landscapes in the Eastern Mediterranean: the QuarryScapes project'. In B. Ooghe (ed.) *Broadening Horizons – Multidisciplinary Approaches to Landscape Study*. Cambridge: Cambridge Scholars Press.
Heldal, T., Storemyr, P., Salem, A., Bloxam, E., Shaw, I. and Lee, R. in press b, 'GPS and GIS Methodology in the Mapping of Chephren's Quarry, Upper Egypt: A Significant Tool for Documentation and Interpretation of the Site', *ASMOSIA* 7. Thassos, Greece.
Henning, D. R. 1998a 'The Oneota Tradition' in W. R. Wood (ed.) *Archaeology on the Great Plains*, 345–414. Lawrence: University of Kansas Press.
Henning, D. R. 1998b 'Managing Oneota: A Reiteration and Testing of Contemporary Archeological Taxonomy', *The Wisconsin Archeologist* 79, 2, 9–28.
Henry-Gambier, D., Bon, F., Gardere, P., Letrouneux, C., Mensan, R. and Potin, Y. 2004 'Nouvelles données sur la séquence culturelle du site de Brassempouy (Landes): fouilles 1997–1998', *Archéologie des Pyrénées occidentales et des Landes* 23, 145–156.
Hesse, R. 1990a 'Origin of Chert: Diagenesis of Biogenic Siliceous Sediments'. In I. A. McIlreath and D. W. Morrow (eds) *Diagenesis*, 227–252. Geoscience Canada Reprint Series 4. Newfoundland: Geological Association of Canada.
Hesse, R. 1990b 'Silica Diagenesis: Origin of Inorganic and Replacement Cherts'. In I. A. McIlreath and D. W. Morrow (eds) *Diagenesis,* 253–276. Geoscience Canada Reprint Series 4. Newfoundland: Geological Association of Canada.
Hill, M. G. 1994 'Paleoindian Projectile Points from the Vicinity of Silver Mound (47JA21), Jackson County, Wisconsin', *Midcontinental Journal of Archaeology* 19, 2, 223–259.
Hillam, J., Groves, C. M., Brown, D. M., Baillie, M. G. L., Coles, J. M. and Coles B. J. 1990 'Dendrochronology of the English Neolithic', *Antiquity* 64, 210–220.
Hoare, R. C. 1810 [1812] *The ancient history of Wiltshire.* London: William Miller.
Hoffmeier, J. K. 1993 'The Use of Basalt in Floors of Old Kingdom Pyramid Temples', *JARCE* 30, 117–123.
Holgate, R. 1995 'Neolithic flint mining in Britain', *Archaeologia Polona* 33, 133–161.

Holleyman, G. 1937 'Harrow Hill Excavations, 1936', *Sussex Archaeological Collections* 78, 230–251.

Holmes, W. H. 1890 'A quarry workshop of the flaked-stone implement makers in the District of Columbia', *The American Anthropologist* 3, 1–26.

Holmes, W. H. 1890 'Excavations in an ancient soapstone quarry in the District of Columbia', *The American Anthropologist* 3, 321–330.

Holmes, W. H. 1891 'Aboriginal Novaculite quarries in Garland County, Arkansas', *The American Anthropologist* 4, 313–315.

Holmes, W. H. 1919, *Handbook of Aboriginal American Antiquities. Part I: Introductory, the Lithic Industries.* Bulletin 60, Bureau of American Ethnology. Washington, D.C.

Howley, J. P. 1974 [1915] *The Beothucks or Red Indians: The Aboriginal Inhabitants of Newfoundland.* Toronto: Coles Publishing Company.

Hughes, R. E. 1994 'Intrasource chemical variability of artefact-quality obsidians from Casa Diablo area, California', *Journal of Archaeology Science* 21, 263–271.

Hughes, R. E. and Emerson, T. E. 1999 'The Mineralogical Sourcing of Prehistoric Cahokia-Style Figurines from the Midcontinental United States,'manuscript on file at the Illinois Transportation Archaeological Research Program, University of Illinois at Urbana-Champaign.

Hughes, R. E., Berres, T. E., Moore, D. M. and Farnsworth, K. B. 1998 'Revision of Hopewellian trading patterns in Midwestern North America based on mineralogical testing', *Geoarchaeology* 13, 7, 709–729.

Ingbar, E. E. 1994 'Lithic Material Selection and Technological Organization' in P. J. Carr (ed.) *The Organization of North American Prehistoric Chipped Stone Tool Technologies,* 45–56 International Monographs in Prehistory, Archaeological Series No. 7, Ann Arbor.

Irving, G. J. 1857 'On the camps at Cissbury, Sussex', *Journal British Archaeological Association* 13, 193–215.

Ismail, M., Yakoub, N. G. R. and Farag, F. undated, *Toward Sustainable Development in Toshka Region – Development of a Geo-Information System Using Remote Sensing and GIS.* Available at: www.mes.eg.net/acrobat_files/3_5.pdf

Jackson, D. K. 1998 'Settlement on the Southern Frontier: Oneota Occupations in the American Bottom', *The Wisconsin Archeologist* 79, 2, 93–116.

Jackson, L. J. 1997 'Caribou Range and Early Paleo-Indian Settlement and Disposition in Southern Ontario, Canada', in L. Jackson and R. Thacker (eds) *Caribou and Reindeer Hunters of the Northern Hemisphere,* 132–164. Aldershot, England: Avebury.

Jaubert, J. (dir.) with Brugal, J.-Ph., Chalard, P., Diot, M.-F., Falguières, Ch., Jarry, M., Kervazo, B., Konik, S. and Mourre, V. 2001 'Un site moustérien de type Quina dans la vallée du Célé. Pailhès à Espagnac-Sainte-Eulalie (Lot)', *Gallia Préhistoire* 43, 1–99. Paris: CNRS Éditions.

Jaubert, J. and Barbaza, M. (dirs.) 2005 – *Territoires, déplacements, mobilité, échanges pendant la Préhistoire,* 561. Actes du colloque du CTHS *Terres et Hommes du Sud,* Toulouse 9–14 avril 2001. Paris: Ed. du CTHS.

Jaubert, J., Kervazo, B., Bahain, J.-J., Brugal, J.-Ph., Chalard, P., Falguères, Ch., Jarry, M., Jeannet, M., Lemorini, C., Louchart, A., Maksud, F., Mourre, V., Quinif, Y. and Thiébaut, C. 2005 'Coudoulous I (Tour-de-Faure, Lot), site du Pléistocène moyen en Quercy. Bilan pluridisciplinaire'. In N. Molines, J-L. Monnier and M.-H. Moncel (dirs.) *Données récentes sur les modalités de peuplement et sur le cadre chronostratigraphique, géologique et paléogéographique des industries du Paléolithique inférieur et moyen en Europe,* 227–253. du Actes Colloque de Rennes, Univ. de Rennes, 22–25 sept. 2003. Oxford: BAR International Series S1364.

Jenness, D. 1932 *The Indians of Canada.* Ottowa: National Museums of Canada Bulletin 65, Anthropological Series 15.

Julig, P. J. 1994 'The Cummins Site Complex and Paleo-Indian occupations in the northwestern Lake Superior region', *Ontario Archaeological Reports,* 236. Toronto: Ontario Heritage Foundation.

Julig, P. J. 2002 'The Sheguiandah Site: Archaeological, geological and palaeobotanical studies at a Paleo-Indian site on Manitoulin Island, Ontario'. Canadian Museum of Civilization, Mercury Series, *Archaeological Survey of Canada Paper* 161.

Julig, P. J. and McAndrews J. 1993 'Les cultures paléoindiennes dans la région des grands lacs en amérique du nord: contextes paléoclimatique, géomorphologiques et stratigraphiques', *L'Anthropologie* 97, 4, 623–650.

Julig, P. J., Long, D. G. F. and Hancock, R. G. V. 1998 'Cathodoluminescence and petrographic techniques for positive identification of quartz-rich artifacts from Late Paleo-Indian sites in the Great Lakes Region', *Wisconsin Archeologist* 19 (1), 68–88. Madison: Wisconsin.

Julig, P. J., Long, D. F., and Hancock, R. G. 1999 'Cathidoluminesence and Petrographic Techniques for Positive Identification of Quartz Rich Artifacts from Late Paleo-Indian sites in the Great Lakes Region', *Wisconsin Archeologist* 79, 1, 68–88.

Julig, P. J., Long, D. F. G., Hancock, R. G. V. and Pavlish, L. A. 2002 'Provenance Studies of Late-Palaeoindian Quartzite Artifacts in the Great Lakes Region of North America'. In Erzsébet Jerem and Katalin T. Biró (eds) *Proceeding of the 31st International Archaeometry Congress, Volume 2, (Archaeometry* 98), 749–756. Oxford: BAR International Series S1043.

Kay, M. 1999 'Microscopic Attributes of the Keven Davis Blades'. In M. Collins (ed) *Clovis Blade Technology: A ComparativeStudy of the Keven Davis Cache, Texas*, 126–143. Texas Archaeology and Ethnohistory Series. Austin, Texas: University of Texas Press.

Keeley, L. 1980 *Experimental Determination of Stone Tool Uses*. Chicago: University of Chicago Press.

Klaric, L. 1999 'Le site de Garet à Serreslous-et-Arribans (Landes): un gisement aurignacien de plein air', *Archéologie des Pyrénées Occidentales et des Landes* 18, 101–112.

Klemm, R. and Klemm, D. 1993 *Steine und Steinbrüche im Alten Ägypten.* Berlin-Heidelberg: Springer Verlag.

Knauth, L. P. 1994 'Petrogenesis of Chert'. In P. J. Heaney, C. T. Prewitt and G. V. Gibbs (eds) *Silica: Physical Behavior, Geochemistry and Materials Applications*, 233–258. Reviews in Mineralogy volume 29. Washington DC: Mineralogical Society of America.

Knight, I. and Morgan, W. C. 1977 *Stratigraphic subdivisions of the Aphebian Ramah Group, Northern Labrador*, Geological Survey of Canada, paper 77–15, 31.

Knight, I. and Morgan, W. C. 1981 'The Aphebian Ramah Group, northern Labrador,' *Proterozoic basins of Canada Paper*, Geological Survey of Canada, paper 81–10, 313–330.

Korlin, G. and Weisgerber, G. 2006 *Stone Age-Mining Age.* Bochum: Deutschen-Bergbau Museum.

Kornfeld, M., Harkin, M., and Durr, J. 2001 'Landscapes and Peopling of the Americas', in J. Gillespie, S. Tupakka and C. deMille (eds) *On Being First: Cultural Innovation and Environmental Consequences of First Peopling*, 149–162 edited by Gillespie, J., Tupakka, S. and de Mille, C. The Archaeological Association of the University of Calgary, Calgary.

Kuhn, S. L. 1989 'Hunter-Gatherer Foraging and Strategies of Artifact Replacement and Discard', in D. Amick and R. Mauldin (eds) *Experiments in Lithic Technology*, 33–47. BAR International Series no. 528. Oxford: Archaeopress.

Kuhn, S. L. 1994 'A Formal Approach to the Design and Assembly of Mobile Toolkits', *American Antiquity* 59, 3, 426–442.

Kurčatov, V. in press 'Stone raw material varieties from Azmak – Neolithic and Chalcolithic layers', *Annuary of Department of Archaeology* 7. Sofia.

Lacombe, S. 1998 'Stratégies d'approvisionnement en silex au Tardiglaciaire. L'exemple des Pyrénées centrales françaises', *Bulletin de la Société Préhistorique Ariège-Pyrénées* LIII, 223–266.

Lacombe, S. 2005 'Territoires d'approvisionnement en matières premières lithiques au Tardiglaciaire, remarques à propos de quelques ensembles pyrénéens'. In J. Jaubert and M. Barbaza (dirs) *Territoires, déplacements, mobilité, échanges pendant la Préhistoire*, 329–353. Actes du colloque du CTHS *Terres et Hommes du Sud*, Toulouse 9–14 avril 2001. Paris: Ed. du CTHS.

Lane-Fox, Col. A. 1869 'An examination into the character and probable origin of the hillforts of Sussex', *Archaeologia* 42, 53–74.

Lane-Fox, Col. A. 1876 'Excavations in Cissbury Camp, Sussex', *J. Anthrop. Institute* 5, 357–90.

Langevin, É. 1990 *DdEw-12: 4000 ans d'occupation sur la Grande Décharge du lac Saint-Jean*, MSc Thesis, Université de Montréal, Montréal.

Langlais, M. and Sacchi, D. 2006 'Note sur les matières premières siliceuses exploitées par les magdaléniens de la grotte Gazel (Aude, France)'. In C. Bressy, A. Burke, P. Chalard and H. Martin (eds) Notions de territoire et de mobilité: exemples de l'Europe et des premières nations en Amérique du Nord avant le contact européen, 71–75. Actes deux sessions présentées au Colloque de l'EAA, Lyon, 8–12 septembre 2004, *ERAUL*, 116, Liège.

LaPorta and Associates, L. L. C. 2000 *Phase i Cultural resources survey – supplement, characterization of prehistoric quarry development, Smiths Basin site, town of Hartford, Washington County, New York.* Submitted to Spectra Environmental, Latham, New York. NYSOPRHP no. 96pr0303. Copy on file with LaPorta and Associates, L.L.C.

LaPorta and Associates, L. L. C. 2001 *Data recovery plan and educational program for prehistoric quarry investigation and mitigation at the Smiths Basin site, town of Hartford, Washington County, New York.* Submitted to Spectra Environmental, Latham, New York. NYSOPRHP no. 96pr0303. Copy on file with LaPorta and Associates, L.L.C.

LaPorta, P. C. 1994 'Lithostratigrapic Models and the geographic Distribution of Prehistoric Chert Quarries within the Cambro-Ordovician Lithologies of the Great Valley Sequence, Sussex County, New Jersey'. In C. A. Bergman and J. F. Doershuk (eds) *Recent Research into the Prehistory of the Delaware Valley*, 47–66. Journal of Middle Atlantic Archaeology, Vol. 10.

LaPorta, P. C. 1996 'Lithostratigraphy as a Predictive Tool for Prehistoric Quarry Investigations: Examples from the Dutchess Quarry Site, Orange County, New York'. In C. Lindner and E. V. Curtin (eds) *A Golden Chronograph for Robert E. Funk*, 73–83.

LaPorta, P. C. 2009 *The Stratigraphy and Structure of the Cambrian and Ordovician Chert-Bearing Carbonates of the Wallkill River Valley: The Stratigraphic Nature of the Chert and their Archaeological Potential,* PhD dissertation, The Graduate Center, City University of New York, three-volume set (including plates).

Lazenby, M. E. and Colleen M. E. C. 1980 'Prehistoric sources of chert in Northern Labrador: field work and preliminary analysis', *Arctic* 33, (3), 628–645.

Le Brun-Ricalens, F. and Seronie-Vivien, M. R. 2004 'Présence d'un silex d'origine nord-pyrénéenne (Chalosse?) en Haut-Quercy dans l'Aurignacien du Piage (Lot, France) et implications', *Paléo* 16, 129–136.

LeBlanc, D. 2004 *Caractérisation géochimique de matières premières lithiques: Analyse de la quartzite de Mistassini (colline Blanche, rivière Témiscamie) et de la calcédoine du lac-Saint-Jean (île aux Couleuvres, lac Saint-Jean)*, MSc Thesis, Université du Québec à Chicoutimi, Chicoutimi.

Lech, J. 1981 'Flint Mining Among the Early Farming Communities of Central Europe: Part I', *Przeglad Archeologiczny* 28, 5–55.

Lech, J. 1983 'Flint Mining Among the Early Farming Communities of Central Europe: Part II', *Przeglad Archeologiczny* 30, 47–80.

Lech, J. 1995 *Flint Mining: dedicated to the Seventh International Flint Symposium* Warsaw: Archaeologia Pologna 33 Special Theme.

Lelouvier, L. A. 1996 *Le Magdalénien initial du gisement du Cuzoul (Vers, Lot.). Approche techno-économique de l'industrie lithique de la couche 23,* Mémoire de maîtrise, Université de Paris X-Nanterre, 96.

Lenoir, M., Obry, J. and Seronie-Vivien, M. R. 1997 'Occurrence of allochtonous flint in an Upper-Paleolithic site near Bordeaux'. In A. R. Millan and A. Bustillo (eds) *Siliceous rocks and culture,* 385–390. Monografica Arte y Arqueologia, universidad de Granada.

Levi-Sala, I. 1986 'Use-Wear and Post-Depositional Surface Modification: A Word of Caution', *Journal of Archaeological Science* 13, 229–244.
Levi-Sala, I. 1996 *A Study of Microscopic Polish on Flint Implements*. BAR International Series 629. Oxford: Archaeopress.
Lewis, A. 1994 'Bronze Age mines at the Great Orme'. In T. D. Ford and L. Willies (eds) *Mining Before Powder.* Matlock Bath: Peak District Mines Historical Society.
Lewis, J. 2005 *Monuments, ritual and regionality: the Neolithic of northern Somerset* BAR British Series 401. Oxford: Archaeopress.
Lezin, C. 2000 *Analyses des faciès et stratigraphies intégrée: application aux évènements du passage Lias-Dogger sur la plate-forme du Quercy.* Thèse 3è cycle, 317. Université Paul Sabatier, Toulouse.
Lindgren, C. 1995 'Prehistoric quartz quarries and quarrying in Eastern Middle Sweden'. In *Flint Mining: dedicated to the Seventh International Flint Symposium.* Warsaw: Archaeologia Pologna 33, Special Theme, 89–98.
Linnamae, U. 1975 *The Dorset Culture: A Comparative Study in Newfoundland and the Arctic.* Technical Papers of the Newfoundland Museum, Number 1.
Loebel, T. J. 2005 '*The Organization of Early Paleoindian Economies In the Western Great Lakes*', PhD Dissertation, University of Illinois-Chicago, Chicago.
Long, D. G. F., Julig, P. J. and Hancock, R. G. V. 2002 'Characterization of Sheguiandah quartzite and other potential sources of quartz-arenite artifacts in the Great Lakes region'. In P. J. Julig (ed.) The Sheguiandah Site: archaeological, geological and paleobotanical studies at a Paleo-Indian site on Manitoulin Island, Ontario. (Chapter 10) Mercury Series, *Archaeological Survey of Canada.* Paper 161, 265–295.
Longworth, I. and Varndell, G. 1996 *Excavations at Grimes Graves, Norfolk 1972–1976, and Fascicule 5: Mining in the Deeper Mines.* London: British Museum Press.
Loring, S. 2002 'And They Took Away the Stones from Ramah: Lithic Raw Material Sourcing and Eastern Artic Archaeology'. In W. W. Fitzhugh, S. Loring and D. Odess (eds) *Honoring our Elders: A History of Eastern Arctic Archaeology*, 162–185. Arctic Studies Center, National Museum of Natural History. Washington, DC: Smithsonian Institution.
Lothrop, J. C. 1988 *The Organization of Paleoindian Lithic Technology at the Potts Site*, PhD Dissertation, State University of New York, Binghampton.
Lucas, A. and Harris, J. R. 1999 *Ancient Egyptian Materials and Industries* (4th ed., originally published 1962). Dover: New York.
Luedtke, B. E. 1976 *Lithic Material Distributions and Interaction Patterns During the Late Woodland Period in Michigan*, PhD Dissertation, University of Michigan, Ann Arbor.
Lundelius, E. L. Jr. 1998 'Vertebrate Fauna at the Gault Site', *TARL Research Notes* 6, 17.
Maliva, R. G., Knoll, A. H. and Simonson, B. M. 2005 'Secular Changes in the Precambrian Silica Cycle: Insights from Chert Petrography', *GSA Bulletin* 117, 835–845.
Mallory-Greenough, L. M., Greenough, J. D. and Owen, J. V. 2000 'The Origin and Use of Basalt in Old Kingdom Funerary Temples', *Geoarchaeology* 15, (4), 315–330.
Martijn, C. and Rogers, E. S. 1969 *Mistassini-Albanel: Contributions to the prehistory of Québec*, Travaux divers, no. 25, Centre d'étude nordiques, Université Laval, Québec.
Mason, R. J. 1981 *Great Lakes Archaeology.* New York: Academic Press.
Mason, R. J. 1986 'The Paleo-Indian Traditions', *The Wisconsin Archaeologist* 67(3–4), 181 206.
Matthiessen, P. (ed.) 1989 *George Catlin: North American Indians*. New York: Penguin Books.
Maxfield, V. A. and Peacock, D. P. S. 2001 *The Roman Imperial Quarries, Survey and Excavation at Mons Porpyrites 1994–1998, 1, Topography and Quarries*. Egypt Exploration Society, London.
McAdams, W. 1882 'Antiquities'. In *History of Madison county, Illinois,* 58–64. Edwardsville, Illinois: W. R. Brink and Company.
McGhee, R. 1976 'Differential Artistic Productivity in the Eskimo Cultural Tradition', *Current Anthropology* 17(2), 203–220.

McGhee, R. 1987 'Prehistoric Arctic Peoples and their Art', *American Review of Canadian Studies* 17(1), 5–14.

McGhee, R. 1996 *Ancient People of the Arctic*. Vancouver: Canadian Museum of Civilization and UBC Press.

McK Clough, T. H. 1973 'Excavations on a Langdale axe chipping site in 1969 and 1970', *Transactions of the Cumberland and Westmorland Antiquarian and Archaeological Society* New Series, LXXIII, 25–46.

McK Clough, T. H. and Cummins, W. A. 1988 *Stone Axe Studies, Volume 2*. London: Council for British Archaeology Research Report No. 67.

Meltzer, D. J. 1988 'Late Pleistocene Human Adaptations in Eastern North America', *Journal of World Prehistory* 2, 1–52.

Meltzer, D. J. 1989 'Was Stone Exchanged Among Eastern North American Paleoindians?' In C. J. Ellis and J. C. Lothrop (eds) *Eastern Paleoindian Lithic Resource Use*, 11–39. Boulder: Westview Press.

Meltzer, D. J. and Dunnell, R. G. 1992 *The archaeology of William Henry Holmes*. Washington and London: Smithsonian Institution Press.

Merlet, J. -C. 1992–1993a 'Le gisement paléolithique du Moulin de Bénesse', *Archéologie des Pyrénées Occidentales et des Landes* 12, 7–26.

Meyers, W. J. 1977 'Chertification in the Mississippian Lake Valley Formation, Sacramento Mountains, New Mexico', *Sedimentology* 24, 75–105.

Minchak, S. A. 2007 *A Microwear Study on Clovis Blades from the Gault Site, Bell County, Texas*. MA Thesis, Texas A&M University, College Station, Texas.

Moorehead, W. K., Taylor, J., Leighton, M. and Baker, F. 1929 *The Cahokia Mounds*. Urbana: University of Illinois Press.

Moores, R. G. 1991 'Evidence for Use of a Stone-Cutting Drag Saw by the Fourth Dynasty Egyptians', *JARCE* 28, 139–148.

Moreau, J.-F. 1998 'La question de l'interculturalité en archéologie: l'exemple d'une région du Subarctique oriental', *Material History Review / Revue d'histoire de la culture matérielle* 47, 33–45.

Moreau, J.-F., Girard J. and Vereault, L. 1987 'Aspects de la préhistoire de la Péribonca, à l'embouchure du lac Tchitogama', *Saguenayensia* 29, (3), 4–13.

Murray, G. W. 1939 'The Road to Chephren's Quarries', *The Geographical Journal* 94, (2), 97–111.

Myers, A. 1989 'Reliable and Maintainable Technological Strategies in the Mesolithic of Mainland Britain'. In R. Torrence (ed.) *Time, Energy, and Stone Tools*, 78–91. Cambridge: Cambridge University Press.

Nagle, C. 1982 1981 'Field Investigations at the Fleur de Lys Soapstone Quarry, Baie Verte, Newfoundland'. In J. S. Thomson and C. Thomson (eds) *Archaeology in Newfoundland and Labrador 1981*, 102–129. Annual Report No.2, Newfoundland Museum, Historic Resources Division, Department of Recreation and Youth, Government of Newfoundland and Labrador.

Nagle, C. 1984 *Lithic Raw Material Procurement and Exchange in Dorset Culture along the Labrador Coast*. PhD Dissertation, Department of Anthropology, Brandeis University.

Nelson, M. C. 1991 'The Study of Technological Organization', *Archaeological Method and Theory*. 3, 57–100.

Nicoll, K. 2004 'Recent environmental change and prehistoric human activity in Egypt and Northern Sudan', *Quaternary Science Reviews* 23, 561–580.

Nolan, David J., and Conrad, Lawrence A. 1998 'Characterizing Lima Lake Oneota', *The Wisconsin Archeologist* 79, 2, 117–146.

Normand, C. 1986 'Inventaire des gîtes à silex de la Chalosse (1984–1985)', *Bulletin de la Société de Borda* 402, 133–140.

Normand, C. 1987 'Le gisement paléolithique de plein air du Vignès à Tercis (Landes)', *Bull. de la Soc. d'Anthropologie du Sud-Ouest* XXII, 2, 71–80.
Normand, C. 1991 'Un gisement préhistorique de plein air à Saint-Lon-les-Mines (Landes)', *Archéologie des Pyrénées Occidentales* 11, 5–22.
Normand, C. 1992–93b 'Un atelier de taille de pièces à dos à Tercis (Landes)', *Archéologie des Pyrénées Occidentales et des Landes* 12, 27–51.
Odell, G. H. 1996 'Introduction' in G. H. Odell (ed.) *Stone Tools: Theoretical Insights into Human Prehistory*, 1–6. New York: Plenum Press.
Palumbo, G. and Teutonico, J. M. (eds) 2002 *Management Planning for Archaeological Sites*. Los Angeles, CA: The Getty Conservation Institute.
Park, R. W. 1998 'Size Counts: the Miniature Archaeology of Childhood in Inuit Societies', *Antiquity* 72, 269–81.
Parker Pearson, M., Cleal, R., Marshall, P., Needham, S., Pollard, J., Richards, C., Ruggles, C., Sheridan, A., Thomas, J., Tilley, C., Welham, K., Chamberlain, A., Chenery, C., Evans, J., Knusel, C., Linford, N., Martin, L., Montgomery, J., Payne, A., and Richards, M. 2007 'The Age of Stonehenge', *Antiquity* 81, 617–639.
Peacock, D. P. S. 1992 *Rome in the Desert: A Symbol of Power*. Inaugural Lecture, University of Southampton.
Peacock, D. P. S. and Maxfield, V. A. 1997 Survey and Excavation – Mons Claudianus 1987–1993, 1, Topography and Quarries. *FIFAO* 37, Cairo.
Pélissié, Th. 1982 *Le Causse jurassique de Limogne-en-Quercy: stratigraphie, sédimentologie, structure,* Thèse 3e cycle, Université Paul Sabatier, Toulouse, 281.
Penman, J. T., and Gundersen, J. N. 1999 'Pipestone Artifacts from Upper Mississippi Valley Sites', *Plains Anthropologist* 44, 167, 47–57.
Pertula, T. K., Emerson, T. E. and Hughes, R. E. 2004 'Catlinite Pipe' in T. Pertulla (ed.) 41HO64/41HO65, Late 17th to Early 18th Century Sites on San Pedro Creek in Houston County, Texas, *Bulletin of the Texas Archeological Society* 75, 96–99.
Pétrequin, P., and Pétrequin, A-M. 2000 *Ecology d'un outil: la hache de Pierre en Irian Jaya (Indonésie).* Nouv. éd. Paris: CNRS.
Pétrequin, P., Errera, M., Pétrequin, A-M. and Allard, P. 2006 'The Neolithic quarries of Mont Viso, Piedmont, Italy: initial radiocarbon dates', *European Journal of Archaeology* 9(1), 7–30.
Pitt-Rivers, Lt Gen. A. 1884 *Report on the excavations in the Pen Pits at Penselwood, Somerset*. London: HMSO.
Pitts, M. 1996 'The Stone Axe in Neolithic Britain', *Proceedings of the Prehistoric Society* 62, 311–371.
Plumet, P. 1981 'Matières premières allochtones et réseau spatial paléoesquimau en Ungava occidental, Arctique québécois', *Géographie physique et Quaternaire* 35, 1, 5–17.
Porter, J. 1961 'Hixton Silicified Sandstone: A Unique Lithic Material Used by Prehistoric Cultures', *Wisconsin Archeologist* 42, 2, 78–85.
Porter, J. W. 1974 *Cahokia Archaeology as Viewed from the Mitchell Site: A Satellite Community at A.D. 1150–1200*. Unpublished PhD dissertation, Department of Anthropology, University of Wisconsin.
Proctor, C. V. Jr., Brown, T. E., McGowen, J. H., Waechter, N. B. and Barnes, V. E. 1981 *Austin Sheet*. Francis Luther Whitney Memorial Edition, 1974, revised 1981, reprinted 1995.
Rawlings, M. 1995 'Archaeological sites along the Wiltshire section of the Codford-Ilchester water pipeline', *Wiltshire Archaeological and Natural History Society Magazine* 88, 26–49.
Renouf, M. A. P. 1999 *Ancient Cultures, Bountiful Seas: The Story of Port au Choix*. Historic Sites Association of Newfoundland and Labrador.
Richards, J., Hughes, R. E. and Emerson, T. E. 2005 '*Sourcing Aztalan's Ear Spools*' paper presented at the 23rd Annual Meeting of the Wisconsin Archaeological Survey, Madison, April 23.

Richards, R. H. and Locke, C. E. 1940 *Textbook of Ore Dressing*. New York: McGraw-Hill.

Ritchie, W. A. 1929 'Hammerstones, Anvils, and Certain Pitted Stones'. In L. H. Morgan *Research and Transactions of the New York State Archaeological Association* VII, 2.

Röder, J. 1965 'Zur Steinbruchsgeschichte des Rosengranits von Assuan', *Archäologischer Anzeiger* 467–552.

Roubet, C. 1989 'Report on Site E-82-1: A Workshop for the Manufacture of Grinding Stone at Wadi Kubbaniya'. In F. Wendorf, and R. Schild (eds) *The Prehistory of Wadi Kubbaniya*, vol. 3, 588–608. Dallas: Southern Methodist University Press, Dallas.

Ruggles, D. L. 2001 '*Mobility, Styles, and Exchange Among Upper Great Lakes Late Paleoindians*'. PhD Dissertation, Michigan State University, Lansing.

Rutherford, D. E. and Stephens R. K. 1991 *Geological approaches to prehistoric trade: Physical and Chemical Characterization of Metachert from the Ramah Group, Labrador (Ramah Chert)*, 38. Unpublished report, Institute of Social and Economic Research, St. John, Newfoundland.

Saville, A. 2005 'Prehistoric Quarrying of a Secondary Flint Source: Evidence from North-East Scotland'. In P. Topping and M. Lynott (eds) *The Cultural Landscape of Prehistoric Mines*, 1–13. Oxford: Oxbow Books.

Scott, D. and Thiessen, T. D. 2005 'Catlinite Extraction at Pipestone National Monument, Minnesota: Social and Technological Implications'. In P. Topping and M. Lynott (eds) *The Cultural Landscape of Prehistoric Mines*, 140–154. Oxford: Oxbow Books.

Scott, D. D., Thiessen, T. D., Richner, J. J. and Stadler, S. 2006 *An Archaeological Inventory and Overview of Pipestone National Monument, Minnesota*. Lincoln, Nebraska: National Park Service, Midwest Archeological Center Occasional Studies in Anthropology No. 34.

Seeman, M. F. 1994 'Intercluster Lithic Patterning at Nobles Pond: A Case for "Disembedded" Procurement Among Early Paleoindian Societies', *American Antiquity* 59, 2, 273–288.

Seitzer-Olausson, D. 1980 'Starting from Scratch: The History of Edge-Wear Research from 1838 to 1978', *Lithic Technology* 9, 48–60.

Semenov, S. A. 1964 *Prehistoric Technology: an Experimental Study of the Oldest Stone Tools and Artefacts from Traces of Manufacture and Wear*. Translated by W. M. Thompson. New York: Barnes and Noble.

Séronie-Vivien, M. and M.-R. 1987 'Les silex du Mésozoïque nord-aquitain: approche géologique de l'étude des silex pour servir à la recherche préhistorique', *Bulletin de la Société Linnéenne de Bordeaux*, suppl. au 15, 132.

Séronie-Vivien, M. R. (dir.) 1995 *La grotte de Pégourié, Caniac-du-Causse (Lot)*, 334. Préhistoire Quercinoise, Cressensac.

Seronie-Vivien, M. R., Benoist, F., Boulestin, B., Bourhis, J. R., Duday, H., Guadelli, J. L., Le Gall, O., Ionnnidès, N., Marinval, P., Marquet, J. C., Martin, H., Solari, M. E. and Vernnet, J. L. 1995 'La grotte de Pégourié, Caniac-du-Causse (Lot), Périgordien, Badegoulien, Azilien, Âge du Bronze', *Préhistoire Quercinoise* supplément 2, 334.

Seronie-Vivien, M.-R. 2003 'Origine méridionale de silex recueillis dans le paléolithique supérieur de la région Périgord-Quercy'. In *Les matières premières lithiques en préhistoire*, 305–306. Table ronde internationale d'Aurillac (Cantal), du 20 au 22 Juin 2002.

Shackley, M.S. 1995 'Source of archaeological obsidian in the Greater American Southwest: an update and quantitative analysis', *American Antiquity* 60, 531–551.

Shaffer, N. R., and Tankersley, K. B. 1989 'Oxygen Isotopes as a Method of Determining the Provenience of Silica-Rich Artifacts', *Current Research in the Pleistocene* 6, 47–49.

Shaw, I. M. E. and Bloxam, E. 1999 'Survey and Excavation at the Ancient Pharaonic Gneiss Quarrying Site of Gebel el-Asr, Lower Nubia', *Sudan and Nubia* 3, 13–20.

Shott, M. J. 1993 *The Leavitt Site: A Parkhill Phase Paleo-Indian Occupation in Central Michigan*, University of Michigan Museum of Anthropology Memoirs no. 25, Ann Arbor.

Siever, R. 1957 'The Silica Budget in the Sedimentary Cycle', *American Mineralogist* 42, 821–841.

Sigstad, J. S. 1970 'A Report of the Archeological Investigations, Pipestone National Monument, 1965 and 1966', *Journal of the Iowa Archeological Society* 17 (whole volume).

Simán, K. 1995 'The Korlat-Ravaszlyuktető workshop site-north eastern Hungary', *Archaeologia Pologna* 33, 41–58.

Simonnet, R. 1981 'Carte des gîtes à silex des Pré-Pyrénées'. In Actes du XXIe congrès préhistorique de France, septembre 1979, Cahors-Montauban, vol. 1, 308–323. Paris: Société Préhistorique Française.

Simonnet, R. 1996 'Approvisionnement en silex au Paléolithique supérieur; déplacements et caractéristiques physionomiques des paysages, l'exemple des Pyrénées centrales'. In *Pyrénées Préhistoriques Arts et Sociétés. Actes du 118e Congrès National des Sociétés Historiques et Scientifiques*. 117–128. Pau, 25–29 Octobre 1993. Ed. C.T.H.S.

Simonnet, R. 1998 'Le silex et la fin du Paléolithique supérieur dans le bassin de Tarascon-sur-Ariège', *Bulletin de la Société Préhistorique Ariège-Pyrénées* LIII, 1–42.

Simonnet, R. 2002 'Le silex dans le bassin sous-pyrénéen de la Garonne: compléments', *Préhistoire, Art et Sociétés, Bull. de la Société Préhistorique Ariège-Pyrénées* 57, 113–170.

Simons, D. B., Shott, M. J. and Wright, H. T. 1984 'The Gainey Site: Variability in a Great Lakes Paleo-Indian Assemblage', *Archaeology of Eastern North America* 12, 266–279.

Simons, E. L. and Rasmussen, D. T. 1991 'Vertebrate paleontology of Fayum: History of Research, faunal review and future prospects'. In R. Said (ed.) *The Geology of Egypt*, 627–638. Balkema, Rotterdam: Brookfield.

Slivitzky, A., Saint-Julien, P. and Lachambre, G. 1991 *Synthèse géologique du Cambro-Ordovicien du nord de la Gaspésie (ET 88–14)*. Quebec: Ministère de l'Énergie et des Ressources.

Stanford, D. 1991 'Clovis Origins and Adaptations: An Introductory Perspective'. In R. Bonnichsen and K. L. Turnmire (eds) *Clovis: Origins and Adaptations*, 1–13. Corvallis: Center for the Study of the First Americans.

Stocker, T. L. and Cobean, R. H. 1984 'Preliminary report on the obsidian mines at Pico de Orizaba, Veracruz'. In J. E. Ericson and B. A. Purdy (eds) *Prehistoric quarries and lithic production*, 83–95. Cambridge, London and New York: Cambridge University Press.

Stocks, D. 2003 *Experiments in Egyptian Archaeology – Stoneworking technology in Ancient Egypt*. London and New York: Routledge.

Storemyr, P. 2006 'Reflections on Conservation and Promotion of Ancient Quarries and Quarry Landscapes', *Proceedings of the first QuarryScapes symposium,* Antalya, Turkey, 31–35. Available at: http://www.quarryscapes.no/workshops.php

Storemyr, P. and Heldal, T. in press, 'Ancient Stone Quarries: Vulnerable Archaeological Sites Threatened by Modern Development', *ASMOSIA* 7, Thassos, Greece.

Storemyr, P., Bloxam, E., Heldal, T. and Salem, A. 2002 'Survey at Chephren's Quarry, Gebel el-Asr, Lower Nubia 2002', *Sudan and Nubia* 6, 25–29.

Storemyr, P., Heldal, T., Bloxam, E. and Harrell, J. A. 2003 *Widan el-Faras Ancient Quarry Landscape, Northern Faiyum Desert, Egypt: Site Description, Historical Significance and Current Destruction*, Report No. 2002.062, Zurick: Expert-Center for Conservation of Monuments and Sites.

Storemyr, P., Heldal, T., Bloxam, E. and Harrell, J. A. in press, 'New Evidence of Small-Scale Roman Basalt Quarrying in Egypt: Widan el-Faras in the Northern Faiyum Desert and Tilal Sawda by El-Minya', *ASMOSIA* 7. Thassos, Greece.

Taçon, P. S. C. 1983 'An Analysis of Dorset Art in Relation to Prehistoric Cultural Stress', *Études/Inuit/Studies* 7(1), 41–65.

Taçon, P. S. C. 2004 'Ochre, Clay, Stone and Art: The Symbolic Importance of Minerals as Life-Force among Aboriginal Peoples of Northern and Central Australia'. In N. Boivin and M. A. Owoc (eds) *Soils, Stones and Symbols: Cultural Perceptions of the Mineral World,* 31–42. London: UCL Press.

Tankersley, K. B. 1990 'Late Pleistocene Lithic Exploitation in the Midwest and Midsouth: Indiana, Ohio, and Kentucky' in K. B. Tankersley and B. L. Issac (eds) *Early Paleoindian Economies of Eastern North America*, 259–299 Research in Economic Anthropology, Supplement 5, JAI, Greenwich, Connecticut.

Tarrino, A., Yusta, I. and Aguirre, M. 1998 'Indicios de circulación a larga distancia de sílex en el Pleistoceno superior. Datos petrográficos y geoquímicas de materiales arqueológicos de Antoliñako Koba', *Boletín de la Sociedad Española de Mineralogía* 21–A, 200–201.

Temple, W. C. 1966 *Indian Villages of the Illinois Country: Historic Tribes*. Scientific Papers, No. 2. Springfield: Illinois State Museum.

Teyssandier, N., Renard, C., Bon, F., Deschamps, M., Gardère, Ph., Lafitte, P., Normand, C. and Tarrino, A. 2006 'Premières données sur le site de Marseillon (Banos, Landes): un nouveau gisement solutréen de plein air en Chalosse?', *Archéologie des Pyrénées Occidentales et des Landes* 25, 105–120.

Thomson, C. 1984 'A Summary of Four Contract Archaeology Projects in Newfoundland and Labrador 1983'. In J. S. Thomson and C. Thomson (eds) *Archaeology in Newfoundland and Labrador 1983*, 82–97. Annual Report No. 46, Historic Resources Division, Department of Recreation and Youth, Government of Newfoundland and Labrador.

Thomson, C. 1985 'Dorset Shamanism: Excavations in Northern Labrador', *Expedition* 27, No. 1, University of Pennsylvania.

Thomson, C. 1986 'Investigations on the Baie Verte Peninsula, Newfoundland'. In J. S. Thomson and C. Thomson (eds) *Archaeology in Newfoundland and Labrador 1985*, 196–217. Annual Report No. 6, Newfoundland Museum, Historic Resources Division, Department of Recreation and Youth, Government of Newfoundland and Labrador.

Thomson, C. 1989 'Maritime Archaic and Middle Dorset Occupations at Fleur de Lys: Preliminary Results of 1986 Investigations on the Baie Verte Peninsula'. In J. S. Thomson and C. Thomson (eds) *Archaeology in Newfoundland and Labrador 1986*, 250–259. Annual Report No. 7, Newfoundland Museum, Historic Resources Division, Department of Recreation and Youth, Government of Newfoundland and Labrador.

Topping, P. 1996 'Grime's Graves mined for ritual reasons', *British Archaeology* 18, 2.

Topping, P. 2003 *Grime's Graves*. Site guidebook. London: English Heritage.

Topping, P. 2004 'The South Downs flint mines: towards an ethnography of prehistoric flint extraction'. In J. Cotton and D. Field (eds) *Towards a New Stone Age: aspects of the Neolithic in south-east England*, 177–190. CBA Research Report 137. York: Council for British Archaeology.

Topping, P. 2005 'Shaft 27 Revisited: an Ethnography of Neolithic Flint Extraction'. In P. Topping and M. Lynott (eds) *The Cultural Landscape of Prehistoric Mines*, 63–93. Oxford: Oxbow Books.

Topping, P. forthcoming. 'Prehistoric extraction: further suggestions from ethnography'. In A. Saville (ed.) *Flint and Stone in the Neolithic Period*. Oxford: Oxbow (Neolithic Studies Group Seminar Papers).

Topping, P. and Lynott, M. 2005 'Miners and Mines'. In P. Topping and M. Lynott (eds) *The Cultural Landscape of Prehistoric Mines*, 181–191. Oxford: Oxbow Books.

Torrence, R. 1983 'Time Budgeting and Hunter-Gatherer Technology', in G. Bailey (ed.), *Hunter-Gatherer Economy in Prehistory*, 11–22 Cambridge: Cambridge University Press.

Torrence, R. 1986 *Production and Exchange of Stone Tools: Prehistoric Obsidian in the Aegean*. Cambridge: Cambridge University Press.

Tringham, R., Cooper, G., Odell, G., Voytek, B. and Whitman, A. 1974 'Experimentation in the Formation of Edge Damage: A New Approach to Lithic Analysis', *Journal of Field Archaeology* 1, 171–196.

Turq, A. 2000 *Paléolithique inférieur et moyen entre Dordogne et Lot*, 456. Paléo, Les Eyzies, SAMRA éd. (suppl. 2).

Valdeyron, N., Chalard, P. and Martin, H. 1998 'La grotte de la Herse à Livernon (Lot)', *Préhistoire du Sud-Ouest* 5, 31–37.

Vaughan, P. C. 1985 *Use-Wear Analysis of Flaked Stone Tools.* Tucson: University of Arizona Press.

Vaughan, P. C. 1984–1986 'A Sampling Method for Use-Wear Analysis of Large Flint Assemblages', *Early Man News* 9–11(1), 183–186.

Vermeersch, P. M. (ed.) 2002 *Palaeolithic Quarrying Sites in Upper and Middle Egypt.* Egyptian Prehistory Monographs, Leuven University Press.

Vermeersch, P. M., Paulissen, E. and Van Peer, P. 1995 'Palaeolithic chert mining in Egypt', *Archaeologia Pologna* 33, 11–30.

Vialou, D., Renault-Miskovsky, J. and Patou-Mathis, M. 2005 *Comportement des hommes du Paléolithique moyen et supérieur en Europe: territoires et milieux,* 255. Actes du colloque du G.D.R. 1945 du CNRS, Paris, 8–10 janvier 2003, ERAUL, Liège.

Wahby, W. F. 2004 'Technologies Applied in the Toshka Project of Egypt', *The Journal of Technology Studies* 30, (4), 86–91.

Wahish, N. 2006 'Marketing Toshka', *Al-Ahram Weekly*, 16–22 February 2006, no. 782.

Waldorf, D. C. 1993 *The Art of Flintknapping (fourth edition).* Branson, MO: Mound Builder Books.

Walter, J. 2003 *Étude pétrographique du quartzite de la colline Blanche (région de la rivière Témiscamie),* Unpublished report, présenté dans le cadre du cours de 6SCT604, Université du Québec à Chicoutimi, 42.

Walthall, J. A., and Benchley, E. D. 1987 *The River L'Abbe Mission.* Studies in Illinois Archaeology No. 2. Springfield: Illinois Historic Preservation Agency.

Warren, S. H. 1919 'A stone axe factory at Graig Lwyd, Penmaenmawr', *Journal Royal Archaeological Institute* 49, 342–365.

Weisgerber, G., Slotter, R. and Weiner, J. 1980 5000 *Jahre Feuersteinbergbau.* Bochum: Deutschen Bergbau-Museum.

Wendorf, F. (ed.) 1968 *The Prehistory of Nubia,* vols. 1–2, Dallas: Southern Methodist University Press.

Whittaker, J. C. 1994 *Flintknapping: Making and Understanding Stone Tools.* Austin: University of Texas Press.

Willett, E. H. 1875 'On flint workings at Cissbury, Sussex', *Archaeologia* 65, 337–348.

Willies, L. 1994 'Firesetting technology'. In T. D. Ford and L. Willies (eds) *Mining Before Powder.* Matlock Bath: Peak District Mines Historical Society.

Wilmsen, E. 1970 *Lithic Analysis and Cultural Inference: A Paleo-Indian Case.* Anthropological Papers no. 16, Tuscon: University of Arizona Press.

Wilson L. and Pollard A. M. 2001 'The Provenance Hypothesis'. In D. R. Brothwell and A.M. Pollard (eds) *Handbook of Archaeological Sciences,* 507–517. New York: Wiley.

Wintemberg, W. J. 1940 'Eskimo Sites of the Dorset Culture in Newfoundland: Part II', *American Antiquity* 4, 309–333.

Winwood, Rev. H. H. 1884 'The result of further excavations at Pen Pits', *Proceedings Somerset Archaeology and Natural History Society* 30, 149–152.

Wisseman, S. U., Emerson, T. E., Hynes, M. R. and Hughes, R. E. 2004 'Using a Portable Spectrometer to Source Archaeological Materials and to Detect Restorations in Museum Objects', *Journal of the American Institute for Conservation* 43, 2, 129–138.

Wisseman, S. U., Moore, D. M., Hughes, R. E., Hynes, M. R. and Emerson, T. E. 2002 'Mineralogical Approaches to Sourcing Pipes and Figurines from the Eastern Woodlands, USA', *Geoarchaeology* 17, 7, 689–715.

Witthoft, J. 1952 'A Paleo-Indian Site in Eastern Pennsylvania: An Early Hunting Culture' *Proceedings of the American Philosophical Society* 96, 464–495.

Woolworth, A. (compiler) 1983 'Red Pipestone Quarry of Minnesota: Archaeological and Historical Reports', *Minnesota Archaeologist* 42 (whole volume).

Young, G. M., Long, D. G. F., Fedo, C. M. and Nesbitt, H. W. 2001 'The Paleoproterozoic Huronian Basin: product of a Wilson cycle accompanied by glaciation and a meteorite impact', *Sedimentary Geology*, 141–142 and 233–254.

Zilhão, J. and Aubry, T. 1995 'La pointe de Vale Comprido et les origines du Solutréen', *L'Anthropologie* 99, 125–142.